The Speed Bag Bible

The Ultimate Speed Bag Training Program

by Alan H. Kahn

First Edition

Third Printing

Published by   Rehabilitation & Sports Consulting

Waco, Texas

The Speed Bag Bible

The Ultimate Speed Bag Training Program

by Alan Kahn

Published by

Rehabilitation & Sports Consulting
Post Office Box 21103
Waco, Texas 76702-1103

Library of Congress Catalog Card Number: 94-92116
ISBN 0-9641827-6-9   3rd Printing

First Edition
Copyright © 1994, Alan Kahn
Printed in the United States of America

Speed Bag...

...Just Hit It !

In Memorandum

Alan Kahn
Author

"Mr. Joe"
1929 - 1996

Cornell Kahn
Brother

The Book is Dedicated To:

Mr. Joe Sckrycki
Grand Rapids, MIchigan

Dr. Charles R. Schroeder
Memphis, Tennessee

Grand Master Kyong Sik Song
Dallas, Texas

And, of course,...Mom

Acknowledgements

No book ever gets completed by itself. This book was over six years in the making and I would like to thank the following for their inspiration, guidance and support.

Mr. Joe Skrycki spent 35 years as a police officer in Grand Rapids, Michigan. I had the occasion to meet "Mr. Joe" as the director of the Seidman Center, a small youth center located in mid-town Grand Rapids. It was here that I first saw and heard the magical sound of the speed bag. Mr. Joe was then coach of the Seidman Center Boxing Team. Under his leadership for nine years, they won a combined 140 regional, state and national boxing championships. But he was much more than a boxing coach. He coached little league teams, basketball, football and many other sports. He coached the late great Buster Mathis to several title shots against both Ali and Frazier.

He was a friend and father to hundreds of kids who gathered daily at the center. Together with his lovely wife Mary, no kid was ever turned away. There are a lot of kids who became much better adults because of Mr. Joe, including this author. I am dedicating this book to him, and all the kids who ever shadowed the doors of the Seidman Youth Center. Sadly, Mr. Joe died on November 11, 1996. He will be greatly missed.

Dr. Charles R. Schroeder, Ph.d, was a full professor of exercise physiology at the University of Memphis (formerly Memphis State University.) He is a speed bag *master*, and through him I watched and learned. His book "Boxing Skills", published by Regmar Publishing, 1973, had a chapter dedicated to the speed bag. As a member of the first M.S.U. boxing class, I pestered "Doc" at least a thousand times to "...show me how you did that again.." And he always did.

Today he is retired and sailing the seven seas. A teacher, friend and great practical joker, he always said "...if you know something, pass it on." Well, Doc, I'm trying. On behalf of the original "Schroeder's Raiders", I dedicate this book to him.

a master at work

Grand Master Kyong Sik Song, of Dallas Texas, is a master of three major martial art styles, Tae Kwon-Do, Hapkido and Kung Fu. He is also a "Moo Sa", which is a weapons expert. I began training in his system, Oriental Heritage Total Concept (O.H.T.C.) at the age of 34. He guided my training over numerous physical challenges (surgeries), enabling me to attain the rank of Black Belt in Hapkido. As a Grand Master of the Martial Arts and licensed acupuncturist, he is dedicated to teaching the right way of the martial arts. He has also authored numerous books about the martial arts. On behalf of my entire O.H.T.C. family, I also dedicate this book to him.

There are numerous other people to thank who were instrumental in producing this book. My wife Elizabeth (Libby) took almost every picture that appears. I also acknowledge several of my speed bag students who kept encouraging me to "..put it in writing". Also, thanks to my friends Joe Franco, drummer extraordinare, for creating my demonstration music, and John Brown, Ringside Boxing for his help and guidance.

My doctor once told me I wasn't suppose to live this long, and now it seems to take a lot of them to keep me going. I want to thank neurosurgeon Dr. Michael Dorsen M.D, of Austin Texas, and neurosurgeon Dr. Marcial Lewin M.D., Orthopedic surgeons Dr. Brett Miller and Dr. Bill Berryhill M.D. , all of Waco, Texas ...for continually fixing all the parts. Also, Mr. Lynn Glass, LAT, ATC of HealthSouth Sports Medicine Clinic, for the many hours of encouragement and patience. Also, thanks to Dr. Douglas Tippen, M.D., Ph.d. for being a great work-out partner and good friend. Cure Cancer, Douglas - I dare you. Last, I must recognize Mr. Doug Heir, esq. National, World and Olympic Champion and the "*world's best overall wheelchair athelete*", for your friendship and the inspiration to "follow your dream."

If not for the people above, this book would not have been finished . Thank you all!

CONTENTS

Now in the Third Printing!

contents

contents

INTRODUCTION

The speed bag is normally associated with the sport of boxing, where it is often shown in a boxing related interview, movie or training program. And it has been a staple in boxer training facilities for hundreds of years. But it has also shown up in health clubs, fitness facilities and basements or garages of many homes. Unfortunately, there is not much information available on *how it works*, and the "secrets" of its use are pretty much passed by word of mouth, one user to another. But not everyone has access to an *experienced* user who can, or will, take the time to teach. I am amazed at the number of fitness facilities I have visited where the equipment is available…but no one, staff or patrons, really knows how to use it. What is it for? How many striking "techniques" are there? How are they named? What is the best method to progress from a beginner to advanced ability? This book was developed to answer all these questions.

BENEFITS of Speed Bag training

Speed bag training offers a variety of benefits. By its very design, it is 'hit' by the fists and elbows smoothly and repeatedly in flowing combinations which **increases eye-hand coordination**. The bag is often going faster than you can "see and react" to, so direct eye control is reduced and your swinging movements must become automatic, which **increases rhythm and timing**. You have to put your hand at the correct spot or you will miss. Learning to target and hit the moving bag **helps develop hand speed**. To keep the bag going at a constant rate of speed also requires using **equal and controlled power (or force)**, with no wasted motion, (swinging harder or faster changes the bag speed and reduces your control.)

Besides the previous physical skills, there are some obvious fitness benefits. The actions of doing this require the user to hold the arms and hands up for extended periods of time, **building shoulder & arm strength and endurance**. This in turn helps to **shape, tone and define the muscles** involved. Punching repetitively for a length of time, such as 3 minutes can have **cardiovascular benefits**, taxing the heart and lungs, and often leave you winded. With practice, you can extend this to 15 minutes or longer, helping to **increase aerobic capacity**.

And one of the greatest benefits is the "experience" of using it - or the *training experience* itself! Like a "hanging drum" It allows the user a vast amount of **creative capability**. With a little practice, you can develop all kinds of different rhythms, allowing for **a great deal of self-expression**, exactly as though you are playing a set of drums. The hypnotic beating of the bag, peppered with accents and afterbeats, can be an artform. With proficiency, you can execute various fist-elbow combinations, blending them into a fascinating workout and listening experience, both alone and too music. No other exercise equipment allows for as much **free expression** and **enjoyment during use** as the speed bag. In fact, my own personal journey through this began as a frustrated drummer trying to get a workout! Now I creatively rock with the hotest music out there, just like I am in the band. With a little practice - you can too!

Who can benefit from Speed Bag Training ?

Of course, these benefits are important to combatant sports (boxing, martial arts), and self-defense. But they are also vital to a lot of other people who will never step into the boxing ring. In fact, I think it is one of the most unique physical training devices ever invented, for the competitive athlete, the non-competitive athlete, the fitness enthusiast, (especially home based fitness programs..), and the physically challenged or disabled.

If you are an **ATHLETE**, and play any sport that requires you to put your hands rapidly at a point in space to hit, catch, or block a moving object, (such as a moving ball, fist or foot...), you can benefit from regular speed bag training. These actions often require split second timing, quick and accurate, (even automatic), reactions. The speed bag will fine tune your reaction time, which translates to *all* sports. It will also help you learn to keep your hands up in the a "ready" position. Affected sports include the "big 4" of basketball, football (american), baseball and volleyball, as well as: Handball, Softball, Lacrosse, and all racket sports (tennis, racquetball, ping-pong). Simply put, If you "get in the game"- speed bag training can help you play better.

For the **FITNESS ENTHUSIAST**, the speed bag gives a tremendous upper body work-out. It can build strenth, endurance. It shapes and tones the muscles of the shoulders and arms. It has aerobic and cardiovasular benefits. It can be a super "high rep" warm-up, or finish to your regular work-out. Like other exercise, it can help burn fat, expend energy and melt away unwanted pounds. With understanding you can "modify" several aspects of your training, and manipulate the benefits to suit your own purposes, such as emphasizing "muscle strength" training, or "speed" training, or a "high rep/cardiovascular" session. Of course, many training benefits overlap. And the speed bag is a simple, cheap and effective fitness activity, easily adapted for the privacy of your home, which also effects the next group.

For the **DISABLED OR PHYSICALLY CHALLENGED** looking for an in-expensive home activity to increase, maintain or re-gain their upper extremity coordination, strength, endurance or sense of accomplishment, the speed bag is an excellent choice. I think it is a secret weapon in the field of rehabilitation, because it has great potential in this area. It is beneficial for people in a wheel chair, because **it is not necessary** *to stand to hit a speed bag. It works perfectly well sitting down.* Also, The visual movement of the bag and auditory sounds can offer valuable cues for people with neurological or movement disorders, to help guide and maintain more fluid, rhythmic control of movements. And - let us not forget stress reduction! Punch the bag a few times, and let off a little steam.

About this book

This book (and videotapes) is the result of personal journey by a confessed speed bag fanatic. First, I wanted to completely understand how it works, and master all the punching and elbow-striking techniques. Second, I wanted to develop a method to teach all of this to someone else.

But an effective teaching method...one that did not focus on me (or the individual teacher) to be present, was elusive. Often students found it difficult to remember the order of the fists and elbows within the different techniques. Another problem centered on explaining sometimes complicated physical skills that are most noticeable perceived by sound and rhythm. You must hear the results of your efforts.

The answer was born when I began visualizing the speed bag less as a piece of exercise equipment and more as its musical cousin-the drums, an instrument I played for many years. The method I have developed and used in this book is directly related to the teaching method for playing the drums, which has a well defined path of training progression. Let me briefly describe this similarity. When you begin the drums, you will need the "striking instruments"...the 2 sticks. For the speed bag, we have two fists and two elbows. Drum students learn basic sticking techniques-known as *rudiments*, in the order of simple to complex. Similarly for the speed bag, we will cover 24 separate striking techniques, from simple to complex. Finally, the drummer will learn to read musical rhythms which will guide him through practice exercises that teach each sticking rudiment, and then how it is used with all the previous rudiments.

These written practice exercises will guide him through all the sticking techniques. For the speed bag, I created an abbreviated representation (symbol) for each technique that shows exactly which parts (fists or elbows) are hitting the bag, and the exact order of their contact. Skill-by-skill, I have laid out practice exercises that will teach you each technique and how it is used. I have even included the number of rebounds between techniques as well as the rhythm counting method. When needed, I have included some "secrets" to make things easier. Through a gradual course of skill acquisition, I will guide you to the point of complete improvision. Speed bag mastery is not as difficult as it looks!

How to use this Book

I wrote this book with the intention of developing a complete and *comprehensive* guide to training with a speed bag. Think of it as an ENCYCLOPEDIA. Whether you only want to develop a few basic skills for an occasional work-out, or you are a speed bag fanatic (as myself), desiring to reach complete understanding and total mastery, this book will help. But….it is not "light reading" or something you can breeze through. With each technique you learn, the combination possibilities multiply. So do the numbers of practice exercises offered and time you may need to practice. Only *you* know your level of ability and what you want to gain from this book, so I offer the following advice:

Everyone, of any level or experience:

Regardless of your present ability, *please at least read chapter three concerning how the techniques are named and abbreviated.* In 25+ years of using the bag, I have never seen "standardized" names for the techniques. So, if you have different names for the striking movements, you will need to understand *my* symbols to make sense out of the written exercises. The little time you spend with this chapter will save you lots of time trying to figure things out later.

For The Experienced Speed Bag User:

If you already have the equipment and basically understand the rhythm of the speed bag, than you might skip chapters one and two. If you know several techniques already, then quickly scan the "skills" chapters and look to find skills you do not recognize. But be sure and read the sections about LINKING techniques on different sides of the bag, because many of the practice combinations use linking symbols to indicate when the fists "pass through the bag" to hit from another side. Linking is discussed more and more, from chapters five through nine. (The more techniques you know, the more linking possibilities there are.) As you learn more and more you can go back and fill in anything you skipped… but I hope you do not waste several work-outs trying to figure out something in chapter nine that was thoroughly developed in chapter five or six. The written exercises are the key to your advancement. Even if you are excellent on the speed bag, you will need a certain amount of ability to tackle the written exercises in chapter 10 (advanced skills) and chapter 11 (echo combinations).

For The beginner with no experience:

Take heart! You have no bad habits to unlearn, so you can begin the correct way right from the start. For total understanding and fastest results read all the preliminary information found in chapters one, two and three. (If you do not have your equipment yet, be sure and read chapter one.) Start learning the techniques in chapter four and work through the exercises one-by-one in the order given. I developed all the practice exercises **specifically for beginners**. Each written exercise only includes the new skill, and those previously learned. The accompanying text will oftentimes discuss specific fist movements and *"secrets" to making things easier*. Jumping ahead will more than likely be very confusing. **There is also an optional beginner work-out *"guideline"* on page 32, outlining the easiest way to get started.**

Learn at your own pace. After learning a few new techniques, relax and hit for fun. After a while, or a few work-outs, pick it up and try a few more techniques or practice exercises. There is never a shortage of things to learn on the bag. Technique chapters four and five may seem the most difficult because almost everything is new to you. Chapters 6-9 will build on the earlier information. But you will be drawing a crowd long before that! Also, look through chapter 13, "teaching" to pick up a few extra learning tips that may help. *(After you go through chapters four and five, you may want to try your hand at hitting to music, which is discussed in chapter 11, page 165. It adds a lot of creative variety to your work-out.)*

For Martial Artists:

Martial artists usually want to work various attacking movements together in combinations of two, three or four at a time. These training needs differ from "regular" speed bag striking, (where the object is to keep the bag going in a non-stop, continuous manner…sometimes for 15 or 20 minutes at a time.)

If your are NOT familiar with the speed bag, (and many are not) than at least read chapters two and three, to get a basic background of how the speed bag works and how I write techniques and combinations. After that, chapter 12, "Special Training and Martial Arts" is focused on your training needs. I have offered many practice exercises *specifically* for martial art techniques. These include various punches, open hand techniques and kicking. Once you understand the method used for showing combinations, you will quickly get up to speed. **WARNING: This chapter is intend for *trained* martial artists. If you are not a martial artist, and have not had proper instruction in the techniques shown in chapter 12, please do not attempt them.** *This is especially true for kicking*.

For Coaches & Trainers

If your main focus is teaching or coaching others on the speed bag you will need to know the facts about rhythm and technique execution, but you do not have to be a great practitioner yourself. Read chapters two and three carefully and scan all the technique chapters (4-9). For helping advanced students, you will need to be familiar with the topics covered in the "advanced" chapters (ten and eleven). Chapter 13 is especially for teaching and gives some inside tips on what problems to look for, what causes them and how to overcome them. If you are also a martial arts instructor, then also see chapter 12.

You do not have to use this entire book to get the benefits you want from hitting the speed bag. You can get a great work out with just a few techniques.

Chapter 1

Speed Bag Equipment

Introduction:

Three separate pieces of equipment are needed to use a speed bag; a rebound board, a swivel attachment, and the bag itself **[FIG 1A]**. Most of the time, they are initially purchased together as part of package deal. They can be set up in a couple of ways, either attached to a wall or on a freestanding frame. I will address each of these later in the chapter. But first, there are some important factors to know about each piece, and a little planning before you setup your equipment can save lots of maintenance headaches down the road.

Rebound Board

The rebound board (sometimes called the "drum") is usually a piece of wood at least 24in x 24in, which holds the swivel and allows the bag to bounce. Industrious types can make their own out of plywood or solid board and some angle iron for the hanging brackets. Inexpensive rebound boards tend to be of light weight pressed wood. For better performance, add a 1/2 or 3/4 inch piece of plywood to the top (this can be seen in FIG 1A, over the top of the black board.) A heavier board holds up better, especially with larger bags - and will not rattle as much. They also yield a softer, lower sound, which is an integral part of the training experience.

Fig 1A Speed Bag Equipment

Whatever kind of board you use, there are a few important features to consider when hanging it. The first is the height of the board. You need the belly of the bag about level with your mouth. You will find it is best to attach the swivel (next section), place a bag on it and hold it up to the wall. Then extend it up until the belly of the bag is in the correct position, and mark the wall. This sets the board for your height with that size bag. (A later section will address attaching the wall brackcts.)

Another important factor of the rebound board is making sure it is level with each adjustment. An uneven board can interfer with the pace of the bag. Place a level on top of the board or under the bottom when you slide it up in the adjustment brackets, which allow 8-9 inches of change. Also, it is best to have the end of the board extend beyond the end of the rebounding bag. (see section on *Speed Bags* .)

Safety is also a concern. Do not allow <u>anyone</u> to swing on the board. Beside the fact that the person can get hurt when it (and the wall) comes down on their head, it can really mess up your board!

Once the board is properly hung, upkeep is pretty easy. Keep a set of wrenches around to snug up the bolts before each use. They often work loose. Make sure it is tight and does not vibrate. Excessive vibration kills the natural rebounding of the bag. Always make sure your "rebound" surface (the under part of the board) is smooth. Any chips or protrusions can damage the bag or leave splinters in you hand. Also, when hitting the bag, do not lay anything on top of the board. Because of vibration it will soon be on your head. A larger board is shown in Fig 1L.

Swivel

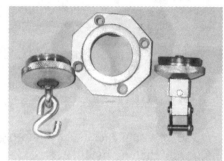

Fig 1B Swivels

The Swivel is the attachment point of the bag to the center of the board. They come in several types **[Fig 1B]** ; the ball-hook (seen on the left) or universal hinge with 360° ball bearings (chain link style) seen on the right. Many people favor one or the other type, but only advanced practitioners can tell any difference in swivel performance. Both are fast and efficient, but the ball-hook type makes changing bags easier. The bag can also fly off the end if mis-hit, so I recommend putting a narrow piece of tape over the opening to keep it on. The ball-hook is also the *loudest* of all, so if you noise is a concern you might want another type.

It is often difficult to attach or detach the speed bag to the most chain-link styles, so they are great for places where bag theft may be a concern. And they are much quieter. Newer models are variations of these **[Fig 1C]** and have some different types of methods to both attach a bag and allow its movement.

Fig 1C   Newer Swivels

Swivel choice is a matter of preference or availability. I am often asked which type I personally prefer, and the answer is the ball-hook. In my own experience (and opinion) it gives the truest rebound angle *when punching from all sides* non-stop (not just the front.) It is the only one that does not seem to influence the bags rebound due to its own mechanics. The chain-link swivel occassionally seems to influence (change) the rebounding angle of the bag which causes problems when hitting from all sides. The bag also seems to "float" along the bar of the newer swivels, especially if mis-hit slightly. This can influence bag speed and create timing problems. Again, this is mostly when hitting from all areas, especially sideways. One last point about swivel choice is brand interchangeability, or *lack of it*. The threaded parts of one brand most likely will not fit the other. Most attempts to <u>*make* them match up</u> may result in ruining them both. Because of that, I often buy swivels in pairs.

<u>The swivel is the site of most wear, tear and repair</u>. The best swivels can be broken down into two pieces...one part, the swivel base, (the center circular piece with four holes in it) that stays permanently attached to the board and the other part that can either remain hanging on the board, or be unscrewed to keep with the bag. BOTH pieces can cause problems so a little planning here can help avoid aggravating repair jobs later.

The site of swivel base-to-board attachment is the *number one site of problems*. I strongly recommend that you attach the swivel to the board with long bolts that pass through the rebound board and fasten on top. <u>*Do not*</u> use screws that may come with the board or swivel. This area endures all the board vibration and the force of your punching. Screws will eventually come loose and soon this process will strip the screw holes. Retightening will become a constant event. Bolts will solve this problem. The swivel bolts can be seen on top of the board, directly over the swivel, in FIG 1A.

The moving portion of the swivel, either the ball-hook or chain link, can also cause problems. If it is threaded and screws on to the base attachment, then be sure to screw it very tight. It can vibrate loose and unscrew, causing "play" in the swivel. Any play in the swivel kills the natural bouncing of the bag…even worse than a loose board. During a workout, if all of your skills and control seem to disappear, check the swivel. Something is loose. So keep a pair of vice-grips handy. Also, the constant banging of the ball-hook against the housing may eventually wear down the housing. If this piece is threaded and screws on to the part attached to the board, then it is easily replaced. Some economical speed bag "package deals" found in most department stores include a ball-hook swivel. They are usually made of very soft metal, and do not seem to last long. As the ball beats against the housing, the housing will wear and be pushed back. Eventually the ball-hook will fall out and you will need to purchase another swivel. I recommend you avoid this swivel, and purchase a profession model as shown. Cheap swivels always come back to haunt you, and many a speed bag workout has been foiled by a swivel problem. ☹

Swivel upkeep usually involves occasional tightening of the bottom piece and light lubrication of the ball-hook. Do not use a gummy grease because it will slow down the movement, not speed it up. Use a light weight machine oil sparingly. Too much will drip down the swivel onto the bag and your hands.

Speed Bags

A *Speed bag* is actually made up of two separate parts. An external leather covering and an internal air-bladder **[FIG 1D]**. They are connected together at the air nozzle on the bottom. Generally, we should not see the air-bladder unless we have a problem, which will be discussed in a later section.

Speed bags come in an assortment of shapes and sizes. The 13" x 10" and 12" x 9" are among the largest and require more punching force to move and keep them going.

Fig 1D Bag & Bladder

The middle sized bags such as 11"x 8" or 10"x 7" are best for learning because they offer sufficient speed yet they are easier too control. They are also more forgiving of mis-hits than the smaller ones.

The smallest bags, 9"x 6" or 8"x 5" and especially the 7"x 4" are lightening fast and extremely difficult for learning. they are best left for the experienced user.

Several of these different speed bag sizes and shapes are shown in **[FIG 1E]**. The two <u>middle bag sizes</u> were used in this book. The larger 11"x 8" is the size for all the *technique* photo's. The front cover and action photo's in the advanced chapter feature the 9" x 6" size bag.

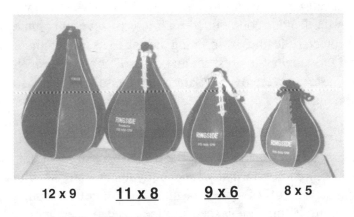

12 x 9   <u>**11 x 8**</u>   <u>**9 x 6**</u>   8 x 5

Fig 1E Different Size Speed Bags

A beginner should start on a mid-size bag (11x8) for they offer good control but will not hurt the hands with extended use. For training purposes, the larger bags are better for strength and endurance. The smaller bags really focus on speed and coordination. Photo **[FIG 1F]** illustrates the relationship between bag size and purpose. Note the dramatic difference in size (you sure will in speed…).

Some bags have an external "welted" seams, which is a raised bead down the bag, and some do not. Seams do not effect performance but the external seams can hurt bare knuckles .

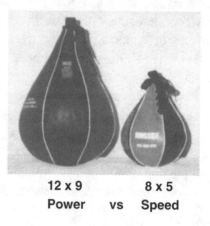

One of the most important features about the bag is adjusting it to the proper height for the user. This can be a major roadblock to advancement. *Struggling to use an improperly adjusted bag has probably caused many people to give up in frustration*. **The belly of the bag needs to be even with your nose or mouth**. It is usually OK to have the bag slightly *higher* than it needs to be, but over an inch or so can ruin your swing motions. With the bags in FIG 1F a full three inches of board adjustment may be needed to properly align the bag if changing

12 x 9   8 x 5

Power vs Speed

Fig 1F Bag Focus

from one to the other. I do not recommend standing on tip toes to hit a bag that is too high, or bending into a half-squat to hit one that is too low.   (**see "teaching" chpt-13, for more on bag height problems**.)

Fig 1G 11 x 8

You may also need to consider the size and sturdiness of your board when selecting the proper bag. An 11 x 8 bag will reach the end of a 24-inch diameter economy board **[Fig 1G]**. The larger bags will extend past the end of this board. This can damage the bag and interfere with proper rebounding. If you want to use the larger bags, consider getting a 30 or 36 inch board.

Speed Bags are a hardy piece of equipment and can usually withstand many powerful punches. It is also excellent for martial art kicking techniques. However, do not allow anyone to idly blast away at it as hard as they can. I have seen people throw a punch at a speed bag with so much force that their momentum carried them into the bag, which smacked them right in the face. This always draws a reaction from any casual observers.

Care for the external leather covering is very important. Never hit it with hand jewelry of any type (including wedding rings), or watches. It can instantly damage your bag, the jewelry or your hand. Keep it dry and wipe off any perspiration. This can cause your hands to slip off (particularly in elbow striking techniques.) After a workout, you can keep the leather conditioned with any of several commercially available oils or creams. You can also help protect the leather by inflating the bag to its proper air-pressure level, which is usually printed on the bag. Slightly lower air-pressure makes it softer and slower. Slightly more air-pressure makes the bag harder and faster. Severe over-inflation will cause the leather seams to pull apart or rip open, as well as damage the bladder .

A small hand pump is all you need for inflation but do not push the needle in too vigorously, or you may push the air badder knob into the bag. I do *not* usually deflate the bag after each session, because the air valve is a potential site for problems. They do not normally leak, but you run that risk with every push of the needle. Every so often, or if I expect a layoff of a week or more, I will deflate it slightly, or just until the leather creases. Constantly deflating it completely seems to increases the leather cracking.

There is a simple way to guess at the correct pressure if you do not have a guage. Using a hand pump, inflate the bag until there are no creases and the leather is smooth. With both hands, squeeze the bag with the thumbs. It should "give" and bend in slightly to medium pressure. When you punch it at medium speed, you should also feel it give when the fist connects. The bag should *not* feel rock hard and the seams should not be straining or pulled apart. Air-bladder protrusions are caused by constant over-inflation.

Air-Bladder Problems

The air-bladder inside the bag can be a source of problems. It may develop a leak from the air-valve or a pinhole in the rubber. It can also suddenly rip open. It is usually easy to tell the difference. If the bag has a leak, then it will inflate but slowly go soft. Air valves are notorious for this. Sometimes you can even hear the air escaping, and feel it either at the valve hole or through a seam. A pinhole leak can be patched. A major rip - or blowout - usually occurs on a punch, and the bag goes flat instantly. (You run this risk with an extremely over-inflated bag.) A ripped bladder will not inflate. If the air-valve is leaking or if the bladder is ripped you have to replace the bladder with a new one.

All these problems can be repaired, but prepare for a little work. The bag must be totally deflated, and the front lacings undone to get inside. A leather "tongue" covers and protects the top of the air-bladder. Pull it up and peel back the leather, exposing the air bladder. If a pinhole is located on the flat rubber surface (…and usually it is **not**), you can use a rubber patch. But if the hole is located on the *bladder seam*…(which it usually is…) forget about patching it. Since the bag is now open, just replace the bladder. This may have to be ordered, since most department or sporting good stores do not always carry speed bag bladders. To replace it you must dig down and remove the air-valve stem, which is usually attached to the bottom of the bag by a knob. (If it was not, the valve stem would sink inside when the needle is inserted.) Remove this, and attach the new bladder to the bottom of the bag. Be sure the valve is seated correctly and sticking out the hole at the bottom of the bag.

Fig 1H Inflate Bladder

Regardless of whether you patched a leak or installed a new bladder, fill it slightly *before* lacing the bag up **[Fig 1H]**. Check and make sure all is well. Otherwise you have to unlace the whole thing again.

Fortunately, these problems do not occur very often, and most bladder problems are caused by repeated over-inflation. But just in case, *I usually buy several bags at a time* when they are on sale. Properly maintained, with surprisingly little care, your speed bags can last for years.

Gloves & Hand Wraps

Hand protection is very important. As an avid speed bag user, you may spend 30 minutes or more each day hitting the bag. The hands bear the brunt of all this repetitive contact and they are the site of most injuries. Injuries (addressed in chapter 2) usually center around "sore hands", or broken, bleeding skin over the contact areas on the knuckles. If you are a speed bag novice, you are particularly vulnerable.

There are several options for hand protection, either gloves or hand wraps **[Fig 1i]**. Both are recommended for unconditioned hands, particularly if striking a bag with either plastic or leather external

beaded seams. Gloves are the easiest method and there are several types of speed bag gloves available. Your choice is a matter of personal preference. Purchase a set that have some type of padding to offer some shock absorption. (I have seen people use a cheap pair of cloth or cotton gloves, but these do not have padding and offer little protection.) If you use a pair of the popular "training" gloves (usually used for lifting weights), look for a pair with <u>soft</u> leather and <u>no seams</u> over the contact areas. I like a few types of weight training gloves that have an attached wrist support strap. Some training gloves have a solid steel bar in them, laying across the palm. The bar is suppose to help build shoulder endurance and give something to grab and maintain a tight fist. It does not effect the bag unless the bottom of the gloves wear out and the bar protrudes. Then it can damage your bag.

Fig 1i Gloves and wraps

"Hand wraps" are another method of protection, but are a little more troublesome because they take more time to get on and off. They also tend to get loose, particularly over the fingers, and may have to be rewrapped. (I actually prefer wraps because they bind tighter and keep the small hand bones from jarring so much. The cloth covering also protects the skin over the knuckles.) The most common brands have some type of thumb loop and self adhesive bindings to secure them. The technique for wrapping your hands is not so important for speed bag practice. Put your thumb through the loop and *begin the wrap across the back of your hand* **[Fig 1J]** . This helps draw it tight when you make a fist.

Next, extend your fingers and make several wraps around the hand and knuckles. Make sure to cover the fingers to the center knuckles, especially the little "pinkie" finger. It does not have to be as professional as for extended heavy bag use of more serious contact training. Pull the wraps snug but not so tight as to cause pain or cut off circulation. I prefer hand wraps for short workouts. For the photo's in this book I did not wear wraps to better emphasize the fist position and contact points.

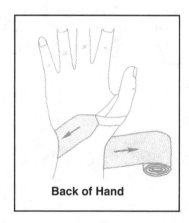

Back of Hand

Fig 1J Start hand wrap

The Home Set-Up

One of the greatest benefits of the speed bag is that it is perfect for a home workout. All the equipment can usually be purchased for less than $100.00. When planning the workout area, keep in mind that a speed bag set up comes in two main "styles". First, there is one that attaches to a wall or second, a free standing bag stand. There are pro's and con's to each type

Probably by far the most popular is the type that attaches to the wall. These are great for garage areas, as shown in **[FIG 1A]**, or a spare room **[FIG 1K]**. They take up less space (no floor area) and are the most stable. Most wall setups have two sets of brackets. One set attaches to the board. (shaped like a "U") and a set of slotted steel brackets that attaches to the wall by three long screws The 'slot' allows for 8-9 inches board height adjustment

Hanging the Wall Mounted Rebound Board.

These brackets (and the wall) support all the rest of the equipment. They **MUST** be attached to studs or framing in the wall. Butterfly bolts in the sheetrock will not support the weight or vibration. The "economy" speed bag frame and holes in the board are usually made for wall studs set on 16 inch centers. They are light enough to be set directly on the wall, but I recommend protecting the wall with a wood frame. You can do this by running 1x4 boards either vertically or Horizontally, as shown in **[FIG 1K]**.

The vertical frame requires *two* boards, each slightly longer than the black vertical hanging slots. There are three screw holes in each metal bracket.

The horizontal frame is best if the studs are not standard 16in. *Three* boards (one for each screw hole) need to be about 52 inches long to span 3 studs.

You may first want to determine the *lowest point* of adjustment you want for board. Do this as earlier described

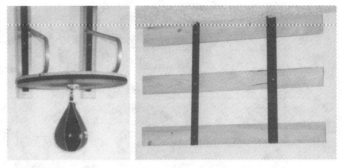

2 - Vertical   3 - Horizontal

Fig 1K Wood support Framing for hanging brackets

with the board and bag. This will generally correspond to the bottom hole on the wall bracket. *Be sure to allow enough adjustment for different size bags or height of other people. (Remember, as you get better you will probably go to a smaller faster bag.)* In a room with an 8 foot ceiling, I always put the top of the boards up against the ceiling. Make sure everything is level, and all screws and bolts are tight.

Of course, there are heavier-duty professional models available, often with easy board height adjustment **[FIG 1L]**. These usually weigh quite a bit more and require a very strong wall. They are often placed on center support columns or concrete walls. These may be overkill for the home area, but health clubs or locations with high volume usage are better off with this type of equipment.

Free Standing Frame

Fig 1L Heavier duty platform

The second option for the home workout area is a free standing frame **[FIG 1M, pg 8]**. These can be purchased either individually as shown, or as a package feature along with a heavy bag. They are ideal if (1) there is no place for a wall unit or (2) there is no place for a heavy bag, and you want to use one of these also. These are excellent for apartment dwellers, since they are portable and do not put holes in the walls. There are a few drawbacks to these free standing units. First, located on the floor, they take up more space. Also, they are usually fairly tall and require free space all the way to the ceiling. Along with this, they are prone to sway, or "react" to the bag being hit.

However, this model has some unique characteristics that make it ideal for certain types of training that might otherwise be very difficult or impossible with a basic wall unit. For instance, these floor units usually have more height adjustment, which can bring the bag either up and down to more extreme levels of height very quickly. This makes it a reasonable choice for locations with a wide variety of people, including very tall adults as well as small children, or persons in wheelchairs.

Floor units need some type of weight to hold them steady, especially over the board. I have found a method to help by using two or three common luggage straps with a ratchet adjustment mechanism. I prefer the type with end "S" hooks, which can attach into the angle iron of the stand **[collage]**. First set the board to the height you want. Then, from the center piece of angle iron just over the board (the board is usually attached to it), hook one strap in and go down to the left base (floor) unit. Do the same to the right base unit. Tighten both equally until there is no slack in the straps. These help hold the board and greatly reduce sway. For additional support, another strap can be used down the tall vertical frame pole.

Fig 1M Free Standing Frame   **Fig 1M** Secure standing frame with straps

Rehabilitation & Speed Bag

You do not have to stand up to hit a speed bag and it is an excellent activity for upper body range of motion and eye-hand coordination for those who may be physically challenged or temporarily disabled. It is also financially more feasible than most "rehabilitation" equipment. For people in wheelchairs, hanging a wall frame *lower* is an alternative, as well as using a free standing frame. Hitting the speed bag can even be performed with someone actually supporting the arms up under the elbows, or moving the forearms and fists (see "Teaching" chapter.) It may be especially useful in movement disorders that respond to an external visual or auditory stimuli to help guide and smooth out tremulous or spastic movement.

Proper installation, adjustment and use of your equipment will reward you with years of trouble free service and enjoyment. Improper setup may completely retard your progress, perhaps even causing you to quit. It can cause aggravating and expensive repairs, or worse, cause personal injury. Do not take any piece for granted. For several equipment adaptions for advanced workouts, please see appendix A.

Several photographs in this chapter were furnished by Ringside, inc. I am very appreciative of their support. Ringside inc. may be contacted at: Ringside Inc. , P.O. Box 14171, 9650 Dice Lane, Lenexa, Kansas, 66215   phone 1-877-4-Boxing.   I am proud to have them distribute The Speed Bag Bible.

CHAPTER 2

Stance, Swing, Rhythm & Contact

Stance

The "classic" speed bag stance has the front of the body open, facing the bag. The elbows are raised out from the sides, upper arms almost parallel to the floor [Fig 2A]. Dropping the elbows will almost assuredly bring your hands down and make them arrive late on a punch. Anchor the hands close to the face; fists at the outside corner of the mouth or chin.

Ideally, adjust the height of the rebound board so the "belly" (fattest part) of the bag is about level with your mouth (usually just below the brand name). It can be slightly higher or lower with higher being the better of the two. Distance yourself so either striking arm is bent at the elbow upon striking, yet be far enough away so the bag will not strike your nose on the rebound. (Don't laugh; it happens to almost everyone occasionally.)

Fig 2A   Basic Stance & position

Punching Motion

The speed bag is fixed to the swivel in the center of the board. Although it bounces all around the swivel, its position stays fixed. We must move around to bring the fists and elbows into the bag at the right moment. Because of this, our body (chest and shoulders) will sway left and right, in and out, to set up for the next technique. I find it helpful to view all techniques in their relation to our chest. Generally, all punches and elbow strikes will be moving either "in" toward the center of the chest, or "out" from the center of the chest. The arms and legs work together in an easy flowing pattern that makes each technique motion automatically set up for the next technique. Let's look at the general movements of the arms and legs separately.

Holding the elbow out in the proper position, the fists move in small circles from the elbow; between eye and chest level only. As the fists move we will rotate the body, especially the shoulders, so we can lean "into" each technique. The elbow strikes are powered by the shoulders quickly circling in a short, crisp movement ending with the fist at eye level. Always hit the belly, or fattest part, of the bag. When moving, it is best to connect the bag while it is angled slightly away from the straight position.

Footwork

The feet shuffle; shifting forward, sideways and backwards slightly to help bring the body into alignment. Most of the leg motions will be from the knees. Generally, a knee will bend "in" when the *same side fist* strikes in toward the chest. For example, when the right fist moves "in" toward the chest, the right knee will bend in also. (The "inward" knee motion is a lot like the action of the back leg when swinging a baseball bat). Continuing, the knee will straighten as we punch "out", or away from the center of the chest. Normally, one knee is bending while the other is straightening out. You will also notice some swiveling of the hips as you move. Most people quickly "feel" the correct arm and body motion after a few techniques and begin shuffling "to the beat", like dancing.

Every step or shuffle should feel comfortable. If the motion does not feel right....it's not. Do not fight it. The general motions of the fists will be described for each technique in this book, along with the knee movements when needed.

The speed bag yields instant reinforcement to your technique. A crisp, sharp sounding rebound and bag movement occur after a correct strike. A poor technique yields a weak sounding rebound and the bag does not go in the intended direction, or squirts off circling around the swivel. Late punches strike the bag from the bottom in an upward direction, easily detected by the metallic sound of the swivel being driven upwards. Sometimes, if we are really "off", the bag will come flying off a ball-hook swivel. Slow hands may be caught by the rebounding bag.

"Breakdowns," or loss of control, invariably occur as part of the learning process. Most are caused by a few basic swinging errors, which include: "pawing" the bag in an up and down motion, rather than striking into it. People who "paw" the bag usually do not move their feet or body, but stand riveted in one place staring rigidly at the bag. "Giant swingers" do just the opposite. They swing the arms in exaggerated movements or over-rotate the body. Over-swinging adds more force and the bag races out of control. A "half-moon" swing results when only one-half of the punch is made. The hand stops below the bag at stomach or waist level, and is then quickly re-circled for the next strike. Unfortunately it is either late or too fast. These problems mostly stem from a few basic causes: The hand position dropping too low, usually due to sinking elbows **[Fig 2B]**, and the swing trying to compensate, or lack of the proper body motions. Also, hard swinging invariably causes breakdowns. Universally, the remedy is proper position, correct swing mechanics; and slowing down. Never try to go fast! Control is the key. Once gained, speed follows automatically. It is similiar to driving a car. No one learns to drive at 90 mph, and the speed bag is not learned by hitting hard or fast.

Fig 2B Elbows
too Low

Rhythm 101

Speed bag emphasizes speed and rhythm. Individual techniques link these together in fascinating combinations but speed and rhythm are separate entities. First, **bag speed** is detemined mostly by the force of your striking. The harder you punch, the faster the bag will go. But trying to punch hard will create larger wasted motion, and your fists will not keep up with the bag. *You never want to try and keep up with the bag, but rather have the bag be controlled by the speed of your fists*. We do not have to punch <u>hard</u> to keep the bag going a good speed. We want to punch "fast" with short, crisp fist motions. Fast fists can deliver great power in short distances. The key to this is **control**. Small circular movements will give more control and develop faster striking ability, which will result in very powerful strikes. With practice, this becomes a smooth, relaxed movement.

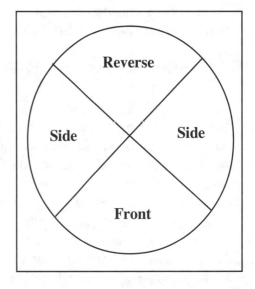

Fig 2C Areas of the Speed bag

Second, **rhythm** is mostly determined by direction. The bag can be hit from different "areas" and travels in any direction around a 360° axis **[Fig 2C]**. It rarely bounces exactly front-to-back or side-to-side, but varies depending on the general direction of contact; and here lies the *secret*. The most important factor concerning rhythm is "the direction of the NEXT strike." A strike coming from the <u>same</u> direction as the last one will always occur after an odd number of bounces; either one, three or five. Three is the usual and five is great for learning. Three bounces, or rebounds, between strikes produces a very definite sounding "triplet" rhythm. This triplet rhythm can be counted as "**1-2-3**...**1-2-3**...". A strike coming from the <u>opposite</u> direction of the last one must occur on an even count, either two or four.

Many advanced combinations change direction several times. Individual differences can occur if a strike comes from a slightly different angle, imparting a different direction to the bag. For example a fist entering from the "side" may contact the bag closer to the "front-side" border, or on the "rear-side" border. The resulting angle of rebound (...path the bag travels) is much different for each one of these points. When this happens, the next technique *may* follow after EITHER an even (two) or odd (three) number of rebounds. But....it is all under your control. Actually, this does not happen very often, and I will alert you to the these situations. Most people pick it up easily.

Of course, the most fascinating aspect is the rhythmic "beat", or sound of the bag slapping the board. This is called a rebound and there are definite accents in the sound. The bag slaps the rebound board much louder just after the fist connects. The rebounds that occur while the bag is *swinging* (in between the techniques) are softer. Accents differ according to the techniques used, but normally the <u>last</u> strike in a technique is the loudest. When going slow, you can count the rebounds (or...the "beat") as the bag slaps the board. This often helps in learning new techniques or combinations and I often include this "count" underneath the written exercises. Direction changes create "stutters" in the rhythm, like musical syncopation. Put all this together and the speed bag generally makes *two different types* of rhythms. One, is *the triplet rhythm*...(as mentioned above) when the bag is hit from the same side. The second type, called *the double bounce rhythm*, has a definite "**1**-2-**1**-2" driving beat, caused by "...the next strike" coming from the opposite side. These accents and interbeats allow for <u>the most unique aspect</u> of speed bag training...individual self expression through the rhythms you create. As we learn the different techniques, you will hear the various rhythms of the bag. (In chapter 11, we will even play with this "beat" to *create* specific rhythm patterns, called *echoing*, as well as discuss ways to hit the bag to music!) With practice, the speed and rhythm of the bag will be directly under our control, never the other way around.

The speed bag is not hit by sound alone. When hitting, you will notice that the moving bag creates "after images" and the faster it goes the more images appear. You can not pick out the bag fast enough to hit it when it is moving. The secret is to deliver the fist or elbow to the exact point underneath the swivel at the right time. Focus the eyes in the center of the non-moving bag, which is the general striking area. You will soon learn how to focus the eyes, but when all else fails, swing at the one in the middle!

Contact Areas on the Fists and Elbows

Normally when we punch something we hit with the *front* of the fist and make contact over the large knuckles of the hand. When punching a speed bag, we will not only punch straight to the front but we will also punch in various different directions around a spherical bag. We will hit the front of the fist as well as other areas around the hand. The different points of contact on the fist are shown in **[FIG 2D]**. It does not matter if you are wearing gloves, hand wraps or hitting bare handed, the contact points will be over these areas. It is not necessary to maintain a strongly "clenched" fist when hitting the speed bag. The hand should be closed tight enough to keep the fingers touching the palms, but not much tighter.

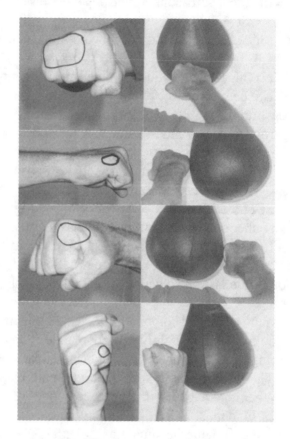

The size and movement of a speed bag gives many opportunities to use the elbows as a striking surface. They can easily be added into a speed bag routine, and there are numerous elbow striking techniques included in this book. There are two general points of contact between the elbows and the bag **[FIG 2E]**. The back, or tricep side of the elbow contacts the bag when the elbow is swung in

Fig 2D Fist Contacts on Bag

an "Outward" or "Downward" direction (top and bottom pictures). The forearm point of the elbow hits the bag during an "Inward" moving elbow strike (center photo.) The bag may hit on the exact point of these surfaces or vary a little in either direction.

Training Injuries...("oh, my aching hands")

The speed bag is one of the safest training devices around, but there are a few injuries that seem so common that they can almost be expected. The repeated poundings on the hands will take some getting used to. Most injuries, thankfully, are minor but knowing what to expect,-what causes the problem and how to correct it is the best defense. Sore hands and skin abrasions are the most common injuries and they often occur together. Both are usually the result of several correctable situations.

During even a modest speed bag work-out, the fists hit the bag hundreds of times. The small bones in the hands are jarred repeatedly in punching, especially when contacting the *sides* of the hands,

OUTWARD

INWARD

DOWNWARD

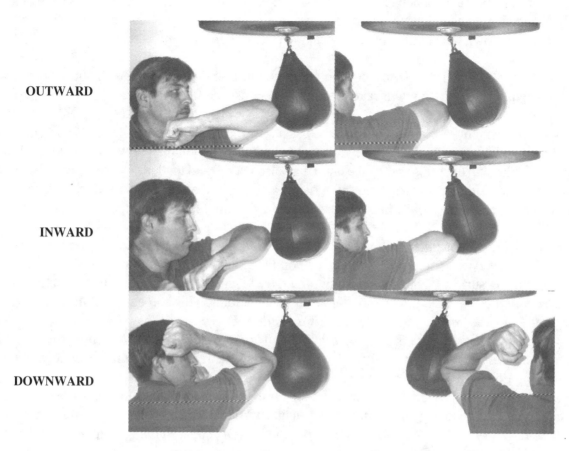

Fig 2E Elbow motions & contact points on Bag

which happens a great deal when punching a speed bag **[FIG 2D]**. Many of the striking techniques make contact on the large knuckle of the little finger, and all reverse and side techniques make contact on the large knuckle of the index finger. The hand, even when clenched in a fist, has very little support to protect from forces in these directions. The best prevention is to give support to the bones by wrapping the hands or wear gloves. (Gloves do not support the bones, but they do absorb some of the punching force.) Punching with a "loose" fist, (fingers not touching the palms) adds to this problem. This is often seen on the speed bag. Try not to let the fists go loose between punches. The biggest cause of sore hands is punching too hard. It will take some experience to punch _fast_ rather than hard, and all the excess force goes into the bones of the hand. (Oddly enough, I have seen people improve because of this condition. When training with sore hands they will not hit as hard, because their hands hurt, and they learn to punch without a lot of excess force. I do not recommend this method, however.)

Another cause of sore hands <u>and</u> skin abrasions (shredding the skin) is an over-inflated bag. The more air it has, the harder it is. Repeatedly smacking a rock hard bag iis asking for injury. Also, the fist often _slides_ on a hard bag. You will not necessarily feel it, but when this happens repeatedly, it will shred the skin on an unprotected hand. You will notice slightly reddened abrasions over the large knuckles, especially those shown in **[FIG 2D]**. They will burn, which is the first warning sign. Repeating beatings will expand this deeper until it begins to bleed. Now it is an open wound, directly in the area of the most bag contact. Even worse, it will get bigger **fast**. If it gets to this point, not even gloves will protect the wound and you are looking at a week or more for healing. These wounds can really hurt. Not only when you train, but when you do everything else! Protecting this from infection is very important. Get it treated quickly and let it heal.

Another factor that leads to these injuries is the type of bag you use. Generally, I have found genuine calfskin or kangaroo leather to be much more forgiving than vinyl. But, calfskin leather bags usually have an externally beaded, or "welted" seam which is sometimes plastic and sometimes leather. The leather seams will get beaten down flat, but the plastic ones do not. I prefer the leather seams.

One last factor that can lead to open cuts on your knuckles is poor punching technique. Swinging in an up and down half-moon motion will rake the knuckles across the face of the bag, not punch into it.

Besides these hand maladies, you may run across a few other annoying problems. If you practice a lot of reverse punching, and especially sideways techniques, you may have the wrist area around the thumb to get sore. The skin over this area of the hand may also get red and tender. This usually goes away with time. Reverse and side techniques bend the wrist at an awkward angle as you swing back toward yourself. That is one reason why I like handwraps, since they can tighten around the wrist for support.

When practicing a lot of elbow techniques, you may find the skin areas around the elbow can break down much like the knuckles of the hand. Particularly on Downward Elbow Strikes, which tend to slip the elbow down the bag surface rather than push in directly. Downward techniques will also contact the fist on the *middle joint* of the little finger, not the large knuckle joint. This can get painful. Be sure and protect this area. *One little known potential injury as a result of Downward Elbow Strikes is to the nose of someone wearing eyeglasses.* **The thumb of your fist moving in the downward direction can (…and will) contact your glasses.** **Take them off**. I will always add a reminder of this prior to practice combinations using downward elbow movements.

The elbow techniques, particular the outward-elbow strikes, can give the shoulders a real stretch. If you have any type of chronic shoulder injuries, particularly rotator cuff problems, be sure and warm up *completely*. A re-injury here can stop you training for months. (Of course, It is a good idea to go through a complete whole body warm-up before physical training of any type.)

Most of these conditions are minor and should not cause real problems, unless you continue to do what is causing them. *Punching through the pain usually causes more pain.* And they can occur at any level of ability. Even after thirty years of continuous speed bag usage, if I do not hit for several weeks and then give it a good two hours, my hands will get sore. (Perhaps I should have given it a good twenty minutes, but I am a speed bag fanatic. When the urge hits, I may stay under the board for hours at a stretch. When I forget to wrap my hands I usually end up regretting it.)

Martial Artists can look for a few other types of problems, because the open hand techniques (Ridge Hand and Knife Hand Striking) have the fingers extended. You must keep the fingers firmly together in these techniques, or the fingers will get banged together with great force. The speed bag is a great place to learn how to do these techniques properly.

In summary, knowing what can cause injuries, and how to prevent them is important. The hands will take a certain amount of training to become adapted to repeated speed bag work-outs. We are not asking them to hit something one or twice…but thousands of times in the course of regular training. Sore and aching hands need help. The best treatment for any of the above is rest and protection.

Chapter 3

TECHNIQUE NAMES AND ABBREVIATIONS

One of the most difficult things for most people to determine on the speed bag is the difference between a "technique" and a "combination". When viewing an experienced practitioner hit the bag everything runs together. Where does one technique stop and another begin?

TECHNIQUES AND COMBINATIONS

A technique is one independent striking skill that can be made in one smooth motion. Since we have two fists and two elbows, a single technique may include up to all four parts in the motion. There are techniques that use one fist, both fists, a fist and an elbow, both fists and one elbow, or both fists and both elbows. The key to all this is the number of rebounds that occur. Within a **technique**, the bag will only rebound <u>once</u> between the connecting parts. Any time two or more rebounds occur before we hit the bag again, it is a combination. **Combinations** are created by performing techniques with two or three rebounds in-between them. This is often difficult to determine on a moving bag.

I have developed a method of naming and representing speed bag techniques which immediately tell you what happens to make a technique. Their names will indicate (1) The area of the bag struck (front, back, side), (2) the striking parts, (fists or elbows), and the order in which they hit, (3) the number of striking parts (single, double, triple or four), and (4) the direction of elbow movement (out, in or down), when necessary.

When only the fists are used the technique is a **"punch"**, and the name tells both the area of bag struck and the number or fists contacting the bag. As an example, the "Front Double Punch" means both (double) fists striking from the front, and the "Reverse Single Punch", means a single (one) fist striking in the reverse (back of bag) position. Whenever the fists are "rolling" over each other the technique is called **"Fist Rolling"**, and the area of the bag is given. As an example, "Front Fist Rolling" indicates a fist roll to the front of the bag.

When a technique includes an elbow hitting the bag, it is <u>always</u> called an **"Elbow Strike"**. The name will also include both the <u>direction</u> of the elbow movement and the number of striking parts. As an example, the "Outward-Triple Elbow Strike" tells you the elbow motion is outward from the center of the body, and three (triple) parts will strike the bag. Likewise, a "Downward-Double Elbow Strike" refers to the elbow striking the bag in a downward direction, with two parts (an elbow and fist) striking the bag. In this manner, you can always remember how the elbow moves, and how many striking surfaces make contact in the technique.

Every technique will be fully described by explanation and photographs. Also, the abbreviated name of the technique will be given. I have broken down each technique name into an abbreviated symbol which precisely mirrors the technique name, the parts striking <u>and</u> the exact order of the fists and elbows contacting the bag. It's important to understand this simple method of abbreviating the techniques, for they are used to develop the practices exercises.

TECHNIQUE ABBREVIATIONS

R (FSP)

Fig 3A

Each technique abbreviation has two lines and some, when needed, have three. The following examples will simply illustrate how they work. **[Fig 3A]** demonstrates the right hand performing a "Front Straight Punch". Notice the "**R**", for right arm, on top and **(FSP),** which is the first letters from <u>F</u>ront <u>S</u>traight <u>P</u>unch. The top line <u>always</u> refers to the arm used, either left or right. The technique name is <u>always</u> in parenthesis.

As another example, **[Fig 3B]** refers to the left arm performing an "<u>O</u>utward-<u>S</u>ingle <u>E</u>lbow <u>S</u>trike". The top line (L) reflects the "left arm" and the technique name abbreviation is **(O-SES).**

L (O-SES)

Fig 3B

L-R (FDP)

Fig 3C

Double punches, which use both fists, are shown in **[Fig 3C]**. The top line "L-R" reflects both arms and the order (left-right) that they connect. The **(FDP)** indicates the <u>F</u>ront <u>D</u>ouble <u>P</u>unch.

Other techniques use <u>both</u> an elbow and fist. In this case, a third, or bottom, line is added to reflect the <u>exact order</u> that the elbow and fist strike the bag- as shown in **[Fig 3D]**. This represents the <u>L</u>eft arm (top line) executing the <u>O</u>utward-<u>D</u>ouble <u>E</u>lbow <u>S</u>trike (middle line). The bottom line, (e-f) indicates the order they contact the bag, first the Left <u>e</u>lbow, then the Left <u>f</u>ist. It isn't necessary to use more than one "L" in the top line.

L (O-DES) e-f

Fig 3D

More complex techniques utilize an elbow and <u>both</u> fists striking the bag. In this instance, the top and bottom line combine with each other and reflect both the <u>arm and the part</u> connecting, as shown in **[Fig 3E]**. The middle line **(O-TES)** reflects the technique name, <u>O</u>utward-<u>T</u>riple <u>E</u>lbow <u>S</u>trike. Notice the top line "L" (left arm) is over the bottom line "e" (elbow). The next "L" aligns over the "f" (fist). The slash (\) in both lines indicates an arm change and lastly the "R" (right arm) aligns over the "f" (fist). These accurately reflect the "left elbow, left fist then right fist" order of striking the bag.

L-L\R (O-TES) e-f \ f

Fig 3E

As a final example, **[Fig 3F]** displays an "<u>O</u>ut and <u>D</u>ownward **4 way** Elbow Strike **(O-D 4way)**. The top and bottom line precisely show the order of contact, With "Le" meaning Left elbow and "Lf" for left fist. The slash "\" in both lines (arm change), then "Re" indicating <u>R</u>ight <u>e</u>lbow and finally "Rf" <u>R</u>ight <u>f</u>ist.

L-L\R-R (O-D 4way) e-f \ e-f

Fig 3F

This system of visually displaying techniques allows you to quickly understand how each technique is formed and executed. Every new striking skill will have its abbreviation used in the practice exercises that follow, showing how to use that technique alone and in combination with previous ones.

Practice Exercises for combinations

Each technique has practice exercises written to help you learn how to use that technique with all the other techniques. The more techniques you know, the more combinations are possible. These exercises are simply lines of technique abbreviations put together in sequence. However, there are several other symbols or abbreviations used to show you exactly what is happening. For instance, the bag rebounds off the board every time it is struck. A **rebound** is defined as every time the bag hits the board. The number of rebounds is important for learning and I indicate each rebound that occurs with the symbol ('). For instance '' indicates two rebounds, and ''' indicates three rebounds. A sample combination could be written as:

```
        L       R      R-L       L-L\R
     (FCP)'''(FSP)'''(FDP)'''(O-TES)
                                e-f \ f
```

This combination has four techniques. A <u>Front Circle Punch</u> (FCP) by the left hand (L, top line), followed by the <u>Front Straight Punch</u> (FSP) by the right fist (R, top line), followed by a right-left (R-L, top line) Front Double Punch (FDP), followed by an <u>Outward-Triple Elbow Strike</u> (O-TES), created by striking with the Left-elbow, Left fist, Right fist. (Le,-Lf \ Rf, top and bottom line.) There is three rebounds (''') between these four techniques.

One quick glance at the written abbreviations shows how much more efficient this method is than the five line paragraph needed to describe it. In this way I can also highlight various physical "mechanics" or key features to help you understand. I will repeat the same exercise below to demonstrate:

```
        L       R      R-L       L-L\R
     (FCP)'''(FSP)'''(FDP)'''(O-TES)
                                e-f \ f
      1-2-3              1-1-2-3  1-1-1-2-3
```

[Here the differences in type appearance lets me show some important points in this combination.] ...Notice the (FDP), and how the *second fist* (larger **L**) returns to lead the next technique (O-TES), and the elbow (**e**) makes first contact. It helps to bring the left fist under and past your right ear to get into position to do this. Also, notice the count line underneath. The bolded (**1**) are the fist or elbow contacts on the bag and the larger underlined (**1**) are the loudest, most noticeable rebounds....

Once you develop skill with the techniques and understand the abbreviations, then you will quickly become efficient at reading the exercises. As we progress through more and more techniques, (from all sides of the bag) there are many key points, or *secrets* I will point out to make it easier. As you learn to hit the bag, I also want you to be able to create your own combinations. At that point, this method of writing speed bag techniques and combinations will help you record what **you** create. Think of it as writing rhythm music. I encourage you to take the book with you to your practice area if you need help remembering different techniques.

This Book was written as a "workbook".
Keep it by your speed bag and use it as a
guide for your workouts.

PRACTICE TIPS

The practice exercises are the only way I have of expressing physical skills (techniques) that are occurring very fast on a rapidly moving target. The actual physical movements are not that difficult when learned **slowly**. It is very important to get the feel of the "*Basic Rhythm*" and motions of the bag. Once you do, you will be able to practice <u>all</u> of the techniques and exercises while looking at this book <u>without</u> the bag! That is what I mean by **slowly**. Simply visualize the bag about a foot in front of your nose, put your arms in the ready position and move your arms and body in the exact punching motions. With practice you will also "hear" the rhythm it makes. Or do this in front of a mirror and use the point of your nose as the target. You can even count the beats as they hit. Your friends and neighbors may think you are a little nuts waving your fists and elbows around in front of your face, but this simple practice method is <u>always available</u>,...and it works. It easily lets you feel the exact motions needed for the techniques and combinations. Lastly, it also lets you practice at *your own speed*, not the bags speed, which is usually too fast for learning....especially if you are a complete beginner.

<u>Abbreviation Review for Practice Exercises</u>

Top Line	**L** or **R**	Arm used. Always Left or Right.	L-L\R
Middle Line	**(First Letters)**	Abbreviated Name of Technique	**(O-TES)**
Bottom Line	**e** or **f**	<u>e</u>lbow or <u>f</u>ist	elbow-(e) Fist-(f)
Rebounds	**'**	Each time bag hits the board	''' = 3 rebounds
Count line	**1-2-3....**	Counting the "beat" of the bag on board.	
Linking Symbols	[1/2] or [8]	indicates fist(s) changing sides of the bag.	

Chapter 4

Seven Beginning Techniques

This chapter will focus on four fist punching techniques and three elbow striking techniques that are performed from the front of the bag **[Fig 4A]** and flow together smoothly in combinations. The four punching skills are the "Front Circle Punch", The "Front Straight Punch", the "Front Double Punch", and "Front Fist Rolling". The three elbow strikes are the "Outward-Single Elbow Strike", "Outward-Double Elbow Strike", and "Outward-Triple Elbow Strike". Many speed bag practitioners will learn most of these without special instruction. These seven skills are often seen in demonstrations or in the movies. When learned equally well with either arm leading, they can created hundreds of different rhythm striking combinations. As we learn each technique and its abbreviation, several practice exercises will demonstrate how it is used. Following the practice exercises given with each skill, you will quickly learn to flow from one to another. To make it easier I have included the number of bag rebounds (') after each punch. Also included underneath is the counting rhythm used. Count the fist striking as "one". Let's begin our speed bag training by learning these techniques in there natural progression.

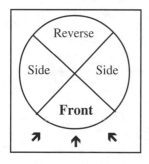

Fig 4A   **Front Area**

The Front Circle Punch (FCP)

The Front Circle, represented by (FCP), is the easiest repetitive punch to learn and is the most often used entry and exit movement to more advanced techniques. You will find that this movement always "circles" your hand back to the start position **[Fig 4B-1&2]**.

Start from the ready stance, and elbows held out from the body-even to the point of parallel. The (FCP) is performed by making a very small circle with the fist from its start position just below the eye, striking the bag on the <u>outward point of the large knuckle</u> of the little finger, and returning to the start position. This movement should be initiated from the <u>elbow</u>, not the shoulder. Lean into the punch slightly by placing the shoulder of the punching arm a little closer to the bag and placing the weight on the same side leg.

Fig 4B-1   **Front Circle Punch**

19

As an example, the right shoulder will lean into the bag and you will straighten the right leg while shifting your weight on it.

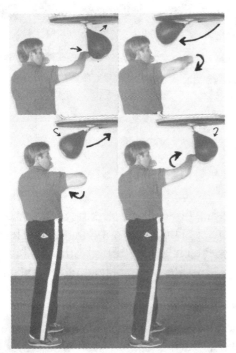

Fig 4B-2 Front Circle Punch

The first rebound off the fist will sound louder (more accented) than the others and a noticeable "**ONE**-two-three, **ONE**-two-three" triplet rhythm is heard. The bag will move away from your fist striking the rebound board for the first and loudest bounce, then bounce toward your face and strike the board for the second bounce. It will then bounce back to the other side for the third and softest rebound, with the fist making contact again on "one". You will soon *feel* this repetitive triplet rhythm. It is the foundation from which all other rhythm variations grow. This is a smooth, non-stop movement. Perform it <u>slowly</u> and softly at first.

#1 One fist separately

       L   *L*   *L*   *L*
(FCP)'''(FCP)'''(FCP)'''(FCP)....change hands
count   *1*-2-3   *1*-2-3   *1*-2-3   *1*-2-3

#2 Alternating fists

     L   *L*   *R*   *R*
(FCP)'''(FCP)'''(FCP)'''(FCP)....Continue
count *1*-2-3 *1*-2-3 *1*-2-3 *1*-2-3

#3 Continually alternating fists

     L   *R*   *L*   *R*
(FCP)'''(FCP)'''(FCP)'''(FCP)....Continue
count *1*-2-3 *1*-2-3 *1*-2-3 *1*-2-3

Front Straight Punch (FSP)

Represented by (FSP), this is the next most commonly used punch and approximates the classic straight right cross in boxing. Starting from the ready stance, slightly rotate the right shoulder back, creating the proper angle of attack, and aim the front of the fist directly into the bag. The fist will move across your face

Fig 4C Front Straight Punch

as it moves to the target, and will strike the fist on the <u>front</u> of the last two or three knuckles. Lean slightly into the speed punch by bending the same side knee in toward the bag [**Fig 4C**].

This is best done by swiveling in on the foot and raising the heel slightly off the ground, which will bend the knee. (As an example, for a Front Straight Punch by the right fist, the front of the right fist moves toward the bag as you swivel on the ball of your right foot, slightly lifting up the heel an bending the right knee.) See **[Fig 4C]**   Practice exercises include:

#1 Each fist separately

      R   *R*   *R*   *R*
    (FSP)'''(FSP)'''(FSP)'''(FSP)…..Change hands
count   *1*-2-3   *1*-2-3   *1*-2-3   *1*-2-3

At this point, the fist must "circle back" to the start position, creating a Front Circle Punch (FCP). If this is followed, quite naturally with a (FCP) by the same fist (right in this example), then the left shoulder will automatically rotate into the proper angle for a left straight punch.

As described above, the (FSP) and (FCP) universally follow each other in a very rhythmic motion. The body easily leans with and into each movement as you shift your weight from side to side. The fists should always be up and in front of the face. It is vital that the entire motion of the fists be executed smoothly at the same speed. The fist performing the punch is <u>always</u> moving. It only pauses momentarily (and always around the chin level), when the other fist is moving. The natural body movement always sets you up for the next punch in the sequence. The next practice sequence combines these two techniques.

#2 FSP and the FCP together

     R   *R*   *L*   *L*   *R*   *R*   *L*   *L*
** (FSP)'''(FCP)'''(FSP)'''(FCP)'''(FSP)'''(FCP)'''(FSP)'''(FCP) **
    1-2-3 *1*-2-3 *1*-2-3 *1*-2-3 *1*-2-3 *1*-2-3 *1*-2-3 *1*-2-3

** These two movements and the rhythm they make are the <u>BASIC RHYTHM</u> **[Fig 4D-1&2]**

Fig 4D-1 The Basic Rhythm

The count is always a triplet "**1**-*2*-*3*" with the fist connection on "**1**" being accented. The legs will usually straighten on the Front Circle Punch and bend with the Front Straight Punch. The majority of the weight shift occurs as the Front Circle Punch connects the bag.

Common mistakes are over-swinging the arms, swaying the body too much, hitting too hard or fast, and pausing the fist too low (caused by dropping the elbows to close to the body). In Fig. 4D-1&2, the punching pattern began with the Right (FSP) and followed a RRLL sequence. This could also be written beginning with the Front Circle Punch as:

R   L   L   R
(FCP)'''(FSP)'''(FCP)'''(FSP)… Or a RLLR sequence, and it still indicates the same *Basic Rhythm* pattern. This is important for all new skills will be **entered** from this rhythm and only the <u>last</u> punch before a new skill, either the (FSP) or the (FCP) need be identified. Also, all new techniques will **exit** into this rhythm and only the <u>first</u> punch of the Basic Rhythm needs to be indicated.

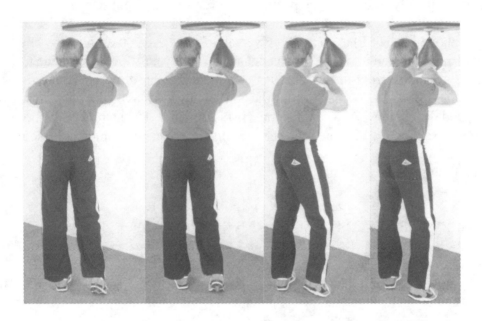

Fig 4D-2 The Basic Rhythm from behind

Mastering this sequence is an important key on the speed bag. This basic punching pattern can be varied by using several (FCP)'s in succession. Several practice rhythms to learn this are written below.

R   R   L   L   R   R   R
(FCP)'''(FCP)'''(FSP)'''(FCP)'''(FSP)'''(FCP)'''(FCP)…continue

L   L   L   R   R   R   R   L
(FCP)'''(FCP)'''(FCP)'''**(FSP)**'''(FCP)'''(FCP)'''(FCP)'''**(FSP)**…repeat.

Practice with these until you can easily break into a smoothly flowing LL-RR basic rhythm pattern at any time in the sequence, from either (FSP) or (FCP). It may be easier to learn by counting the rebounds as you practice but you should quickly feel this rhythmic tempo.

From this point the counting underneath will not be written in every practice exercise but only when needed to emphasize the rhythm. The (') to indicate bag rebounds will always be used.

The Front Double Punch (FDP)

The Front Double Punch, represented by (FDP) is a double striking technique in which both fists strike the bag with only one rebound inbetween. It is performed by circling both fists into the bag almost at the same time. The motion is similar to throwing a left and right Front Circle Punch together, or a left Front Circle and right Front Straight Punch together. The key factor is the distance between the fists and moving <u>both fists together as one motion</u>. This is not two separate movements. The bag is struck by the leading hand on the large knuckle of the little finger, and makes only one rebound before the second (or following) fist strikes **[FIG 4E]**.

The bag may strike the second fist on the large knuckle of the little finger <u>or</u> the front of the last two or three knuckles. This will

Fig 4E Front Double Punch

create two noticeable louder rebounds, with the second accent slightly louder than the first. When done correctly, the last (or second) fist to strike the bag naturally ends up in front. After the Front Double Punch, the bag will rebound 3 times before the next punch.

Several practice patterns are:

#1 From Basic Rhythm, same arm leads the FDP

$$L \quad \textbf{\textit{L-R}} \quad R \quad L \quad \textbf{\textit{L-R}} \quad R$$
Basic LLRR…(FSP)'''**(FDP)**'''(FCP)'''(FSP)'''**(FDP)**'''(FCP)…repeat
count   *1*-2-3   *1*-**1**-2-3   *1*-2-3

Notice how the (FDP) naturally follows the (FSP) and that the last fist to strike the bag "**R**" in the (FDP) quickly circles back to re-strike the bag. Also notice the larger "**1**" in the count line under the (FDP). This indicates the loudest sounding rebounding within the technique.

#2 From Basic Rhythm, alternating lead fist of FDP

$$L \quad \textbf{\textit{L-R}} \quad R \quad L \quad L \quad R \quad \textbf{\textit{R-L}} \quad L \quad R \quad R$$
Basic LLRR..(FSP)'''**(FDP)**'''<u>(FCP)</u>'''<u>(FSP)</u>'''<u>(FCP)</u>'''<u>(FSP)</u>'''**(FDP)**'''(FCP)'''(FSP)'''(FCP)..repeat

Notice the 4 single punches, <u>underlined</u>, or basic rhythm, between the (FDP)'s. This naturally changes the leading fist of the double punch. In the previous patterns, the (FDP) occurs after a (FSP) but it can also be performed after a (FCP), as we will see in the next sequence.

#3 Changing the lead hand of FDP *with only one punch between*

$$L \quad \textbf{\textit{L-R}} \quad R \quad \textbf{\textit{R-L}*} \quad L* \quad \textbf{\textit{L-R}} \quad R \quad \textbf{\textit{R-L}} \quad L$$
Basic LLRR…(FSP)''' **(FDP)**'''(FCP)''' **(FDP)**'''(FCP)''' **(FDP)**'''(FCP)''' **(FDP)**'''(FCP)…basic

To this point only one fist, the <u>last</u> fist of the FDP, (**R** & **L***) re-circled back to the bag for a single punch. For the next sequence, both fists will re-circle in a continuing fashion.

#4 Continuous Front Double Punching, changing lead hand

$$L \quad \textbf{\textit{L-R}} \quad \textbf{\textit{R-L}} \quad \textbf{\textit{L-R}} \quad \textbf{\textit{R-L}} \quad L$$
Basic LLRR…(FSP)''' **(FDP)**''' **(FDP)**''' **(FDP)**'''(<u>**FDP**</u>)'''(FCP)…Basic

Again we see the *last* fist of the (**FDP**) leads the next technique. The smooth changing of the fists in front of the face occurs automatically and the second fist ends up slightly lower than the leading fist. Practice the above exercises until you can perform the (FDP) anytime in the basic pattern leading with either hand.

Front Fist Rolling (F-Roll)

This skill, represented by (F-Roll), is the fastest sounding of all striking techniques. From the ready position step closer into the bag with one leg, <u>overlap</u> the fists about an inch and simply roll them over each other in continuous "front circles". Do not be afraid to step in close, because your fists are up protecting your face. The bag will be angled toward the back of the board. *The secret is to keep the fists in close to the face so a "V" pocket is formed by the angle of the elbows to the fists* **[Fig 4F]**. The elbows must be kept high…even slightly above parallel. As the fists circle each other, the bag will strike the large knuckle of the little fingers, or the side of the hand. It should not strike the wrists. Any mis-hits will be directed into the center of the "V" pocket.

Fig 4F Front Fist Rolling

The rotating fists connecting after one rebound create a very fast sounding "machine gun" effect. In this technique, the "leading" fist is the first fist in the rolling sequence, and the "exiting" fist is the last fist written over the roll. Each has a different effect on the counting method, so I have added some extra help in identifying them by making the fist under discussion **<u>underlined</u>** in the top line. Exiting the fist roll is a little more difficult than beginning it, because we must retreat back a step or the bag may catch the nose (OUCH!).

When you exit this technique, the bag will rebound three times before the next strike. Several practice rhythms are:

#1 <u>Same hand</u> leading and exits a Front Fist Roll after the Front Circle Punch

R	R	R	<u>**R**</u>-L-R-L-<u>**R**</u>	R	R	R	**R**-L-R-L-**R**	R
(FCP)'''	(FCP)'''	(FCP)'''	**(F-Roll)**'''	(FCP)'''	(FCP)'''	(FCP)'''	**(F-Roll)**'''	(FCP)...change leading hand

count   *1*-2-3 *1-2-3-4-5*-2-3   *1-2-3-4-5*-2-3

To identify the leading and exiting fist, note the larger "<u>**R**</u>", for the right fist appears at the beginning and end of the fist roll. When the <u>same</u> fist enters and exits, an odd number of bounces (5) occur in the Roll, as indicated by the bottom counting line, and you can count them as they hit. This makes it easy to know when to exit....and "retreat" a step back. Do it when the last fist ("5" in this example) connects. Also, the last fist connecting in the roll may be slightly louder then the others (the larger **5**). It is important to notice that the "exiting" fist circles back for the next technique, in this example a (FCP). This occurs naturally.

Fig 4F **Front Fist Rolling Sequence**

#2 from Basic Rhythm, same hand leading and exits after the Front Straight Punch.

	<u>R</u>	**R**-L-R-L-**R**	R	L	L	R	**R**-L-R-L-**R**	R
Basic LLRR...	(FSP)'''	**(F-Roll)**'''	(FCP)'''	(FSP)'''	(FCP)'''	(FSP)'''	**(F-Roll)**'''	(FCP)....

count   *1*-2-3 *1-2-3-4-***5***-2-3

After the (FSP), the right fist (<u>**R**</u>) leads into the Fist Roll. The initial motion is the same as a Front Circle Punch, but both fists move into the fist roll. Also, notice the RLLR basic rhythm inbetween the fist rolls. In #1 and #2 the (F-Roll) followed <u>*either*</u> the Front Circle Punch or the Front Straight Punch.

The last two exercises exited the fist roll with the same fist that began it. Now let's exit the Roll with the <u>opposite</u> fist. This is be done after an *even number of rebounds* as seen in the count line.

#3 from Basic Rhythm, <u>opposite</u> hand exits.

R   **R**-*L*-*R*-**L**   *L*   *R*   **R**-*L*-*R*-**L**   *L*

Basic LLRR…(FSP)'''**(F-Roll)**'''(FCP)'''(FSP)'''**(F-Roll)**'''(FCP)…repeat

  count   *1*-*2*-*3*   *1*-*2*-*3*-**4**-*2*-*3*   *1*-*2*-*3*-**4**-*2*-*3* *1*-*2*-*3*

Here we see the right fist (larger **R**) began the roll and the left fist (larger **L**) exited after four rebounds. Once again the last fist connecting in the roll may be the loudest. Notice how the Fist Roll easily fits into the basic rhythm pattern with only two punches between the rolls.

In reviewing the above three exercises, the fist making the last single punch <u>before</u> the Fist Roll started, or leads into the Roll. It is also possible to use the other fist to begin rolling.

#4 Opposite hand leading into Roll.

L   **R**-*L*-*R*-*L*-*R*   *R*   *L*   **L**   **R**-*L*-*R*-*L*-*R*   *R*   *L*

Basic LLRR…(FCP)'''**(F-Roll)**'''(FCP)'''(FSP)'''(FCP)'''**(F-Roll)**'''(FCP)'''(FSP)..repeat

Notice the left Front Circle Punch "**L**" is followed by the opposite "**R**" right hand to begin the Roll.

With the above four practice patterns, we can now enter or exit a Front Fist Roll with either hand. Remember several things about the Front Roll…first, you always <u>exit</u> with the same fist which began the Roll on an odd count and exit with the opposite fist on an even count. With practice, you will not have to count. Second, the last fist in the fist roll almost always circles back to lead the next technique. Also, I have used 4 & 5 bounce fist rolls due to space. You can perform the fist roll for as long as you wish. Try and work this technique up to at least ten or more continuous rebounds.

The next techniques will begin to use the elbows. Before beginning the Elbow Strikes, let's look at several combinations using **all** <u>the previous fist techniques together.</u>

#1 Front Double Punch-to-Front Fist Rolling

L   *L*-*R*   ***R*-*L*-*R*-*R***   *R*   *R*-*L*   ***L*-*R*-*L*-*R*-*L***   *L*

Basic LLRR…(FSP)'''(FDP)'''**(F-Roll)**'''(FCP)'''(FDP)'''**(F-Roll)**'''(FCP)…BASIC

#2 Front Fist Rolling-to-Front Double Punch

R   ***R*-*L*-*R*-*L*-*R***   *R*-*L*   *L*

Basic LLRR…(FSP)'''**(F-Roll)**'''(FDP)'''(FCP)….repeat

#3 Continuous Front Double Punch-to-Front Fist Rolling

R   *R*-*L*   *L*-*R*   ***R*-*L*-*R*-*L*-*R***   *R*-*L*   *L*-*R*   ***R*-*L*-*R*-*L*-*R***

Basic LLRR…(FSP)'''(FDP)'''(FDP)'''**(F-Roll)**'''(FDP)'''(FDP)'''**(F-Roll)**…

Outward-Elbow Strikes

The next easiest group of *front* techniques to learn are the Outward-Elbow Strikes. They are called this because they have the elbow moving "outward" from the center of the chest into the bag. There are three Outward-Elbow Striking techniques and they follow and easy progression of movement.

Outward-Single Elbow Strike (O-SES)

The Symbol for this technique is (O-SES), and refers to the elbow moving outward from the center of the body. Only the elbow will hit the bag, which will bounce three times before being struck again.

It is performed from the ready stance by bringing the fist across the face and close to (or under) the opposite ear. You will feel some torso rotation in this action and the shoulder of the striking arm will be in closer to the bag. At this point your elbow is just in front of your nose **[Fig 4G]**. Direct the point of the elbow into the bag by making a small outward motion from the shoulder. The bag makes contact just above the elbow joint on the upper arm. The leg of the same side will straighten and your weight will shift to it as the elbow connects on the bag. The striking arm stays bent and the fist stays close to the body so it will not strike the bag. The key is to make the striking motion from the shoulder, circling the elbow into the bag. When the move is completed the fist should return to the correct position by your mouth.

Fig 4G   Outward - Single Elbow Strike

Initially, it may be difficult to begin a technique that leads with the elbow on a non-moving bag. So we will use a preliminary "set up" punch before it to establish the rhythm and speed. Begin slowly. Practice exercises include:

#1 Outward-Single Elbow Strike, one arm

```
    R          R          R          R
 (FCP)'''(O-SES)'''(O-SES)'''(O-SES)…Change hands
 Count     1-2-3      1-2-3      1-2-3
```

#2 from Basic Rhythm, Outward-Single Elbow Strike, same arm,

```
             R     R    L    L    R     R    L    L
Basic RRLL…(FSP)'''(O-SES)'''(FSP)'''(FCP)'''(FSP)'''(O-SES)'''(FSP)'''(FCP)…repeat
```

Notice how the right elbow strike simply replaces the right Front Circle Punch in the Basic Rhythm.

#3 from Basic Rhythm, Outward-Single Elbow Strike, Alternating Arms,

$$\begin{array}{cccc} R & R & L & L \end{array}$$
Basic RRLL...(FSP)'''(O-SES)'''(FSP)'''(O-SES)....repeat

Outward-Double Elbow Strike (O-DES)

The next progression from the last technique is the Outward-Double Elbow Strike, represented by (O-DES). It is a "double strike" because both the elbow and the fist will strike the bag with only one bounce inbetween. It is performed exactly as the last technique, except that the fist will be allowed to extend out from the elbow slightly (not all the way) and contact the bag. *The secret to this technique is*

Fig 4H Outward-Double Elbow Strike

to make only one motion from the shoulder and let the fist naturally follow the elbow. It is not a conscious effort and you do not have to swing the arm harder or faster. When done correctly the bag will be hit by the elbow, rebound once and automatically strike the fist on the large knuckle of the little finger (same spot as the Front Circle) **[Fig 4H]**. It will create a double accented sound exactly like the Front Double Punch. You may notice the fist strike has more force than the elbow, resulting in a faster moving bag.

In time you will adapt to this, but to learn the technique do not emphasize the fist movement. Your weight will shift to the straightened leg when the fist connects after the elbow. After the fist makes contact, it quickly circles back to the ready position, about chin level. As usual, the bag rebounds three times before the next strike.

This is the first skill where the third (or bottom) line will appear under the technique name indicating the order of the striking part, both the lower case (e), for the "elbow" and (f) for the fist. Again, we will begin the sequence with a preliminary punch to establish the speed and rhythm. Begin slow and soft.

#1 Outward-Double Elbow Strike, after Front Circle Punch, Same Arm.

$$\begin{array}{cccccc} R & R & R & R & R & R \end{array}$$
(FCP)'''(O-DES)'''(FCP)'''(O-DES)'''(FCP)'''(O-DES)...change arms
    e-f   e-f   e-f
Count   *1-2-3* *1-**1**-2-3* *1-2-3*

Again we see the larger "**1**" in the count line, indicating a slightly louder rebound.

#2 Continuous Outward-Double Elbow Strikes, same arm

R   R   R   R   R
(FCP)'''(O-DES)'''(O-DES)'''(O-DES)'''(O-DES)…change arms
e-f   e-f   e-f   e-f

#3 From Basic Rhythm, Outward-Double Elbow Strike, same leading arm

R   R   L   L
Basic RRLL…(FSP)'''(O-DES)'''(FSP)'''(FCP)…Repeat
e-f

#4 From Basic Rhythm, Outward-Double Elbow Strike, alternate leading arm,

R   R   L   L
Basic RRLL…(FSP)'''(O-DES)'''(FSP)'''(O-DES)…Repeat
e-f   e-f

Note this technique follows a Front Circle Punch or Front Straight Punch of the same arm and easily replaces the Front Circle Punch in the Basic Rhythm.

Outward-Triple Elbow Strike   (O-TES)

This technique, symbolized by (O-TES), is the next technique and is created by simply adding the other fist onto the last technique. It involves slightly more torso/shoulder rotation. As the shoulder turns to move the fist under the opposite ear the other fist moves with it and they stay close together (much like the Front Double Punch). For example, to perform a left leading (O-TES), the left fist comes across to the right ear. As this happens, the right fist stays close, but slightly below, the left fist. With your left elbow in front of your nose and both fists poised at the right ear, **[Fig 4i-1&2]**, execute the double elbow strike motion, allowing the right fist to follow. The leg action is the same as the last technique, and the right knee will bend in with the right fist movement. The bag will strike the left elbow, rebound once into the left fist and rebound once again to strike the right fist. The bag may contact the right fist on the front, similar to the FSP…or it may hit on the large knuckle of

Fig 4i-1 Outward-Triple Elbow Strike

the little finger, similar to the FCP. Again, the third (last) fist may be a little more forceful, sounding louder then the previous blows and adding speed.

You will hear three distinctly accented bounces because three repetitive blows are made with only one bounce inbetween. The fists will make a small circle back into the ready position and the bag will bounce three times before the next strike. The key, as before, is to perform this as <u>one single motion</u> and keep the swing at the same tempo you established with the Basic Rhythm.

Fig 4i-2 Outward-Triple Elbow Strike from behind

Once again, the lower line will indicate the striking part, either elbow or fist.

Some practice sequences include:

#1 from Basic Rhythm, Outward-Triple Elbow Strike, same leading arm,

```
            L      L-L\R      R     L     L-L\R      R
Basic LLRR…(FSP)'''(O-TES)'''(FCP)'''(FSP)'''(O-TES)'''(FCP)…repeat
                   e-f \ f                 e-f \ f
Count              1-1 -1 -2-3   1-2-3
```

Notice how the last fist "**R**" leads the next technique, and the last fist strike "**1**" is the loudest.

#2 from Basic Rhythm, Outward-Triple Elbow Strike, alternating lead arm   (note <u>Basic Rhythm</u>)

```
            L      L-L\R      R     L     L     R     R-R\L      L     R     R
Basic LLRR…(FSP)'''(O-TES)'''(FCP)'''(FSP)'''(FCP)'''(FSP)'''(O-TES)'''(FCP)'''(FSP)'''(FCP)
                   e-f \ f                                     e-f \ f
```

To this point the (O-TES) has followed a Front Straight Punch of the same arm. Likewise, it can also follow a Front Circle Punch of the same arm

#3 Alternating lead arms with one punch in-between

$$L \qquad L\text{-}L\backslash R \qquad R \qquad R\text{-}R\backslash L$$
Basic LLRR…(FCP)'''**(O-TES)**'''(FCP)'''**(O-TES)**…repeat
$$\qquad\qquad \textbf{e-f}\backslash\textbf{f} \qquad\qquad\qquad \textbf{e-f}\backslash\textbf{f}$$

#4 From Basic Rhythm, Continuous Alternating Outward-Triple Elbow Striking

$$L \qquad L\text{-}L\backslash R \qquad R\text{-}R\backslash L \qquad L\text{-}L\backslash R \qquad R\text{-}R\backslash L \qquad L$$
Basic RRLL…(FSP)'''**(O-TES)**'''**(O-TES)**'''**(O-TES)**'''**(O-TES)**'''(FCP)…basic
$$\qquad\quad \textbf{e-f}\backslash\textbf{f} \qquad \textbf{e-f}\backslash\textbf{f} \qquad \textbf{e-f}\backslash\textbf{f} \qquad \textbf{e-f}\backslash\textbf{f}$$

In the Outward-Elbow Strikes we can see that every <u>single</u> elbow strike has a natural addition of either fist(s) or elbow, extending it to a double strike and then a triple strike. By examining the last few techniques, we find that the Outward-Single Elbow Strike (O-SES) added a fist to create the Outward-Double Elbow Strike (O-DES), and then another fist to form the Outward-Triple Elbow Strike, (O-TES). You could see the triple technique graphically as:

(O-SES) + (FDP) = (O-TES)   Or as   (O-DES) + (FSP) = (O-TES)

In either case, we simply added a technique *that was previously learned*. They were combined through timing to create the new skill. This same pattern will be found for all the new techniques to come. This may seem like a meaningless gesture, but it is useful for understanding all the various triple strikes and 4-way combinations. Every one of them combines skills you have already learned.

We have now completed a simple progression of seven striking techniques from a single fist striking the bag, to double fists, to elbow-fist and then elbow-fist-fist combinations. Most of the practice exercises have shown each skill by itself and how it fits into the basic triplet pattern. These skills can <u>all</u> be mixed together in many combinations to create hundreds of interesting rhythms, peppered with single, double or triple accented main beats and after beats. (But these combinations still have three rebounds between the individual techniques.) The different fist and elbow-fist maneuvers make for a very lively and enjoyable workout. Although you can create your own combinations, a few interesting patterns are offered.

$$R \qquad R \qquad L \qquad L\text{-}R \qquad R\text{-}L \qquad L\text{-}L\backslash R \qquad R$$
Basic LLRR…(FSP)'''(O-DES)'''(FSP)'''(FDP)'''(FDP)'''(O-TES)'''(FCP)…basic
$$\qquad\qquad \text{e-f} \qquad\qquad\qquad\qquad\qquad \text{e-f}\backslash\text{f}$$

$$L \qquad L\text{-}L\backslash R \qquad R \qquad R\text{-}L \qquad L \qquad L\text{-}L\backslash R \qquad R$$
Basic LLRR…(FSP)'''(O-TES)'''(O-DES)'''(FDP)'''(O-DES)'''(O-TES)'''(FCP)..basic
$$\qquad\quad \text{e-f}\backslash\text{f} \qquad \text{e-f} \qquad\qquad\qquad \text{e-f} \qquad \text{e-f}\backslash\text{f}$$

$$R \qquad R\text{-}R\backslash L \qquad L\text{-}R \qquad R\text{-}L \qquad L\text{-}L\backslash R \qquad R\text{-}L\text{-}R\text{-}L\text{-}R \qquad R\text{-}R\backslash L$$
Basic LLRR…(FSP)'''(O-TES)'''(FDP)'''(FDP)'''(O-TES)'''(F-Roll)'''(O-TES)…basic
$$\qquad\quad \text{e-f}\backslash\text{f} \qquad\qquad\qquad\qquad \text{e-f}\backslash\text{f} \qquad\qquad\qquad \text{e-f}\backslash\text{f}$$

OPTIONAL BEGINNER WORK-OUT PROGRAM

Although each technique has practice exercises, they are based on the ability to do the techniques and combinations with three rebounds inbetween. For some people, this is too fast because they cannot *control the bag*, or their own *punching power*. IF you find yourself in this category, the following is an alternative work-out program. It is kind of a "preliminary" to the written exercises, and it features four graduated levels of control.

I. HIT and STOP the bag. Then hit again.

Here you want to assume the proper position, hit the bag with the new technique, then **stop the bag and reposition** before hitting it again. For example, using the Front Circle Punch (FCP), Position the fist by the mouth, then swing and hit the bag with the technique. Let the bag rebound a few times, *then stop the bag* before hitting it again (repeat). **STOPPING** IT IS THE KEY. This allows you to *feel* the proper arm position, punching motion, hear the sound and watch the bag movements - but eliminates the need to "time" your movements, control your punching force, or try and "control" the bag. Try the following practice order as a guide:

1. **EACH ARM ALONE** (or leading) with *each* Technique, do *3 sets* (groups) of *10-15 repetitions* (punches)

   Ex A: FCP or FSP: 3 sets x 15 reps, left arm only, (then 3x15 with right arm)
   Ex B: FDP, 3 sets x 15 reps, left arm leading, (then 3x15 with right arm leading)

2. **ALTERNATING ARMS** Do *3 sets* of *10-15 repetitions*, Left, then Right fist (alternating between)

   Ex: with (FCP), 3 sets x 10-15 reps: ALTERNATING...Left Arm (lead), then Right Arm (lead)

3. **ALTERNATING TECHNIQUES**. EX: Hit (FCP). Stop bag. then hit (FSP). Stop bag. Then back to (FCP) or another technique you know. This works well for techniques that come from different areas of the bag.

II. HIT, let it SWING, then hit again.

Here, do the same thing as the last except after you punch, let the bag swing *until it almost stops*, (a good point is when it is not reaching the rebound board, but still moving, barely). Then, when you see it is in the proper location, hit it again. Be sure and hold the arm/fist in proper position while it swings. This level helps you to maintain arm position, hear the sound, see the bag motion, and also start "timing" your swing movements. You can use the same three Examples, (Single arm, Alternating arms, Alternating techniques). The key is to hit the bag while it is moving. If you miss-hit and the bag goes crooked, just let it swing until it is slow enough to hit again.

III. HIT and COUNT the rebounds..........High number, "7" then to "5"

In the last two levels, YOU chose when to swing. At this level, you will start "timing" your movements to hit the bag at the proper moment and proper position. Start with a fairly high number of rebounds (7 or 5). Punch, maintain position, then swing again after counting the needed number of rebounds. Use the same three examples as above (Single Arm, Alternate Arms, Alternate Techniques). Mix these together. After a few workouts with seven (7) rebounds, try and use five (5). At this level, you will learn punching power & control, because this effects the rebounding speed. Hit "easy" so the bag will go slow. As you gain control, start punching harder and faster.

IV. HIT, count TRIPLET Rhythm   (written exerises)

Now you may be able to complete the written practice exercises (…you can also use five rebounds instead of three).

Chapter 5

REVERSE PUNCHING and LINKING

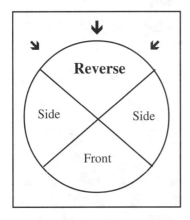

Fig 5A Reverse bag area

The last chapter covered seven striking techniques that all hit the front of the bag. Now let's learn several techniques that will hit behind, or in back of the bag **[Fig 5A]**. I call this the "reverse" position. Striking the back of the bag offers a lot of combination possibilities. In this chapter we will learn the three reverse techniques and the methods for using them in combinations with the front techniques.

Reverse Single Punch   (RSP)

The Reverse Single Punch has the symbol (RSP), and is the first skill that hits another side of the Bag (in this case, behind). It is exactly the reverse of the Front Circle Punch, for we are striking toward our face, not away from it. Assume the ready position and extend the arm out from the elbow. Begin by slowly circling your fist in a small circle <u>toward your nose</u> **[Fig 5B]**. Be sure to initiate movement from the elbow, not the shoulder. The bag will strike the large knuckle of the index finger. You should NOT have to lean *way* back to perform the (RSP).

Fig 5B Reverse Single Punch - Left Fist

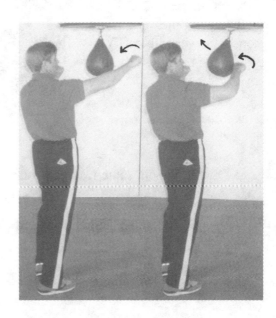

Reverse Single Punch - Right Fist

You will not see the contact point behind the bag **[Fig5B-1]**. A larger bag may come close to your nose, so take a small step to the side…or hit the bag close to the "reverse-side" angle. As before, the bag will rebound three times before striking again. Several practice exercises include:

#1 Single arm Reverse Single Punch

    R   R   R
(RSP)'''(RSP)'''(RSP)….Change hands
   1-2-3   *1*-2-3   *1*-2-3

#2 Alternating hands

  R   *R*   *L*   *L*
(RSP)'''(RSP)'''(RSP)'''(RSP)…..repeat

Fig 5B-1 Contact Area Behind the Speed Bag.

Reverse Double Punch (RDP)

Designated by (RDP), this is exactly the opposite of the Front Double Punch. Assume the ready position with the arms once again extended with both fists behind the bag. You will circle both fists back toward your face, striking the bag on the large knuckles of the index fingers **[Fig 5C]**. Just as the Front Double Punch, move both fists together at the same time. The key is the distance between them. You may need to lean back slightly, but do not overdo it.

Fig 5C Reverse Double Punch

Practice exercises:

#1 Reverse Double Punch, same leading hand

  L-R   *L-R*   *L-R*
(RDP)'''(RDP)'''(RDP)….Change lead hand
 1-**1**-2   *1*-**1**-2   *1*-**1**-2

The larger "**1**" in the count line indicates a slightly louder rebound off the second fist.

#2 Reverse Double Punch, alternate leading hand.

   L-R   *R-L*   *L-R*   *R-L*
(RDP)'''**(RDP)**'''**(RDP)**'''**(RDP)**

#3 Reverse Double Punch, following a Reverse Single Punch

  L   **_L_**   **_L-R*_**   *R*   *R*   **_R-L*_**   *L*
(RSP)'''**(RSP)**'''**(RDP)**'''**(RSP)**'''**(RSP)**'''**(RDP)**'''**(RSP)**

Note in the last sequence, the fist performing the RSP (**_L_**) leads the following RDP and the <u>second</u> fist of each **RDP** (*R** & *L**) leads the next technique

Reverse Fist Rolling   (R-Roll)

This skill, represented by (R-Roll), is the exact opposite of Front Fist Rolling. Overlap the fists <u>slightly</u> and rotate the large knuckles over each other in small circles back toward your face **[Fig 5D]**. At first you may bang your fists together. Because you need to make contact directly behind the bag you will have to lean back to clear your nose. Go slow at first. Practice exercises are:

#1 Reverse Fist Rolling

  R-L-R-L-R
 (R-Roll).....continue for 10-15 strikes

#2 Reverse fist Rolling, Same lead hand exit

   L   *L*   **_L-R-L-R-L_**   **_L_**   *L*
(RSP)'''**(RSP)**'''**(R-Roll)**'''**(RSP)**'''**(RSP)**...repeat
                 *1-2-3-4-**5**-2-3*

Note that after an <u>odd</u> number of strikes in the roll (5), the same fist (larger **_L_**) easily continues to hit. We can exit with the opposite hand after an *even* number of bounces. (Exactly as in Front Fist Rolling)

Fig 5D Reverse Fist Rolling

#3 Reverse Fist Rolling from Reverse Single Punch, opposite hand exits.

   L   *L*   **_L-R-L-R_**   **_R_**   *R*
(RSP)'''**(RSP)**'''**(R-Roll)**'''**(RSP)**'''**(RSP)**
            *1-2-3-**4**-2-3*

We did not practice the last three techniques in the basic striking rhythm. We began with the arms fully extended and made inward circles rather then the normal outward movement. To use these techniques in the *Basic Rhythm* we must learn the method that "links" them together. These linking skills only involve the fists and allow us to flow from one side of the bag to the other.

Linking Skills

To this point every fist or elbow has entered from the <u>same</u> side (either front or reverse). Several "rules of rhythm" come into effect here. Rule of rhythm #1 states that…"any strike coming from the *same* side as the last must be after an odd number of bounces" and we have used only an odd number of bag rebounds. Linking allows us to use rule of rhythm #2, or "a strike coming from the *opposite* direction occurs after an <u>even</u> number of rebounds".

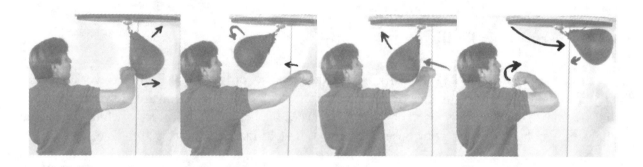

Fig 5E Linking Front and Reverse Techniques " Passing the fist thru the bag "

<u>Linking skills are not punches</u>. It is the method for connecting techniques on opposite sides of the speed bag **[Fig 5E]**. As the fist strikes the bag, instead of circling down and returning to its original position, it is extended *straight through* the striking zone to the other side, and re-circles back in reverse punching position. This "pass through" happens automatically, for the fist passes under the bag as it travels to the rebound board. The only secret is to hit the bag in the correct spot-widest part of the belly, on BOTH sides. If you do not make contact in this area the fist does not have enough room to pass through to the other side. Also, you need to swing straight into the bag, making contact while it is angled *away* from the fist. It is much more difficult if you wait until the bag is straight in line with the swivel. Also, punching in an up-down motion (half-moon swinging) will make linking impossible.

Here is exactly what happens: As the bag is struck from the front, (Front Circle Punch), it travels up to the board, away from you, for the first rebound and the fist passes underneath it (extending the arm). The bag then flies to the front for its second rebound, after which it is restruck from the reverse position. This all happens very quickly, and the punching motions must be smooth. Two rebounds between techniques, instead of three, creates the second main speed bag rhythm, the *Double Bounce Rhythm*. By changing the accented "beats", we hear stutters in the rhythm. It adds variety to the flow of combinations.

Let's learn the two types of linking skills, the one-half figure eight and the full-figure eight. Both can be performed by either or both fists.

The One-Half Figure Eight   [1/2]

In this maneuver, symbolized by [1/2], the fist passes through to the other side <u>and stays there</u> **[FIG 5F]** . It re-circles and strikes from the other direction several times. The linking fists will be identified in **<u>underlined bold</u>**. Notice the difference in the rhythm counting used.

Practice exercises include:

#1A <u>Same arm</u>, [1/2] linking to opposite side - Front to Reverse

Fig 5F One-half [1/2] Linking

$$R \quad\quad R \quad\quad \underline{\textbf{R}} \quad\; \textbf{r} \quad\; R \quad\quad R \quad\quad R$$
(FCP)'''(FCP)'''(FCP)-**[1/2]**-(RSP)'''(RSP)'''(RSP)…Change leading hand
1-2-3 *1*-2-3   *1*-2   *1*-2-3 *1*-2-3 *1*-2-3

The symbol [1/2] equals two rebounds between the techniques, and we could also write this combination using only the techniques as: (FCP)''(RSP). Note the small "r" over the [1/2], which indicates the right fist is passing through to the other side (and the "**l**", for left, below).

#1B <u>Same arm</u>, [1/2] linking to opposite side - Reverse to Front

$$L \quad\quad L \quad\quad \underline{\textbf{L}} \quad\; \textbf{l} \quad\; L \quad\quad L \quad\quad L$$
(RSP)'''(RSP)'''(RSP)-**[1/2]**-(FCP)'''(FCP)'''(FCP)…Change lead
1-2-3 *1*-2-3   *1*-2   *1*-2-3

#2 From Basic Rhythm, [1/2] to Reverse Single Punch and return

$$R \quad\; \underline{\textbf{R}} \quad\; \textbf{r} \quad\; R \quad\; R \quad\; \underline{\textbf{R}} \quad\; \textbf{r} \quad\; R \quad\quad L$$
Basic RRLL…(FSP)'''(FCP)-**[1/2]**-(RSP)'''(RSP)'''(RSP)-**[1/2]**-(FCP)'''(FSP)…Basic

The one-half link can also be performed with <u>both fists</u> after a Front Double Punch. As you do the (FDP), simply extend both fists out-straight *through* the bag-to the other side and re-circle back. The speed bag will strike the first fist, the board, the second fist and then rebound twice before it is hit from the other side. You will hear two accented strikes and one after beat, noted in the counting. Practice Exercises include:

#3 Front Double Punch, Both Fists [1/2], to Reverse Double Punch

$$R\text{-}L \quad\quad \underline{\textbf{L-R}} \quad\; \textbf{B} \quad\; \text{"}R\text{-}L\text{"} \quad\; L\text{-}R$$
(FDP)'''(FDP)-**[1/2]**-(RDP)''(RDP)
1-*1*-2-3   *1*-*1*-2   *1*-*1*-2-3 *1*-*1*-2-3

Note the "B" over the **[1/2]**, which indicates "Both" fists. This combination could also be written as (FDP)''(RDP).

After the **L-R** (FDP) both fists passed under the bag to the other side. They passed through in this L-R order and will naturally be positioned behind the bag to execute the "R-L" (RDP). We'll see the same thing in the next exercise.

#4 Reverse Double Punch, Both fists [1/2] to Front Double Punch * exact techniques note '' rebounds

    L-R   **R-L**   **B**   *"L-R"*   *R-L*   *L-R*   **R-L**   *"L-R"*   *R-L*
(RDP)'''(RDP)-**[1/2]**-(<u>FDP</u>)'''(FDP)   * (RDP)'''(RDP) '' (<u>FDP</u>)'''(FDP)
     *1-**1**-2-3*   *1-**1**-2*   *1-**1**-2-3*   *1-**1**-2-3*

In the above pattern both fists pass **[1/2]** to the front in the same <u>R-L</u> order as the (RDP) and the are automatically in the "L-R" fist order for the (<u>FDP</u>).

#5 From Basic Rhythm, Front Double Punch, Both fists [1/2] to Reverse Double Punch, and return.

           L   **L-R**   **B**   *R-L*   **L-R**   **B**   *R-L*   *L*
Basic LLRR…(FSP)'''(FDP)-**[1/2]**-(RDP)'''(RDP)-**[1/2]**-(FDP)'''(FCP)..Basic

When both fists pass [1/2] under the bag, we do not have to follow automatically with both fists again. We can also use a single punch, as we will see below. (Notice the counting difference)

#6 Reverse Double Punch, [1/2], to Front Circle Punch * exact techniques note '' rebounds

    L-R   **R-L**   **B**   *L*   *R*   *L-R*   **R-L**   *L*   *R*
(RDP)'''(RDP)-**[1/2]**-(FCP)'''(FSP)…Change hands   * (RDP)'''(RDP) '' (FCP)'''(FSP)
   *1-**1**-2-3*   *1-**1**-2*   *1-2-3*   *1-2-3*

Notice the fists passed under the bag in the order of right-left and the last-or second- fist to pass under (*L*) was the fist that circled back into the bag. This is the smoothest transition.

Splitting the Fists

You can also let one fist pass behind and <u>alternate front and reverse punches</u>. I call this "splitting the fists" between the front and back of the bag **[Fig 5G]**. This "split fist" combination is very fast and has the fists going in counter motions. In the next exercise, The Front Circle fist [left] will link [1/2] behind the bag to a Reverse Single Punch…Front Straight Punch [right] combination. You must emphasize control and slow your movements down, for the punches occur after only **two** rebounds-(or four rebounds, if two is too fast). Notice the rhythm counting underneath.

R   L

Fig 5G Split Fist Combination (FSP) '' (RSP)   2 or 4 rebounds

#7   Link [1/2], to "split fist" punching   (note the two '' rebounds)

> *L*   **L**   l   *L*   R   *L*   R   **L**   l   *L*
> (FCP)'''(FCP)-**[1/2]**-(RSP)''(FSP)''(RSP)''(FSP)''(RSP)-**[1/2]**-(FCP)…change leading hand
>   *1-2-3*   *1-2*   *1-2*   *1-2*   *1-2*   *1-2*   *1-2*   *1-2-3*

This last pattern demonstrates a good reason why I use the symbol **[1/2]**. **It indicates the <u>process of changing sides</u>**. Note the two rebounds between the (FSP)''(RSP). The fists are already on different sides. They make opposite circles punching into the bag, each after two rebounds.

It is possible to enter this (RSP)''(FSP) split fist combination by letting one of the fists [1/2] after a Front Double Punch. <u>Either</u> fist can do this. The sequence below features the first fist in the Front Double Punch (larger **L**) linking to the (RSP).

#8 Front Double Punch, lead fist [1/2] to split fists, and return.

> *L*   **L**-*R*   l   *L*   R   *L*   R   **L**   l   *L*
> Basic LLRR…(FSP)'''(FDP)-[1/2]-(RSP)''(FSP)''(RSP)''(FSP)''(RSP)-**[1/2]**-(FCP)…Basic

Splitting the fists is an exciting option that can be used with virtually all the striking techniques. We will completely develop "spit fist" combinations in the chapter of advanced skills.

We have now covered One-Half Figure-8 linking with both Reverse Single Punch and Reverse Double Punch. Finally, let's one-half link to Reverse Fist Rolling. This is the most difficult of all linking, for the fists are rapidly changing directions. You will need to develop good control over reverse rolling. Reverse Fist Rolling can only follow both fists passing through *and the secret is knowing that the next Roll can begin with <u>either</u> the first (lead) or second fist*. The next exercises will demonstrate this concept.

#9 Front Double Punch, both fists link [1/2], to Reverse Fist Roll and exit behind.

>   L   **L-R**   B   *L-R-L-R-**L***   *L-R*
> (FSP)'''(FDP)-**[1/2]**-(R-Roll)'''(RDP)......change leading arm

The reverse roll began with the left fist (larger *L*), which was the <u>first</u> to pass through. To exit the fist roll, the last fist (<u>L</u>) leads the next reverse technique

#10 Front Fist Rolling, both fists link [1/2], to Reverse Fist Rolling and return to the Front.

>   R   *R-L-R-**L**-R*   B   ***R**-L-R-**L**-R* B   *R-L*   *L*
> (FSP)'''(F-ROLL) -**[1/2]**- (R-Roll) -**[1/2]**- (FDP)'''(FCP) ...change leading arm

Here we see a Front Fist Roll, which ends with both fists passing to the other side in a **L-R** fist order to the back of the bag. Here we see the Reverse Roll begins with the second (<u>R</u>) or last fist fist to pass under. Most people will begin the roll with their dominant fist, which seems to be easier.
When you exit the Reverse Fist Roll to the front, you must anticipate this move and almost flex both arms together. Any hesitation will strand one of the fists behind the bag. Linking to and from fist rolling is tricky and we will explore it more in the advanced chapter. For now, learn to do exercise #9 & #10 smoothly.

The most important thing to remember about the one-half figure 8 is that the fist(s) move to the opposite side, re-striking after 2 rebounds, <u>and stay there for several techniques</u>.

The Full Figure-8 Link [8]

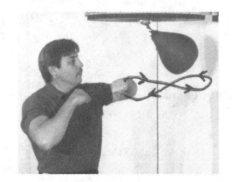

Fig 5H Figure-8 [8] Linking

The full Figure-8, symbolized by [8], indicates the fist(s) passing through the bag to the opposite side and <u>returning to the original position</u>. This is not a different movement than the one-half link, only the fist *immediately* returns to the original position with only one technique on the opposite side. It is performed by simply extending the arm almost straight out and back from the elbow. When viewed from the side, the fist seems to draw a "figure 8", **[Fig 5H]**, but do not try to draw the "8" with your fist. Once again, *the secret is to hit the lower belly of the speed bag, creating enough room for your hand to pass under the bag*. You should never have to purposely drop or loop your fist <u>under</u> the bag. This usually creates a late return and striking the bag from the bottom of the opposite side, driving it up into the swivel.

As an example, **[FIG 5i]** you execute a Front Circle Punch, pass the fist to the opposite side, make one Reverse Single Punch and bring the fist back to the <u>original position</u> in front of the bag. The speed bag moves from the Front Circle Punch to the board away from you for the first bounce, then rebounds near the face for the second bounce. It is then struck by the Reverse Punch and rebounds by the face for the third bounce and then rebounds for the fourth time away from you. The first and fourth bounce were at the back of the board and the second and third bounce were at the front of the board creating a stuttered double-bounce rhythm with two distinctly perceived accents on the 1st and 3rd rebound (which are directly off the fist). The are several methods for counting this rhythm, which is reflected underneath. In the following practice exercises the linking fist is **<u>underlined bold</u>**.

#1 Single Fist Figure-[8] pass through, from Front Circle Punch   Exact techniques Below

   R   *R*   **R** **r**   *R*   <u>R</u>   <u>**r**</u>   *R*
(FCP)'''(FCP)'''(FCP)-**[8]**-(FCP)…change hands   (FCP)''(**RSP**)''(FCP)
   1-2-3   *1*-2-3   *1*-2-*1*-2   *1*-2-3   └— [8] —┘

       Note that during the [8] **a Reverse Single Punch occurred behind the bag, <u>but was not written</u>.** It is very important to understand this, for it is <u>the</u> major difference between the using the [8] symbol and the [1/2] symbol for written exercises. The above sequence using only the [1/2] would look like:

   R   *R*   **R**   **r** **R** **r**   *R*
(FCP)'''(FCP)'''(FCP)-**[1/2]**-(**RSP**)-**[1/2]**-(FCP)…
   1-2-3   *1*-2-3   *1*-2   *1*-2   *1*-2-3

       This adds more symbols to recognize, and takes more space. *This is why the full Figure-8 symbol means to.. "return the fist to the original position"* **Because of un-written punches within the [8] symbol, I will not use it in the written exercises** and only the use exact techniques. But remember: The [8] symbolizes the <u>process</u> of passing through and returning to the original position.

#2 Single Fist Figure-[8] through the bag, from Reverse Single Punch.

   R   *R*   **R**   **R**   *R*
(RSP)'''(RSP)'''(RSP)''(FCP)''(RSP)…Change hands
                  └— [8] —┘

       Notice the [8] returns the fist to its *original position* behind the bag.

Fig 5i Figure-8 Linking - Left Fist, FCP''RSP

TIP: Keep the elbow up almost parallel to help the fist pass <u>straight</u> through without angling

#3   From Basic Rhythm, <u>Same</u> leading arm [8]

Linking symbols [1/2] & [8]

1. Refer to the "action" of passing fists though the bag

2. Only relevant to *written* speed bag exercises.

         R   <u>**R**</u>   <u>**R**</u>   *R*   *L*   *L*

Basic LLRR…(FSP)'''(FCP)''(RSP)''(FCP)'''(FSP)'''(FCP)…Repeat

       1-2-3   *1*-2-*1*-2   *1*-2-3

              └─ [8] ─┘

#4   From Basic, <u>Alternating Arm</u> [8]

      R   <u>**R**</u>   *R*   *R*   *L*   <u>**L**</u>   *L*   *L*

Basic LLRR…(FSP)'''(FCP)''(RSP)''(FCP)'''(FSP)'''(FCP)''(RSP)''(FCP)…repeat

     1-2-3   *1*-2-**1**-2   *1*-2-3   *1*-2-3   *1*-2-**1**-2   *1*-2-3

* alternate count *1*-2-3   **1** <u>**2**</u>   *1*-2-3   *1*-2-3   **1** <u>**2**</u>   *1*-2-3

* To this point we have always counted <u>every rebound</u> between techniques, both accented "main" beats and "after" beats. It can be very difficult to do this at faster speed…especially when doing **[8]**. This alternative method counts <u>only the accented rebounds</u>, which come directly off the fist. In the above example the "<u>**2**</u>" occurs on the (RSP) executed behind the bag. This amounts to only counting the fist contacts in the Figure-[8] pass through. Counting only the fist contacts becomes most apparent when performing the next exercise, multiple Figure-8 linking.

#5 Multiple Figure-8, <u>same</u> arm   (exact techniques also,   note the unwritten <u>RSP</u> techniques!

  <u>**R**</u> **r** **r** **r**   *R*   <u>**R**</u>   <u>**R**</u>   <u>**R**</u>   <u>**R**</u>   <u>**R**</u>   <u>**R**</u>   **R**

(FCP)-**[8]**-**[8]**-**[8]**-(FCP)'''……or……(FCP)''(RSP)''(FCP)''(RSP)''(FCP)''(RSP)''(FCP)'''

 1-2- **1-2-** **1-2** *1*-2-3   **1** - **2** - **1** - **2** - **1** - **2**   *1*-2-3

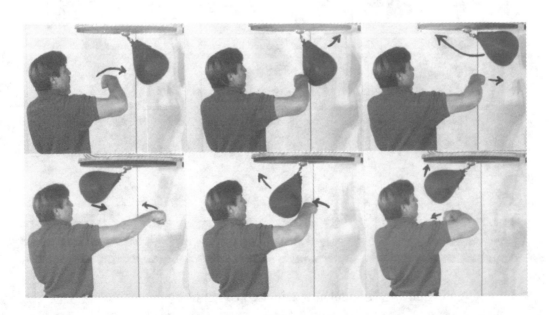

Figure-8 Linking - Right Fist, FCP '' RSP   Can use 2 or 4 Rebounds

So far we have always followed the Figure-8 with the same arm and technique. We can follow the **[8]** with the other arm…or a different technique. These next sequences will demonstrate that the Figure-8 is only passing the fists between the front and back of the bag. Once the fist returns to the front, **ANY** technique can follow.

#6 Opposite hand technique follows [8] Linking with a Front Circle Punch

$$L \qquad L \qquad L \qquad \text{``}R\text{''} \qquad R \qquad R \qquad \text{``}L\text{''}$$
(FCP)'''(FCP''(RSP)'' (FCP)'''(FCP)''(RSP)'' (FCP)…Repeat

└─ [8] ─┘   └─ [8] ─┘

L fist link   R fist link

In this last sequence, each fist performs a (FCP), then links to the (RSP) in the [8] and then returns to the front, but notice the **other fist** [*"R"* & *"L"*] hit after the RSP. The same occurs below.

#7 From Basic Rhythm, Opposite hand-different technique follows [8] with a Front Straight Punch

$$L \qquad L \qquad L \qquad R \qquad R \qquad R \qquad L \qquad L$$
Basic LLRR…(FSP)'''(FCP)''(RSP)''(FSP)'''(FCP)''(RSP)''(FSP)'''(FCP)…Basic

└─ [8] ─┘   └─ [8] ─┘

#8 Single fist Figure-8 pass through followed by a Front Double Punch (FDP)   *note rebounds

$$L \qquad L \qquad L \qquad L\text{-}R \qquad R \qquad R \qquad R \qquad R\text{-}L$$
(FCP)'''(FCP)''(RSP)''(FDP)'''(FCP)'''(FCP)''(RSP)''(FDP)…Repeat

└─ [8] ─┘   └─ [8] ─┘

Just as with the one-half Figure-8, both fists can pass through and return to their original position after a Front Double Punch. When this occurs, a Reverse Double Punch will be used on the back side of the bag **[FIG 5J]**.

FIG 5J **Double Fist Figure-8 Linking - FDP '' RDP**   **Can use 2 or 4 Rebounds**

43

#9 Front Double Punch, Double fist Figure - [8] pass through linking   *note rebounds

L-R   *R-L*   *L-R*   **R-L**   *L-R*   R-L
(FDP)''(RDP)''(FDP) ''' **(FDP)**''(RDP)''(FDP)
1-1-2 *1-1*-2 *1-1*-2-3   └── [8] ──┘
                                            Both Fists

      Passing both fists through and returning is easy, just extend both fists straight out and back. We will do the same in the next exercise.

#10 Continuous Double Fist [8] from Front Double Punch

R-L   L-R   R-L   *L-R*   R-L   *L-R*   R-L   *L-R*
(FDP)''' (FDP)''(RDP)''(FDP)''(RDP)''(FDP)''(RDP)''(FDP)…repeat, change leading fist
     └── [8] ──┘   └── [8] ──┘   └── [8] ──┘
       Both   Both   Both

      After we complete the double fist [8] (or FDP '' RDP) we do *not* have to follow with another Front Double Punch. In the next exercise we will follow with a Front Circle Punch.

> **The secret to passing *both* fists through the bag is to simply extend them out and back. Do not try to loop them under the bag. Go straight through the "belly".** *Do not draw the "8' with the fists.*

#11 Double fist Figure-[8], followed by single fist

     L   **L-R**   **R-L***   ***L***   *R*   **R-L**   **L-R**   *R*
Basic LLRR…(FSP) (FDP)''(RDP)''(FCP)'''(FSP)'''(FDP)''(RDP)''(FCP)…repeat
                 └── [8] ──┘   └── [8] ──┘

      Notice how the last, or second fist (*L*) of the RDP, completes the FCP. **Normally we will lead the next technique with the last fist to pass through the bag**

      You may also follow a Front Double Punch by doing [8] with either the leading (first) fist, or second fist. This greatly widens the variety of possible combinations and builds control. In the next exercise, let the first, or "leading fist" of a double punch link [8]. The second fist of the double punch should hit and draw back slightly. This may feel awkward at first, because the hands will be moving in opposite directions, as in an earlier exercise. Control is the key here, so start soft and slow. Do not try to go fast or hit hard without control.

> **Other Keys to linking**
>
> 1. proper bag height to hit the belly.
>
> 2. Elbow position parallel so fist goes straight, not angled up or down.

#12 Front Double Punch, Lead (first) Fist Figure- [8] pass through   (note 2 or 3 rebounds)

    L   **L-R**   *L*   *L*   *R*   **R-L**   *R*   *R*   *L*
(FCP) ''' (FDP)''(RSP)''(FCP) ''' (FSP) ''' (FDP)''(RSP)''(FCP) ''' (FSP)…repeat

Notice how the first (lead) fist (**L**) of the FDP passed through and returned to the front.

#13   From Basic Rhythm, Front Double Punch, alternating <u>lead</u> fist Figure-[8] pass through

```
              Lead                        Lead
           ┌──────┐                    ┌──────┐
      L    L-R    L    L    R    R-L    R    R
Basic RRLL...(FSP)'''(FDP)''(RSP)''(FCP)'''(FSP)'''(FDP)''(RSP)''(FCP)...repeat
           └── [8] ──┘              └── [8] ──┘
```

Again, notice how the leading fist (<u>underlined</u>) of the FDP passes through. Now let's link [8] with the <u>second</u> fist of the Front Double Punch

#14 From Basic Rhythm, Front Double Punch, <u>Second</u> Fist Figure-[8] pass through.

```
          second              second
        ┌──────┐            ┌──────┐
      L-R    R    R    R-L    L    L
Basic RRLL... (FDP)''(RSP)''(FCP) ''' (FDP)''(RSP)''(FCP) '''.. repeat
        └── [8] ──┘          └── [8] ──┘
```

Here we see the second fist-<u>R</u>-passing through and returning to the front.

#15 Front Double punch, alternating <u>second</u> fist figure-[8], one punch between

```
   L-R    R    R    R-L    L    L
  (FDP)''(RSP)''(FCP) ''' (FDP)''(RSP)''(FCP)....Repeat, change lead fist
```

#16   Front Double Punching, continuous alternating <u>second</u> fist Figure-[8] pass through.
   ** *This is a very quick changing sequence....keep the elbows up!*

```
   second          second
  ┌──────┐        ┌──────┐
  L-R    R    R-L    L    L-R    R    R-L    L
 (FDP)''(RSP)''(FDP)''(RSP) '' (FDP)''(RSP)''(FDP)''(RSP)''
  └── [8] ──┘          └── [8] ──┘
```

Exercise #16 is different than #15 because there is no triplet rhythm (three rebounds) within the sequence when the second fist returns. It immediately leads the next Front Double Punch.

We can mix the [1/2] and the [8] together. You can pass your hands through as many times as you wish and exit whenever you want (or to a certain technique). You may begin linking in the front and exit to a reverse technique or vice-versa. Practice the next sequences to learn this concept. (The fist contacts are the number "<u>1</u>")

#17 Mixing [1/2] & [8] linking, Front-to Reverse, and Reverse-to-Front.   (single punches only)

R　　**R**　　**R**　　**R**　　*R*　　**R**　　**R**　　**R**　　*R*

(FCP)'''(FCP)''(RSP)''(FCP)''(RSP)'''(RSP)''(FCP)''(RSP)''(FCP)'''...change hands

1-2-3　*1*-2　-*1*-2-　*1*-2　　*1*-2-3　*1*-2　*1*-2-　*1*-2　　*1*-2-3

└── [8] ──┘── [1/2]─┘　　└── [8] ──┘── [1/2]─┘

In this last pattern, the fist exits linking to the other side from where it started.

#18 Mixing [1/2] & [8] with Front Double Punch...(2nd fist of FDP links)   (exact techniques only)

L　　*L*-**R**　　**R**　　**R**　　*R*　　**R**　　**R**　　**R**　　*R*-*L*　　*L*

(FSP)'''(FDP)''(RSP)''(FCP)''(RSP)'''(RSP)''(FCP)''(RSP)''(FDP)'''(FCP)...Basic

└── [8] ──┘── [1/2]─┘　　└── [8] ──┘── [1/2]─┘

When you can perform all the linking practice sequences, then you can link by either one-half or full Figure-8 with either fist from all of the techniques we have learned. In fact, it does not matter what technique you use, if it ends with a fist...you can link! This is very important for [1/2] and [8] linking are possible from all the new techniques you are going to learn, with only a few exceptions. This simple maneuver offers a tremendous amount of rhythmic variations and quickly produces solid fist control.

REVIEW OF ALL TECHNIQUES USING [1/2] & [8] LINKING

Before starting any new techniques, let's practice a few linking patterns with the 10 striking techniques we have already learned. They can be done as written or from the Basic Rhythm. They may look complicated, but they are using skills you have already learned. Each should be understandable if broken down by technique abbreviations. These will mix the double bounce and triplet rhythms together, and the linking fist(s) are **underlined bold**. For extra help, I will also write some exercises without the linking symbols and using only the exact techniques.   * Key: notice two or three rebounds!

Review Exercise #1

R　　　**R**　　**r**　*R*　　*R*　　**R**　　**r**　*R*　　　*R*

(FSP)'''(O-DES)-**[1/2]**-(RSP)'''(RSP)'''(RSP)-**[1/2]**-(O-DES)'''(FCP).....change hands

e-**f**　　　　　　　　　　　　　　e-f

Notice the **f** in the bottom line, which indicates the "fist" passing through. Do this After the elbow connects by extending the fist out from the elbow, but try to keep the elbow close to parallel.

exercise #1 with only exact techniques   note " rebounds

R　　　**R**　　*R*　　*R*　　**R**　　*R*　　　*R*

(FSP)'''(O-DES)''(RSP)'''(RSP)'''(RSP)''(O-DES)'''(FCP).....change hands

e-**f**　　　　　　　　　　e-**f**

Review Exercise #2   Figure-8 pass through indicated

```
                                                              ┌─┐[1/2]
                                                              ┌┘ └┐
 L-R     R     R-L-R-L-R     R     R-L     L     L     L     L     L-R
(FDP)''(RSP)''(F-ROLL)'''(FCP)'''(FDP)''(RSP)''(FCP)''(RSP)'''(RSP)''(FDP)
   └─[8]─┘                     └─[8]─┘ └── [1/2] ──┘
```

Notice how the left fist "takes off" in the last sequence while the right fist "holds", or stays in front. Let it rest at chin level. If it drops low, it may be late for the last (FDP).

Review Exercise #3

```
 R      R-L-R-L-R      R      R-L-R-L-R   B   R-L-R-L-R   B   R-L-R-L-R      R
(FSP)'''(F-ROLL)''(RSP)''(F-ROLL)-[1/2]-(R-ROLL)-[1/2]-(F-ROLL)'''(FCP).
```

exercise #3 with exact techniques.   note " rebounds

```
 R      R-L-R-L-R      R         R-L-R-L-R      R-L-R-L-R      R-L-R-L-R      R
(FSP)'''(F-ROLL)''(RSP) '' (F-ROLL) '' (R-ROLL) '' (F-ROLL)'''(FCP).
            └─ [8] ─┘         └─ [1/2] ─┘        └─ [1/2] ─┘
                             Both fists         Both fists
```

Review Exercise #4

```
 L      L-R   B   L-R-L-R-L   B   L-R     R     R     R     R     R-L
(FSP)'''(FDP)-[1/2]-(R-ROLL)-[1/2]''(FDP)''(RSP)''(FCP)''(RSP)''(O-DES)''(RSP)''(FDP)
                                                          e-f
                     └─ [8] ─┘    └─ [8] ─┘
                                            └─ [8] ─┘
```

exercise #4 with exact techniques.   note " rebounds

```
                              ┌──────────────────────────────┐  Left Fist
                              │                               │  Holds
 L      L-R    L-R-L-R-L    L-R     R     R     R     R     R     R-L
(FSP)'''(FDP)''(R-ROLL)''(FDP)''(RSP)''(FCP)''(RSP)''(O-DES)''(RSP)''(FDP)
                                                          e-f
```

In the above sequence the left fist (L) should rest at chin level while the right fist links several times.

The next few sequences will show that either or both fists can link after the Outward-Triple Elbow Strike (O-TES). The most important secret here is to *keep the elbows up* after they contact the bag.

Review Exercise #5

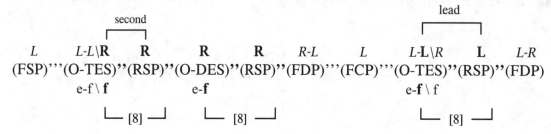

```
                  second                                              lead
                ┌─────┐                                            ┌─────┐
 L     L-L\R      R          R        R       R-L       L     L-L\R    L      L-R
(FSP)'''(O-TES)''(RSP)''(O-DES)''(RSP)''(FDP)'''(FCP)'''(O-TES)''(RSP)''(FDP)
        e-f \ f            e-f                            e-f \ f
          └── [8] ──┘        └── [8] ──┘                    └── [8] ──┘
```

Review Exercise #6

> ### O-TES & Linking
>
> you can pass *either* or *both* fists through to reverse punches after this elbow strike.

```
 L      L-L\R       R       R-R\L      L      L-L\R      R-L     L-R       R
(FSP)'''(O-TES)''(RSP)''(O-TES)''(RSP)''(O-TES)''(RDP)''(FDP)'''(FCP)
        e-f \ f            e-f \ f            e-f \ f
          └── [8] ──┘        └── [8] ──┘      ┬── [8] ──┘
                                          Both Fists
```

Review Exercise #7

```
 L-L\R     B    L-R-L-R-L    B     L-L\R    R-L    R-L-R-L-R       R       R      R-L
(O-TES)-[1/2]-(R-ROLL)-[1/2]-(O-TES)''(RDP)''(F-ROLL)'''(O-DES)''(RSP)''(FDP)
 e-f \ f                            e-f \ f                    e-f
                                                                └── [8] ──┘
```

exercise #7 with exact techniques.   note '' rebounds

```
 L-L\R     L-R-L-R-L    L-L\R     R-L    R-L-R-L-R       R       R      R-L
(O-TES)''(R-ROLL)''(O-TES)''(RDP)''(F-ROLL)'''(O-DES)''(RSP)''(FDP)
 e-f \ f            e-f \ f                    e-f
```

The secret to the last sequence is keeping the elbows up, and noticing that the first (larger) fist to pass through also leads the fist rolls.

Review Exercise #8 (A split fist combination occurs in this sequence)

lead Fist [1/2]

L	L-R	L	L-L\R	L	R	L	L-L\R	R-L	L-R
(FSP)'''	(FDP)''	(RSP)''	(O-TES)''	(RSP)''	(FSP)''	(RSP)''	(O-TES)''	(RDP)''	(FDP)

e-**f** \ f   e-**f** \ f

└── Split Fists ──┘

Exercise #8 is a little tricky because of the split fist combination, underlined, in the middle, beginning with the first fist (**L**) of the (O-TES).

The eight review exercises featured multiple technique-continuous linking, which is the hallmark of exceptional speed bag control…and they are guaranteed to draw a crowd.

Before we move on to more techniques, There is another "secret" to understand about passing the fists through the bag. Remember the *three linking options* that are always possible from *almost* any technique that includes both the fists. [I say "almost" because we will cover a few techniques where this is not possible.] **Simply stated, these options are: (1) lead fist, (2) Second Fist, (3) Both Fists.** These were covered during this chapter and in the practice exercises with the Front Double Punch (FDP), on pages 44 and 45, and the Outward-Triple Elbow Strike (O-TES) in review exercise #5,6,7 - (remember, O-TES is really just a Front Double Punch with an elbow in the front). However **these options are also possible from the Reverse Double Punch (RDP).**

As a matter of fact, as we add new techniques from all around the bag you will see that it makes no difference where the Double Punch originates. We will always have these three linking options. Although I will cover Advanced Reverse Punching in the Advanced Chapter, I will demonstrate this principle here with the Reverse Double Punch (RDP). For clarity, I will not use the linking symbols, and just emphasize the exact techniques. For extra help, I will use brackets or arrows above the linking fists.

From Reverse Double Punch, passing the lead or second fist through the bag.

A. **Lead** (first) Fist links,

lead

R-L	**R**	R-L	**R**
(RDP)''	(FCP) ''	(RDP)''	(FCP)

Notice how the *same* fist **R** always passes to the other side (FCP),

B. **Second** Fist links,

second

R-**L**	**L**	L-**R**	**R**
(RDP)''	(FCP) ''	(RDP)''	(FCP)

Notice how the fists *alternate* passing to the (FCP), first **L** then **R**

In both examples, it works *exactly the same* as the with the Front Double Punch. And we have already done (RDP)''(FDP) in several exercises. However, now we can start joining these options (lead fist, second fist, both fists - from FDP or RDP) together, moving from the front and back of the bag, without stopping. These next few combinations will appear complex, but ***notice which fist is linking***. A little time with these, (*first without the bag*, then on the bag), will reward you with excellent fist control. * I have noted some of the linking fists with "lead", "second" or "both" in the samples. ☺

1. Lead Fist, then <u>both</u> fists, front to reverse linking combination

	lead				lead			Both

L-*R* **L** *L-R* **L** *L-R* **R**-*L* **R** *R-L* **R** *R-L*

(FDP)''(RSP)''(FDP)''(RSP)''(<u>FDP</u>) '' (RDP)''(FCP)''(RDP)''(FCP)''(<u>RDP</u>) '' ....change lead.

2. Second Fist, then both fists, front to reverse Linking combinations

second ... Both ... second ... Both

L-**R** **R** *R-L* **L** *L-R* **R**-*L* **L** *L-R* **R** *R-L*

(FDP)''(RSP)''(FDP)''(RSP)''(<u>FDP</u>) '' (RDP)''(FCP)''(RDP)''(FCP)''(<u>RDP</u>) ''....change lead

3. Lead Fist, Second Fist, Both front to reverse Linking combinations

lead ... second ... Both ... lead ... second ... Both

L-*R* **L** *L-***R** **R** *R-L* **L**-*R* **L** *L-***R** **R** *R-L*

(FDP)''(RSP)''(FDP)''(RSP)''(<u>FDP</u>) '' (RDP)''(FCP)''(RDP)''(FCP)''(<u>RDP</u>) '' ....change lead.

4. Second Fist, Lead Fist, Both front to reverse Linking combinations

second ... lead ... Both ... second ... lead ... Both

L-**R** **R** *R-L* **R** *R-L* *L*-**R** **R** *R-L* **R** *R-L*

(FDP)''(RSP)''(FDP)''(RSP)''(<u>FDP</u>) '' (RDP)''(FCP)''(RDP)''(FCP)''(<u>RDP</u>) '' ....change lead.

These are just a few of the possible combinations possible when linking front to back. Remember, ***any fist combination you can do from the front, you can do from the back***! We will see this throughout all the advanced topics also. It may have been confusing to see the exercises in this chapter written with and without the linking symbols of [1/2] and [8]. The symbols only emphasize the "action" of passing the fist through the bag in written exercises. The most important concept is understanding how techniques on opposite sides of the bag are joined in combinations. With experience, you do not really need to write them, and in most advanced combinations where <u>both</u> fists change to different sides, it is even best not to use them. As we develop the new techniques and combinations, I will often use both methods for clarity.

It is my intention to give you the skills to "Improvise" and freely create your own variations in hitting the speed bag. These combinations are only a few of the hundreds of patterns you have available with just ten techniques - and *fourteen* more to go!

In the next chapter, we will focus on the Inward-Elbow Striking techniques.

Chapter 6

INWARD-ELBOW STRIKING

The next three striking techniques will be based on the elbows striking the bag on an <u>inward</u> motion, similar to the Front Straight Punch. The bag will always strike the point of the elbow on the forearm side. Because of the body rotation needed and lack of force in the movement, it is one of the more difficult moves to learn.

INWARD-SINGLE ELBOW STRIKE (I-SES)

The Inward-Single Elbow Strike, symbolized by (I-SES), is created by directing the forearm point of the elbow into the speed bag. This is done completely by shoulder motion and torso rotation. The fist must remain close to the chest. The same side knee (ie…right arm\right knee) will point in and bend with your upper body motion **[FIG 6A]**. Begin the knee movement by swiveling on the ball of the foot. Resist the tendency to turn your body too far in the movement. After the bag is struck it will rebound three times before being re-struck by another technique.

Fig 6A Inward-Single Elbow Strike

Several practice exercises include:

#1 Basic Rhythm, Inward-Single Elbow Strike, <u>same</u> arm does the elbow strike.

```
              L      L      R      R
Basic LLRR…(FSP)'''(FCP)'''(I-SES)'''(FCP)….Repeat, change leading arm
   Count              1-2-3  1-2-3
```

#2 Basic Rhythm, <u>Alternating</u> Arm, Inward-Single Elbow Strike

L   *R*   *R*   *L*

Basic LLRR...(FCP)'''**(I-SES)**'''(FCP)'''**(I-SES)**...Repeat

      Notice how this technique replaces the Front Straight Punch in the basic pattern. You can use this technique and the Outward-Single Elbow Strike to produce a smooth flowing basic rhythm of just elbows. This will take quick body and shoulder rotations. As soon as the Inward point of the elbow contacts the bag, begin the outward striking move.

#3 From Basic Rhythm, Outward-Single and Inward-Single Elbow strikes

L   *L*   *R*   *R*   *L*

Basic LLRR...(FSP)'''(O-SES)'''**(I-SES)**'''(O-SES)'''**(I-SES)**....continue

      Now, lets combine this movement with the <u>Outward-Double</u> Elbow Strike.

#4 From Basic Rhythm, continuous "Outward & Inward" Elbow Striking (note single or double strikes)

L   *L*   *R*   *R*   *L*

Basic LLRR...(FSP)'''(O-DES)'''**(I-SES)**'''(O-DES)'''**(I-SES)**...Continue

                e-f   e-f

count   *1*-2-3   *1-1*-2-3   *1*-2-3

INWARD-DOUBLE ELBOW STRIKE   (I-DES)

      The Inward-Double Elbow Strike, indicated by (I-DES) is created by striking with the fist and then the elbow, with one bounce in-between. This order is indicated by the bottom line "f" for fist, and "e" for elbow. From the ready position you begin with a Front Straight Punch motion and then follow with an Inward elbow strike <u>of the same arm</u> **[FIG 6B-1&2]**. Like the other double strikes, this is done by one motion, but is somewhat awkward for you must hit the front part of the fist and then keep it close to your chest for the elbow to be thrust into the bag. (You may angle the fist "down" after it connects and raise the elbow up slightly.) Because the body turns so much for the elbow to make contact, we end up in difficult position. There is a tendency to recover with too much force on the next technique. Control is a key factor.

Fig 6B-1 Inward-Double Elbow Strike

Several practice sequences are:

#1 Basic Rhythm, Inward-Double Elbow Strike, <u>same</u> arm

             L   ***R***   *R*   *L*
Basic LLRR…(FCP)'''**(I-DES)**'''(FCP)'''(FSP)…Change Arms
                      f-e
count   *1*-2-3   *1*-*1*-2-3   *1*-2-3

Notice the count line. Normally, the <u>last</u> striking part in a technique will be the loudest. The second "*1*" under the (I-DES) is **smaller**, because the inward moving elbow usually does not generate as much power as the leading fist. Often it will sound softer as a result. This does not change the count used, but it does sound different.

#2 Basic Rhythm,, Inward-Double Elbow Strike, Alternate leading Arm

Fig 6B-2 **Inward-Double Elbow Strike from different Angle**

             L   ***R***   *R*   *L*
Basic LLRR…(FCP)'''**(I-DES)**'''(FCP)'''**(I-DES)**….Repeat
                f-e   **f-e**

This technique can replace the Front Straight Punch in the basic rhythm. Since it is awkward to make the recovering Front Circle Punch, it is easier to recover with an outward-elbow strike. Both the single and the double Outward-Elbow Strikes can be used, as we will see below.

#3 Inward-Double Elbow, Outward-<u>Single</u> Elbow Strikes

             L   ***R***   *R*   *L*   *L*
Basic LLRR…(FCP)'''**(I-DES)**'''(O-SES)'''**(I-DES)**'''(O-SES)
                f-e   **f-e**

#4 Inward-Double Elbow Strike, Outward-<u>Double</u> Elbow Strike

             L   ***R***   *R*   *L*   *L*
Basic LLRR…(FCP)'''**(I-DES)**'''(O-DES)'''**(I-DES)**'''(O-DES)
                f-e   e-f   **f-e**   e-f
count   *1*-2-3 *1*-*1*-2-3 *1*-*1*-2-3 *1*-*1*-2-3 *1*-*1*-2-3

This last sequence seems to be the smoothest combination using the Inward-Double Elbow Strike.

INWARD-TRIPLE ELBOW STRIKE (I-TES)

This technique, symbolized by (I-TES), is created by adding the other fist into the motion…but now we will add the fist to the <u>beginning</u> of the technique, creating an interesting "fist-fist elbow" combination (as the bottom line will indicate). As an example, we would throw the left Front Circle Punch (outward), then the right fist and the right elbow (inward) all in one controlled motion with one rebound in-between **[FIG 6C-1,2&3]**.

This can be an awkward technique. Sometimes it helps to keep the forearm of the elbow striking arm level, so the wrist stays on the same plane as the elbow. Do not allow the elbow to hit the bag above the fist. Keep the fist up and under the chin. Turn your body into the bag and do not swing the arms too much.

Fig 6C-1 Inward-Triple Elbow Strike

Graphically we can view this as (FCP)+(I-DES) = (I-TES), or as (FDP)+(I-SES) = (I-TES). Also, the bag will contact the same areas as in these techniques. It may sound complicated, but I find it easier to do the Inward-Triple Elbow Strike than the previous double elbow motion.

Several practice patterns are:

#1 Inward-Triple Elbow strike, Front Circle Punch

```
              L       L\R-R      R
Basic RRLL…(FSP)'''(I-TES)'''(FCP)…Change leading Arm
                      f \ f-e
count          1-2-3  1-1-1-2-3
```

Notice the count line once more and how the last, or third strike off the inward elbow (*1*) is not the loudest. Again, it is difficult to recover for the (FCP), and all of the outward elbow strikes are easier to use as we will see below.

#2 Inward-Triple Elbow, Outward-Single Elbow Strikes, same lead arm

```
              L       L\R-R      R
Basic LLRR…(FSP)'''(I-TES)'''(O-SES)…Repeat, change leading arm
                      f \ f-e
```

#3 Inward-Triple Elbow, Outward-Double Elbow Strikes, same lead arm

          L   *L\R-R*   *R*

Basic RRLL…(FSP)'''**(I-TES)**'''(O-DES)…Repeat, change lead arm
                 f \ f-e   e-f

Fig 6C-2 Inward-Triple Elbow Strike, From Behind

#4 Inward-Triple Elbow, Outward-Triple Elbow Strikes

        L   **L\R-R**   *R-R\L*   *L*   *R*   *R*

Basic RRLL…(FSP)'''**(I-TES)**'''(O-TES)'''(FCP)'''(FSP)'''(FCP)….Repeat, change leading arm
              f \ f-e   e-f \ f

count   *1*-2-3   *1-1-1*-2-3 *1-1-1*-2-3

#5 Continuous, Alternating <u>Inward</u>-Triple, <u>Outward</u>-Triple Elbow Strikes

        L   **L\R-R**   *R-R\L*   *L-L\R*   **R\L-L**

Basic RRLL…(FSP)'''**(I-TES)**'''(O-TES)'''(O-TES)'''**(I-TES)**…continue
              f \ f-e   e-f \ f   e-f \ f   **f \ f-e**

#6 Continuous Inward-Triple Elbow strikes

        L   **L\R-R**   *R\L-L*   *L\R-R*   *R\L-L*

Basic RRLL…(FSP)'''**(I-TES)**'''**(I-TES)**'''**(I-TES)**'''**(I-TES)**…continue
              f \ f-e   **f \ f-e**   **f \ f-e**   **f \ f-e**

    Sequences 5 and 6 are fairly difficult combinations on the speed bag, due to the large body rotation and arm movements. Take it slow.

Fig 6C-3 Inward-Triple Elbow Strike, different angle

Linking and Inward-Elbow Strikes

You cannot use any linking movements directly after the Inward elbow techniques. Since the elbow is the last "part" to hit the bag, and the fist is close to the chest…it cannot pass through. You can use an Inward elbow technique <u>after</u> a one-half or full-figure 8, as these examples will demonstrate.

#7   Reverse Single punch, [1/2], Inward-Triple Elbow Strike   (exact techniques only at right)

   L   **L**   l   *L\R-R*   *L*   **L**   *L\R-R*

(RSP)'''(RSP)-[1/2]-**(I-TES)**…Basic   or…………………(RSP)'''(RSP)''**(I-TES)**

                 f \ f-e   **f \ f-e**

   1-2-3   *1-2*   *1-1-1-2-3*

#8 Front Circle Figure-[8] pass through, Inward-Triple Elbow Strike

   L   **L**   **L**   *L\R-R*

(FCP)'''(FCP)''(RSP)''**(I-TES)**

                      f \ f-e

   1-2-3   *1-2-1-2*   *1-1-1-2-3*

It will take a little longer to use the Inward elbow strikes as smoothly as the previous techniques. Practice using them with all the others and you will quickly learn how they fit into your rhythm.

In the next chapter we will begin using the elbows in the *"Downward"* direction.

Chapter 7

Downward Elbow Striking

The next techniques will feature a new concept of hitting down into the bag. The motion used for these skills is totally different than any of the previous techniques. It is not difficult…just different. The arm and shoulder actions will be similar to the throwing motion in baseball. The key feature in all these techniques will be the "downward" motion of the elbow connecting the front of the bag. Like the other elbow techniques, there is a single, double and triple strike.

*There is an important safety concern about techniques with "downward" moving fists and eyeglasses. Please - remove them before attempting these techniques. **The thumb of the downward moving fist WILL catch the rim of your glasses**...either knocking them off or driving them into your nose. Perhaps not every time but -don't think "it won't happen to me". It will. Spare yourself the injury and a new pair of glasses* **[Fig 7A].**

Fig 7A

Fig 7B Downward-Single Elbow Strike

Downward-Single Elbow Strike (D-SES)

The Downward-Single Elbow Strike is symbolized by (D-SES). From the ready position, you begin the motion by raising the forearm up and slightly back. When the fist is slightly higher than the head, swing the arm in and down from the shoulder, delivering the point of the elbow into the bag **[FIG 7B]**. The fist stays close to the shoulder and docs not extend out. The leg motion is similar to the Front Straight Punch, and the same side knee will bend in as the elbow comes down. After the elbow hits the bag, the arm returns to the ready position and the bag rebounds three times before the next blow. This movement can naturally follow any "outward" moving technique done by the opposite arm. For example, when throwing a left-outward elbow strike your body is turned to the right. As you deliver the left elbow to the bag in an outward motion, you begin raising the right arm up from the shoulder. After the left elbow hits the bag, your follow through brings the right elbow into the striking position to come "down" into the bag. *The secret is to time the raising and striking of the elbow with the natural flow of your body movement.*

Practice Combinations include:

#1 Basic rhythm, Downward-Single Elbow Strike, same arm leading

               L   ***R***   *R*   *L*
Basic LLRR…(FCP)'''**(D-SES)**'''(FCP)'''(FSP)…Repeat, change leading arm
   Count   *1*-2-3   *1*-2-3

#2 Basic rhythm, Downward-Single Elbow Strike, alternating arms

               L   ***R***   *R*   ***L***
Basic LLRR…(FCP)'''**(D-SES)**'''(FCP)'''**(D-SES)**…continue

Notice how this technique replaces the Front Straight Punch in the basic rhythm. That's because the FSP is an "IN" motion and so is the D-SES. You can also use all three single elbow striking techniques together to create several interesting combinations. A few examples are:

#3 Combining all the Single Elbow Striking Techniques

         L   *L*   ***R***   *R*   *L*   *L*
Basic LLRR…(FSP)'''(O-SES)'''**(D-SES)**'''(O-SES)'''(I-SES)'''(FCP)…Basic

         R   *L*   *L*   ***R***   *R*   *L*
Basic LLRR…(FCP)'''(I-SES)'''(O-SES)'''**(D-SES)**'''(O-SES)'''(FSP)…Basic

The Downward-Single Elbow Strike also combines before, and after, Front Fist Rolling. This next exercise will put the D-SES before the Fist Roll.

#4 Basic rhythm, Downward-Single Elbow Strike, to Front Fist Rolling

             L   ***R***   ***R***-*L*-*R*-*L*-*R*   *R*
Basic LLRR…(FCP)'''**(D-SES)**'''(F-Roll)'''(FCP)…Repeat, change leading arm
   Count   *1*-2-3

This is a little more challenging because of the downward movement of the fist. The secret to get the elbow back "up" to the parallel position as quickly as possible as it connects the bag. It's difficult to begin a fist roll with the elbow in the down position. A little trick is to flex the arm in slightly, bringing the elbow close to the center of your chest. This creates a good body position to turn and let the same side fist (Larger **R**) lead "out" in the circular motion and begin the roll after three rebounds.

In this next exercise, we will simply continue from #4 and follow the Front Fist Roll with another Downward Single Elbow Strike by the other arm.

#5 Basic rhythm, Downward-Single Elbow Strikes, after Front Fist Rolling

	R	*R-L-R-L-***R**	**L**	*L-R-L-R-L-***R**	**L**	*L-R-L-R-L*	**R**
Basic LLRR…	(FCP)'''	(F-Roll)'''	(D-SES)'''	(F-Roll)'''	(D-SES)'''	(F-Roll)'''	(D-SES)'''……repeat
Count		*1-2-3*	*1-2-3-4-5-2-3*	*1-2-3*	*1-2-3-4-5-6-2-3*	*1-2-3*	*1-2-3-4-5-2-3*

The secret to this last sequence is the fist that ends the roll. Notice the first two fist rolls (F-Roll) end with the right fist (**R**), and the following D-SES was by the left elbow (**L**). But the *first* fist roll began and ended with the right fist, and has and odd count (5). The second fist roll has an even number of fist contacts in the roll (6). It was started by the left fist and exited by the opposite right fist (**R**) that started the roll. The third fist roll begins and ends with the same fist (**L**). In all cases, the D-SES is executed by the opposite arm that exits the roll. This is an excellent combination to gain more control of Front Fist Rolling as well as the downward elbow motion.

Downward-Double Elbow Strike   (D-DES)

In the Downward-Double Elbow Strike, identified as (D-DES), the same movement is used, except the fist will be extended out and also hit the bag, after one rebound **[FIG 7C]**. As an example, let's say the right elbow connects in a downward motion. Then slightly extend your right forearm, allowing the right fist to contact the bag, after one rebound. The bag hits

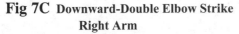

Fig 7C **Downward-Double Elbow Strike**
Right Arm

Downward-Double Elbow Strike
Left Arm

the fist on the ***middle knuckle of the little finger***. Keep a tight fist! The key is to make this one motion, not two separate ones. The leg motion is similar to the last technique with the weight shifting as the elbow comes down. After the fist connects, the arm quickly regains the ready position. The bag will rebound three times before the next technique. The bottom line will indicate the "elbow-fist".

Practice combinations include:

#1 Basic rhythm, Downward-Double Elbow Strike, same arm leading   *** Remove Eyeglasses**

              L   ***R***   *R*   *L*
Basic LLRR…(FCP)'''(**D-DES**)'''(FCP)'''(FSP)…Repeat, change arms
                     e-f
Count   *1*-*2*-*3*   **1-1**-*2*-*3*   *1*-*2*-*3*

The last pattern is counted just like a FDP, with two accented beats in the technique.

#2 Basic rhythm, Alternating arm Downward-Double Elbow Strikes

              L   ***R***   *R*   ***L***
Basic LLRR…(FCP)'''(**D-DES**)'''(FCP)'''(**D-DES**)…continue
                  e-f   **e-f**

    As before, now all the Double Elbow Strikes can be mixed together in a variety of different combinations. Several examples are offered:

Downward-Double Elbow Strike - From Behind

#3 Combining Double Elbow strikes

              L   *L*   ***R***   *R*   *L*
Basic LLRR…(FSP)'''(O-DES)'''(**D-DES**)'''(O-DES)'''(I-DES)…Basic
                  e-f   **e-f**   e-f   f-e

              L   *R*   *R*   ***L***   *L*   *R*
Basic LLRR…(FCP)'''(I-DES)'''(O-DES)'''(**D-DES**)'''(O-DES)'''(FSP)…Basic
                  f-e   e-f   **e-f**   e-f

Linking from the Downward-Double Elbow Strike

You can also use a [1/2] or [8] link following a Downward-Double Elbow Strike. Simply extend the fist through to the reverse position. As you do this the elbow must move back to the parallel position. It is most natural to do this as the fist makes contact. As the fist hits the bag, turn the palm down to the floor. In anticipation of turning the palm down to the floor, you will get the tendency to start the move when the elbow hits the bag. **This is disastrous to eyeglasses.** It puts the downward thumb directly on a crash course with the upper corner of the frames. Try and wait until the fist hits the bag (…and take your glasses off.) This will also help to bring the larger knuckle of the little finger into contact with the bag more than the middle joint. (The middle joint is smaller and can really get sore from a lot of contact, especially on an overfilled bag that is too hard.)

It is very difficult to try and pass the fist through the bag with the elbow in the "down" position. The fist will hit behind the bag in an awkward position and control of the bag is jeopardized. Also, if you return the fist to the front with the elbow in the "down" position, you are pretty much asking for a breakdown. The linking fist is in **underlined bold**.

Several examples include:

#4 Downward-Double Elbow Strike, followed by [1/2] Linking

$$\begin{array}{ccccccc} L & \textbf{R} & \textbf{r} & R & \textbf{R} & \textbf{r} & R \end{array}$$

Basic LLRR…(FCP)'''**(D-DES)**-[1/2]-(RSP)'''(RSP)-[1/2]-(FCP)…Basic

e-**f**

Count		*1-2-3*	*1-1-2*		*1-2-3*	*1-2*	*1-2-3*

#5 Downward-Double Elbow Strike, followed by [8] Linking

$$\begin{array}{cccccccc} ^{*}L & \textbf{R} & \textbf{r} & ^{*}R & \textbf{L} & \textbf{l} & L \end{array}$$

Basic LLRR…(FCP)'''**(D-DES)**-[8]-(FCP)'''**(D-DES)**-[8]-(FCP)…Basic

e-**f**　　　　　　e-**f**

Count		*1-2-3*	*1-1-*2*-1-2*		*1-2-3*	*1-1-*2*-1-2*	*1-2-3*

The secret to Figure-8 linking with the Downward-Double Elbow Strike is getting the elbow in the proper position to come in. Raise the arm up for the elbow strike as the *other* fist begins the circling motion for the FCP, indicated by **L & *R.* This gives you plenty of time to keep the "rhythm" of the movements. Avoid trying to "rush" the elbow up at the last moment. You will probably hit the bag too hard and increase its speed. Strive to keep all the parts moving at the same tempo.

This last exercise has two unwritten RSP's, indicated by the underlined (**1**) in the count line. Exercise #5 without the linking symbols, and just the exact techniques would be:

$$\begin{array}{cccccccc} L & R & \textbf{R} & R & R & \textbf{L} & L & L \end{array}$$

(FCP)'''**(D-DES)**''(RSP)''(FCP)'''**(D-DES)**''(RSP)''(FCP)…Basic

e-**f**　　　　　　　e-**f**

Downward-Triple Elbow Strike   (D-TES)

The Downward-Triple Elbow Strike, (D-TES), is a unique technique that is remarkably easy to do. To create it, we will add the other fist...but we add it before the elbow makes contact, making this a "fist-elbow-fist" combination (as indicated on the bottom line). For example, the left fist will strike the bag in a front circle motion then the right "downward" elbow and fist, all with one bounce in-between **[FIG 7D]**.   We might picture this as (FCP) + (D-DES) = (D-TES).

We will hear three distinctly accented beats with the last one being the loudest. The lower body actions is the same swiveling move as the last technique, and the same knee of the downward moving elbow will bend in. The bag will rebound three times before the next front technique.

* REMOVE GLASSES

Fig 7D Downward-Triple Elbow Strike

Practice combinations include:

#1 Basic rhythm, Downward-Triple Elbow Strike, Same leading arm

<pre>
             L   L\R-R   R   L
Basic LLRR...(FSP)'''(D-TES)'''(FCP)'''(FSP)...Repeat, change leading arm
                    f \ e-f
   Count   1-2-3 1-1-1-2-3 1-2-3
</pre>

#2 Basic rhythm, Downward-Triple Elbow Strike, Alternating Lead arm

<pre>
             L   L\R-R   R   L   L   R   R\L-L   L
Basic LLRR...(FSP)'''(D-TES)'''(FCP)'''(FSP)'''(FCP)'''(FSP)'''(D-TES)'''(FCP)...Basic
                    f \ e-f   f \ e-f
</pre>

In the last two patterns, the downward elbow strike followed a Front Straight Punch. Note how the second, or last fist (**R & L**) to connect in the downward technique circles back to the bag to lead the next technique. The D-TES can also follow a Front Circle Punch, as the next exercise demonstrates.

#3 Basic Rhythm, Downward-Triple Elbow Strike, Alternating arms, one punch between

<pre>
            L   L\R-R   R   R\L-L   L   L\R-R
Basic LLRR…(FSP)'''(D-TES)'''(FCP)'''(D-TES)'''(FCP)'''(D-TES)…continue
            f \ e-f   f \ e-f   f \ e-f
</pre>

We can also let the last fist in a Downward Triple become the *lead* fist for a following Downward Triple Elbow Strike with three rebounds inbetween. Raise the next elbow up as the last fist hits the bag.

#4 Continuous alternating Downward-Triple Elbow Strikes

<pre>
                        last fist leads next
                        ┌─────────┐
            L   L\R-R   R\L-L   L\R-R   R\L-L
Basic LLRR…(FSP)'''(D-TES)'''(D-TES)'''(D-TES)'''(D-TES)….Basic
            f \ e-f   f \ e-f   f \ e-f   f \ e-f
</pre>

The Downward Triple Elbow Strike combines very smoothly with any other front techniques. Several examples include:

#5 Basic Rhythm, Front Double Punch -to- Downward-Triple Elbow Strike

<pre>
            R   R-L   L\R-R   R
Basic LLRR…(FSP)'''(FDP)'''(D-TES)'''(FCP)…Repeat
                            f \ e-f
</pre>

#6 Basic Rhythm, Downward-Triple Elbow Strike -to- Front Double Punch

<pre>
            R   R\L-L   L-R   R
Basic LLRR….(FSP)'''(D-TES)'''(FDP)'''(FCP)…Repeat
                    f \ e-f
</pre>

This technique also combines with any of the other Outward-Elbow Techniques. A few examples are offered in the next exercises.

#7 Downward-Triple Elbow Striking, Outward-*Double* Elbow Strike

<pre>
            L   L\R-R   R
Basic LLRR…(FSP)'''(D-TES)'''(O-DES)…Repeat, change leading arm
                    f \ e-f   e-f
</pre>

#8 Outward-*Double* Elbow Strike, Downward-Triple Elbow Strike

$$L \qquad L \qquad L\backslash R\text{-}R \qquad R$$
Basic LLRR…(FSP)'''(O-DES)'''**(D-TES)**'''(FCP)
$$\text{e-f} \qquad \text{f}\backslash\text{e-f}$$

#9 Downward-Triple Elbow Strike, Outward-Triple Elbow Strike.

$$L \qquad L\backslash R\text{-}R \qquad R\text{-}R\backslash L \qquad L \qquad R \qquad R$$
Basic LLRR…(FSP)'''**(D-TES)**'''(O-TES)'''(FCP)'''(FSP)'''(FCP)….repeat
$$\text{f}\backslash\text{e-f} \qquad \text{e-f}\backslash\text{f}$$

#10 Outward-Triple Elbow Strike, Downward-Triple Elbow Strike

$$R \qquad R\text{-}R\backslash L \qquad L\backslash R\text{-}R \qquad R \qquad L \qquad L$$
Basic LLRR…(FSP)'''(O-TES)'''**(D-TES)**'''(FCP)'''(FSP)'''(FCP)…Repeat
$$\text{e-f}\backslash\text{f} \qquad \text{f}\backslash\text{e-f}$$

Linking from the Downward-Triple Elbow Strike

The Downward-Triple Elbow technique offers the same three linking options as the Front Double Punch, since both fists contact the bag. Either the *lead fist*, *second fist* or *Both* can [1/2] or [8] through, as shown in Chapter 5. Several examples are offered below. Linking fist(s) are **underlined Bold**.

Fig 7E Ex. #11 Left Leading Downward-Triple Elbow Strike, *Lead Fist* pass through [8]

#11 Downward-Triple Elbow Strike, Lead (first) hand Figure-[8] pass through

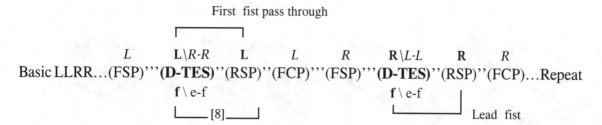

First fist pass through

     L   **L***R-R*   **L**   *L*   *R*   **R***L-L*   **R**   *R*

Basic LLRR…(FSP)'''**(D-TES)**''(RSP)''(FCP)'''(FSP)'''**(D-TES)**''(RSP)''(FCP)…Repeat

        f \ e-f   **f** \ e-f

              [8]   Lead fist

* The underlined (D-TES)''(RSP) techniques are shown in FIG 7E, on the bottom of the last page.

> When you link the *same fist* as the Downward Elbow, try and get that elbow up to parallel quickly after contact. If not, the fist will pass through in a downward angle, and return in an upward angle - hitting the bottom of the bag and driving it up into the swivel.

#12 Downward-Triple Elbow Strike, Last (second) fist [8]

last fist pass through

     L   **L***R*-**R**   **R**   *R*   **R***L*-**L**   **L**   *L*

Basic LLRR…(FSP)'''**(D-TES)**''(RSP)''(FCP)'''**(D-TES)**''(RSP)''(FCP)

        f \ e-**f**   f \ e-**f**

              [8]   2nd fist

#13 Continuous, alternating Downward-Triple Elbow Strikes, separated by second fist [8]
    ** *This is a very quick sequence.   Keep the elbows up.*

     L   **L***R*-**R**   **R**   **R***L*-**L**   **L**   *L*

Basic LLRR…(FSP)'''**(D-TES)**''(RSP)''**(D-TES)**''(RSP)''(FCP)…Basic

        f \ e-**f**   f \ e-**f**

           [8]   [8]

There is a lot happening in sequence #13. As the second fist is linking [8], the arm in front is moving into position for the next Downward motion.

#14 Downward-Triple Elbow Strike, Both fists [8]. (*See Fig.* **7F**, *next page*)

     L   **L***R*-**R**   *R-L*   *L-R*   *R*   **R***L*-**L**   *L-R*   *R-L*   *L*

BasicLLRR…(FSP)'''**(D-TES)**''(RDP)''(FDP)'''(FCP)'''**(DTES)**''(RDP)''(FDP)'''(FCP)…Basic…

       f \ e-**f**   **f** \ e-**f**

The underlined techniques **(D-TES)'' (RDP)** are shown below in FIG 7F

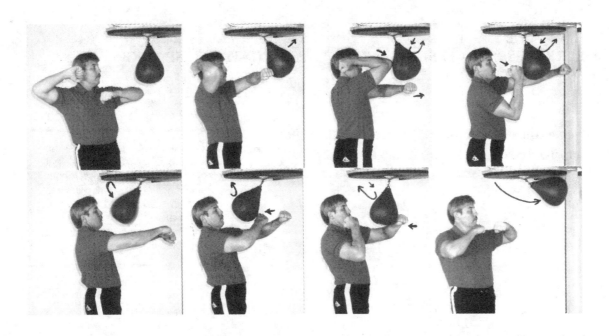

Fig 7F Ex. #14 **Downward-Triple Elbow Strike, Both fists pass through**

#15 Downward-Triple Elbow Strike after single fist Figure-[8] pass through

$$
\begin{array}{ccccccccc}
L & L & L & L\backslash R\text{-}R & R & R & R & R\backslash L\text{-}L & L
\end{array}
$$
Basic LLRR…(FSP)'''(FCP)''(RSP)''**(D-TES)**'''(FCP)'''(FCP)''(RSP)''**(D-TES)**…(FCP)
└── [8] ──┘   f \ e-f   └── [8] ──┘   f \ e-f

#16 Downward-Triple Elbow Strike, after both fists [8].

last fist leads next   last fist leads

$$
\begin{array}{ccccccccc}
L & L\text{-}R & R\text{-}L & L\backslash R\text{-}R & R & R\text{-}L & L\text{-}R & R\backslash L\text{-}L & L
\end{array}
$$
Basic LLRR…(FSP)'''(FDP)''(RDP)''**(D-TES)**'''(FCP)'''(FDP)''(RDP)''**(D-TES)**'''(FCP)
                          f \ e-f   f \ e-f
└── [8] ──┘   └── [8] ──┘
Both Fists   **Both Fists**

In this last exercise, notice how the second (last) fist of the front and reverse double punches lead the next technique. Also, the last fist of the Reverse Double Punch will lead the Downward Triple Elbow Strike . You must anticipate the Downward technique and let the lead fist of the Reverse Double Punch immediately raise up for the downward motion as the second fist connects.

As you can see, Downward-Triple Elbow Striking offers a wide range of enter and exit possibilities. Practice the above sequences, and others you may create, until the downward striking motion feels smooth, comfortable and efficient.

In the next chapter, we will combine the "double elbow strikes" to create several new techniques that will use both fists and both elbows in the same technique.

IT IS MUCH EASIER TO DO THESE TECHNIQUES ON A MOVING BAG.

For Beginners, it may be easier to start a Downward Elbow Strike by simply doing a few easy Front Circle Punches (FCP) and then do the downward technique. This is written below.

$$L \qquad L \qquad L \qquad L\backslash R\text{-}R$$
$$\text{(FCP)'''(FCP)'''(FCP)'''}\textbf{(D-TES)}$$
$$\text{f} \backslash \text{ e-f}$$

Left Leading Downward-Triple Elbow Strike

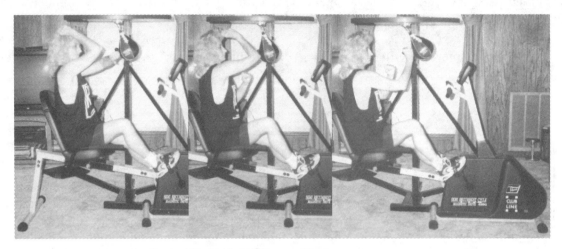

Left leading D-TES on Cycle

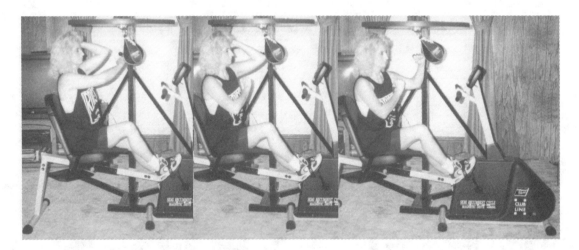

Right leading D-TES on Cycle

Don't Forget Those Glasses!   Take them OFF for Downward Elbow Strikes

Chapter 8

Four-Way Elbow Striking

To this point, we have advanced each elbow striking category to the "triple" strike technique, which includes three contact surfaces, one elbow and both fists, in a variety of combinations. Since we have now covered all the elbow categories (Outward, Inward and Downward), we can begin to address techniques using both elbows and both fists together in one technique.

Four-way striking is a unique category of bag techniques and becomes possible by joining the double elbow strikes into one movement. During this motion, the bag will strike all four contact points - both fists and both elbows, with only one rebound inbetween. This action will create four distinctly accented beats. After a four-way strike, the bag will rebound three times before the next technique, (unless linking follows).

There are two types of Four-way Strikes, the Out-&-Down, and the Out-&-In. These names describe the motion of the elbow strikes used within each technique.

The Out-&-Down Four-Way Elbow Strike   (O-D 4way)

This technique, symbolized by (O-D 4way), is created by executing a *Outward*-Double Elbow Strike and a *Downward*-Double Elbow Strike together as one motion with one rebound between all parts.

Fig 8A-1 Out & Down 4-way Elbow Strike

We can see this as: (O-DES)+(D-DES)=(O-D 4way). This will take some practice and demands control of those two movements. The bag will contact the elbow-then-fist of the first (outward) arm, and then the elbow and fist of the second (downward) arm **[FIG 8A-1&2]**. The same leg of the leading arm will straighten and the weight will shift onto it as the first (outward moving) elbow connects. As an example, when the left arm leads the Out-&-down 4way Elbow Strike, the left knee will be bent as your upper body twists into the ready position. As you rotate to begin the technique, your left leg will straighten and your weight will shift to it. As shown in figure 8A, the "outward" motion begins and the bag first contacts the left elbow, rebounds once into the left fist, rebounds again into the right (downward) elbow and finally into the right fist. As the right (downward) elbow descends, the right knee will bend in towards the bag. (Notice that in the middle of this technique, there is an interesting double strike created by the fist of one arm and the elbow of another.)

Fig 8A-2 Out & Down 4-way Elbow Strike, Different Angle

The key to this technique is the spacing and position of the "outward" fist, and "downward" elbow. They must travel to the bag on the same line. Be sure and leave enough room between them. If the "out" moving fist (left in our example) and "down" moving elbow (right) are too close, then the bag will strike the "down" moving forearm and slide, usually killing the movement. *Also, remove your eyeglasses because the last (downward) fist, can knock them off*. As usual, the bottom line will feature the elbow-and-fist sequence. Several practice exercises include:

#1 Out-&-Down 4way same hand lead.


```
              L          L-L\R-R        R
Basic LLRR...(FSP)'''(O-D 4way)'''(FCP)...Repeat, change lead
                        e-f \ e-f
Count         1-2-3     1-2-3-4-2-3     1-2-3
```


Notice the larger "**4**" in the count line, which indicates the loudest rebound as the bag strikes the right fist "**R**". Also, the last arm (right) of the 4way leads the next (FCP) technique.

#2   Out-&-Down 4way alternating lead arms within Basic Rhythm

$$L \qquad L\text{-}L\backslash R\text{-}R \qquad R \qquad L \qquad L \qquad R \qquad R\text{-}R\backslash L\text{-}L \qquad L$$
Basic LLRR…(FSP)'''**(O-D 4way)**'''(FCP)'''(FSP)'''(FCP)'''(FSP)'''**(O-D 4way)**'''(FCP)…Basic
$$\qquad\qquad\qquad \text{e-f} \backslash \text{e-f} \qquad\qquad\qquad\qquad\qquad\qquad\qquad \text{e-f} \backslash \text{e-f}$$

#3   Continuous, Alternating Out-&-Down 4way Elbow strikes

$$L \qquad L\text{-}L\backslash R\text{-}R \qquad R\text{-}R\backslash L\text{-}L \qquad L\text{-}L\backslash R\text{-}R \qquad R\text{-}R\backslash L\text{-}L \qquad L$$
Basic LLRR…(FSP)'''**(O-D 4way)**'''**(O-D 4way)**'''**(O-D 4way)**'''**(O-D 4way)**'''(FCP)…Basic
$$\qquad\qquad\quad \text{e-f} \backslash \text{e-f} \qquad \text{e-f} \backslash \text{e-f} \qquad \text{e-f} \backslash \text{e-f} \qquad \text{e-f} \backslash \text{e-f}$$
Count   *1*-2-3   1- 2- 3-*4*-2-3   1- 2- 3-*4*-2-3   1- 2- 3-*4*-2-3   1- 2- 3-*4*-2-3   *1*-2-3

Linking and the Out & Down 4way Elbow Strike

As with all the techniques that have both fists in them, you can [1/2] or [8] with either or both fists. It is just like a FDP but with an elbow in the middle. The first fist, which is moving "outward" is the most difficult of the two, but the pass through movement is exactly the same as the FCP. It will feel strange at first, for it will pass through and pause behind the bag as the second (downward) arm completes the technique. In fact, when the first fist makes contact this becomes a Downward-Triple Elbow Strike and linking the second fist is exacty the same as D-TES. Try these practice sequences to learn control. As usual, since there are unwritten punches occuring during the [8] movement, this symbol will not be used. (Take it slow…there is a lot of movement going on.) The linking fist will be larger and **underlined bold** in both the top and bottom line.   * *remove your eyeglasses*

#4   Out-&-Down 4way lead (first) fist figure-[8] pass through, to (FCP)

$$L \qquad L\text{-}\mathbf{L}\backslash R\text{-}R \qquad L \qquad L \qquad R$$
Basic LLRR…(FSP)'''**(O-D 4way)**''(RSP)''(FCP)'''(FSP)
$$\qquad\qquad\quad \text{e-}\mathbf{f} \backslash \text{e-f}$$
$$\qquad\qquad\qquad \lfloor\!\_\!\_\!\_ \text{[8]} \_\!\_\!\_\!\rfloor$$

In the above combination, the **L** fist must wait behind the bag for a moment as the Right Elbow-Fist complete the technique.

#5   Out-&-Down 4way second (last) fist Figure-[8], to (FCP)

$$L \qquad L\text{-}L\backslash R\text{-}\mathbf{R} \qquad R \qquad R$$
Basic LLRR…(FSP)'''**(O-D 4way)**''(RSP)''(FCP)…Repeat
$$\qquad\qquad\quad \text{e-f} \backslash \text{e-}\mathbf{f} \qquad\qquad\qquad\qquad \text{change lead.}$$
$$\qquad\qquad\qquad \lfloor\!\_\!\_ \text{[8]} \_\!\_\!\rfloor$$

#6 Out-&-Down 4way Both fists Figure [8] pass through, to (**FDP**)   (note " rebounds)

```
         L        L-L\R-R    R-L      L-R       R
Basic LLRR…(FSP)'''(O-D 4way)"(RDP)"(FDP)'''(FCP)….Repeat, change lead
         e-f \ e-f
             └─┐
 Both  Fists     └──── [8] ────┘
```

It is important to realize that both fists simply extend out, through the bag, and back to create the Reverse Double Punch (RDP) behind the bag. Be sure and get the right elbow back up to the parallel position after it connects in the downward motion.

Again, any technique covered so far can be used after the reverse technique in the [8], including elbow strikes and fist rolling. In the next example, we will follow the [8] with the opposite fist.

#7 Out-&-Down 4way lead (left) fist figure [8] pass through, opposite fist (right) follow-up

```
                            quick  Split Fist  combo
                       ┌──────────────┐
         L        L-L\R-R     L      R*       R
Basic LLRR…(FSP)'''(O-D 4way)"(RSP)"(FSP)'''(FCP)….Repeat, change arms.
         e-f \ e-f
```

Above the left fist passes through and returns to the front ready position and the right fist (***R****) follows with the FSP after two rebounds. The fists are momentarily split between the front and back of the bag.

I have not shown any [1/2] link sequences, but it can be used just as effectively. Simply substitute (O-D 4way)-**[1/2]-(RSP)**''' within any of the above. You can exit the (RSP) by going to any technique, including another Out-&-Down 4way….As demonstrated below.   * Exact techniques only

#8   [1/2] link, followed by (O-D 4way)

```
                                                   *  L        L-L\R-R
                                                   (RSP)"(O-D 4way)
        L     L      L    1    L-L\R-R      R           e-f \ e-f
   (RSP)'''(RSP)'''(RSP)-[1/2]-(O-D 4way)'''(FCP)….Basic
                         e-f \ e-f
```

The Out-&-In 4way Elbow Strike (O-I 4way)

The Out-&-In 4way strike, symbolized by (O-I 4way), is another sequence combining both fists and elbows into one technique. It is performed by combining an "*Outward*" Double Elbow Strike with an "*Inward*" Double Elbow Strike.

Fig 8B Out & In 4-way Elbow Strike

We can visualize this as: (O-DES)+(I-DES) = (O-I 4way). This creates a unique "elbow fist-fist-elbow" order of attack. As an example, if this technique is initiated with a left arm lead, the left elbow-fist will hit the bag in the "outward" direction and the right fist and right elbow will strike from the "inward" direction….all with only one bounce between **[FIG 8B]**. *The secret is to be sure to use full shoulder, torso rotation and bring the last (inward) elbow crisply into the bag.* This is best done by swiveling on the ball of the same foot as the inward elbow (right foot in this example) and emphasize the heel raising up as you turn. Just as with all the inward movements, it is difficult to recover easily due to the body turn. The following exercises can be used to develop this technique.

#1   Out-&-In elbow strike from (FCP)

L	*L*	*L*	**L-L\R-R**	*R*
(FCP)'''	(FCP)'''	(FCP)'''	**(O-I 4way)**'''	(FCP)…continue
			e-f \ f-e	
Count	*1*-2-3		*1-2-3-4*-2-3	*1*-2-3

#2   Out-&-In 4way followed by (O-DES)

	L	**L-L\R-R**	*R*
Basic LLRR…(FSP)'''	**(O-I 4way)**'''	(O-DES)…Repeat, change hands
	e-f \ f-e	e-f

#3 Combining the Out-&-Down and the Out-&-In 4way strikes

| L | L-L\R-R | R-R\L-L | L-L\R-R | R-R\L-L | L |

Basic LLRR…(FSP)'''(O-D 4way)'''(O-I 4way)'''(O-I 4way)'''(O-D 4way)'''(FCP)…Basic

e-f \ e-f   e-f \ f-e   e-f \ f-e   e-f \ e-f

Although you cannot link off the "in" arm, theoretically you could link with the "out" fist. This is very difficult because of the rotated position after the in-movement. You may want to try it a few times. I use the Out-&-In 4way mostly as the final technique to end a sequence.

You can also link to either of the 4way elbow strikes from a RDP, as shown below, with just the exact techniques written. (no linking symbols) note the two '' rebounds.

| L | L-R | R-L* | L-L\R-R | R-L | L-L\R-R |

(FSP)'''(FDP) '' (RDP) '' (O-D 4way) '' (RDP) '' (O-I 4way)'''…..basic

e-f \ e-f   e-f \ f-e

The key to these combinations is getting into the proper position after the (RDP), especially for the Out-&-Down technique. Get the right arm and elbow up immediately as the left fist (*L**) hits in the RDP.

The Four-Way elbow strikes completes 18 individual striking techniques. In the next chapter we will start looking at the six techniques that utilize the sides of the speed bag.

Out & In   4-way Elbow Strike

Chapter 9

SIDE TECHNIQUES

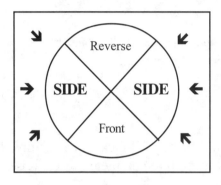

Fig 9A **Side areas of bag**

Striking from the sides of the bag offers a great deal of variety. I have not seen many people develop this area on their own. Martial artists use some of their striking techniques in this manner, but many boxers do not pursue it. In this chapter we will learn to use the sides of the bag as well as the front and back.

There are six techniques from the side, two single punches, three double punches and a triple elbow strike. They are often the most difficult to learn and understand...mostly because of the dramatic effect they have on rhythm and timing. To this point, every individual technique had *all* the striking surfaces come from the same side of the bag. As we will see, several side striking techniques are the exception to this rule. The **key** factor of the side techniques is the entrance of a fist from the side of the bag **[FIG 9A]**. The effect of this motion on the rhythm will be discussed as they occur.

SIDE SINGLE PUNCH (SSP)

This technique, indicated by (SSP), is almost exactly the same as the Reverse Single Punch. The only difference is the contact point on the speed bag. The key to this technique is the starting position of the fist, which must already be extended out to the side of the bag **[FIG 9B-1&2]**. This is easily done from the ready position by extending the arm straight out from the elbow, moving the fist to the side of the bag. *The secret is having the extended arm parallel to the ground.* (This is one reason why I stress keeping the elbows up. Elbow strikes and Side techniques are almost impossible to do with the elbows down.) A Side Single Punch is performed by swinging "in" from the elbow, bringing the fist to contact the bag on

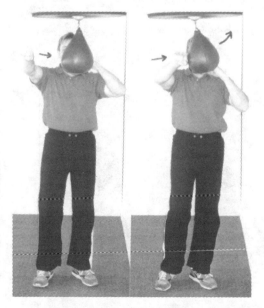

Fig 9B-1 **Side Single Punch**

the large knuckle of the index finger (same spot as the reverse punches). Once the fist strikes the side of the bag, it can re-circle to do it again. This sequence is written as:

#1   Side Single Punch, Same side fist

$$R \qquad R \qquad R \qquad R$$
(SSP)'''(SSP)'''(SSP)'''(SSP)....Repeat,

At this point, to alternate with Side Single Punches, we must use an even number of rebounds, for the alternate side punch comes from... "the opposite side". .

#2 Side Single Punching, alternating fists (Note the two '' between the R & L and L & R)

Fig 9B-2 **Side Single Punch, fist contact**

$$R \qquad R \qquad R \qquad L \qquad L \qquad L \qquad R \qquad R$$
(SSP)'''(SSP)'''(SSP)''(SSP)'''(SSP)'''(SSP)''(SSP)'''(SSP)
1-2-3   1-2-3   1-2   1-2-3   1-2-3   1-2   1-2-3

In the last exercise, each fist entered from the opposite side of the bag. We can advance this to another "split fist" combination, as written below (the elbows must be high to complete this exercise).

#3   Continuous alternating Side Single Punching, "split fists". * (note the '' rebounds)

$$L \qquad R \qquad L \qquad R$$
(SSP)''(SSP)''(SSP)''(SSP)...continue

Fig 9C **Side "Split Fists"**

This side-to-side Split Fist combination **[FIG 9C]** is slightly unstable due to the "angle of entry" of the fists. We can make this easier by altering the angle of the fists to hit straight from the side of the bag...not rear-side. Do this by *dragging* the fists more directly into the side of the bag by letting the shoulders move the arms across, and not flex the elbow completely. Also, angle (bend) the fist *toward your little finger,* which creates a flatter surface for the bag to contact over the thumb, and a more side-to-side rebound.

Splitting the fists between the sides of the bag can create some interesting combinations, just like splitting the fists between the front and back. These combinations will be fully developed in the chapter of advanced combinations.

Of course, we also want to flow from a Side Single Punch to a front punch. This presents a new concept in making combinations. We have always combined techniques from either the same direction (after three rebounds) or the opposite direction (after two rebounds). This new side-to-front combination creates what I call rule of rhythm #3, "mixing directions", and will create some special situations-particularly with the double punch techniques later in the chapter. Since this will include linking, we need to slightly modify the definition of linking.

Side Techniques and Linking

To this point, linking [1/2] or [8] has always meant the fist(s) passed through to the opposite side of the bag. We will now change the definition to "pass through to a different side of the bag." The method of executing this is exactly the same except we will begin linking side-to-front.

The next two exercises will focus on *single fist* side-to-front combinations with the same arm or opposite arms. Each will occur on an even bounce. (note the **two** '' rebounds)

#4 Combining a Side Single Punch with a Front Circle Punch, same arm [1/2]

    R   *R*   *R*   r   *R*   *R*   *R*
 (SSP)'''**(SSP)**'''**(SSP)**-[1/2]-**(FCP)**'''**(FCP)**'''**(FCP)**....Change Hands
   1-2-3   *1-2-3*   *1-2*   *1-2-3*   *1-2-3*   *1-2-3*

The above change feels almost exactly like (RSP)-[1/2]-(FCP). In fact, the only difference is the fist connecting slightly more to the side of the bag than the back.

#5 Combining a Side Single Punch with a Front Circle Punch or Front Straight Punch, opposite arm.

      L   *L*   *R*   *R*   *L*   *L*   *R*   *R*
 A. **(SSP)**'''**(SSP)**''(FCP)'''(FCP)...change   B. **(SSP)**'''**(SSP)**''(FSP)'''(FSP)...Change Hands
    1-2-3   *1-2*   *1-2-3* *1-2-3*

Exercises four and five demonstrate that any front technique following a side punch will occur after an even number of rebounds. Now let's learn how to change from a front punch to a side punch. This will depend on which arm enters from the side, the same or opposite. The next practice patterns are offered to familiarize you with the variations.

#6 Front-Side combination, (FCP)-(SSP) with the same arm [1/2]   exact techniques

    R   *R*   *R*   r   *R*   *R*   *R*
 (FCP)'''(FCP)'''(ΓCP)-[1/2]-**(SSP)**'''**(SSP)**'''**(SSP)**....Change Hands
   1-2-3   *1-2-3*   *1-2*   *1-2-3*   *1-2-3*   *1-2-3*

                                                                       R   R
                                                                  (FCP)''**(SSP)**

Exercise six feels almost like a (FCP)-[1/2]-(RSP). The main difference is the position of the elbow doing the (SSP), which is straight out to your side, not angled in front of the body as in (RSP).

#7 Front-Side combination, (FSP)-(SSP) with the same arm (Odd count)

    R   *R*   *R*   **R**   **R**   **R**
(FSP)'''(FSP)'''(FSP)**'''(SSP)**'''**(SSP)**'''**(SSP)**....Change leading hand

     This last combination has a slightly unnatural movement, swinging "in" to the bag with the (FSP), then quickly swinging "in" again from the side. It takes good control. Exercise #6 and #7 are different because of the angle the bag travels after each technique.

#8 Front-Side combination, (FSP)-(SSP) with the opposite arm (even count)

    R   *R*   *R*   *L*   *L*   *L*
(FSP)'''(FSP)'''(FSP)**''(SSP)**'''**(SSP)**'''**(SSP)**....Change Hands

     Notice the R and L have two rebounds between them.

#9 Front-Side combination, (FCP)-(SSP) with the opposite arm (Odd count)

    L   *L*   *L*   **R**   **R**   **R**
(FCP)'''(FCP)'''(FCP)**'''(SSP)**'''**(SSP)**'''**(SSP)**....Change hands
  1-2-3   *1-2-3*   *1-2-3*   *1-2-3*   *1-2-3*   *1-2-3*

Side Single Punch and Figure-8 Linking

     Doing a Figure-8 link between the *front and side* of the bag with a single fist is only a slightly different than between the front and back. The main difference is the angle of fist entry into the bag.

#10 Side-Front combination, (SSP)-(FCP) with same arm linking figure-[8] pass through

    R   *R*   **R**   r *R*   *R*   **R**   r *R*
(SSP)'''(SSP)'''(SSP)**-[8]-**(SSP)'''(SSP)'''(SSP)**-[8]-(SSP)**....Change hands
  1-2-3   *1-2-3*   *1-2-1-2* *1-2-3* *1-2-3* *1-2-1-2* *1-2-3*

     Here the Right fist is passing "side-front-side" and **there is an unwritten (FCP) in the combination**. The exact techniques are (SSP)''(FCP)''(SSP). **Because of this unwritten punch, the [8] symbol will not be used**. Angle the (FCP) more "out" to the side, and not straight into the bag.

#11 Front-Side combination, (FCP)-(SSP) with same arm linking figure -[8] pass through

    R   *R*   **R**   **R**   *R*   *R*   **R**   **R**   *R*
(FCP)'''(FCP)'''(FCP)''(SSP)''(FCP)'''(FCP)'''(FCP)''(SSP)''(FCP)....Change hands
  1-2-3   *1-2-3*   *1-2-1-2* *1-2-3* *1-2-3* *1-2-1-2* *1-2-3*

     Here the Right fist is passing "*front-side-front*" in the Figure-8. Again, using the symbol "[8]" could be confusing if you did not know the fist goes to the side, because it would be written the same if the fist went to the back of the bag. This is another reason why I avoid using this symbol.

One way to be sure the fist connects the side of the speed bag, and not the back, is to keep the elbow "back" in line with the shoulder. Do not let the upper arm push forward.

Now let's begin using the Side Single Punch in the Basic Rhythm. There are a few ways we can do this, as the following practice exercises will demonstrate.

#12 Basic Rhythm, (FCP) to (SSP) - by same arm [1/2]

           L   *l*   *L*   *L*   *l*   *l*   *R*   *R*   *L*
Basic LLRR...(FCP)-[1/2]-(SSP)'''(SSP)-[1/2]-(FCP)'''(FSP)'''(FCP)'''(FSP)...repeat, change lead

This is similiar to exercise #6. Instead of doing several (SSP) after each other, we can also Figure-[8] link, as the next pattern demonstrates.

#13 Basic Rhythm, (FCP) to (SSP) - by same arm figure-[8] pass through

           R   *R*   *R*   *L*   *L*   *L*   *L*   *R*
Basic LLRR... (FCP)''(SSP)''(FCP)'''(FSP)'''(FCP)''(SSP)''(FCP)'''(FSP)...repeat

#14 Basic Rhythm, (FCP) to (SSP) - by opposite arm

          L   **R**   *r*   *R*   *L*
Basic LLRR...(FCP)'''(SSP)-[1/2]-(FCP)'''(FSP)....repeat, change leading hand

The key to this combination is anticipating the SSP with the opposite fist (**R**).

#15 Basic Rhythm, (FSP) to (SSP) - by opposite arm

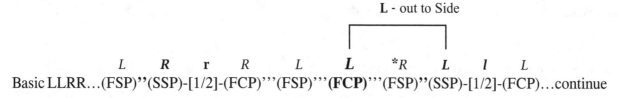

L - out to Side

          L   **R**   *r*   *R*   *L*   **L**   **R*   *L*   *l*   *L*
Basic LLRR...(FSP)''(SSP)-[1/2]-(FCP)'''(FSP)'''**(FCP)**'''(FSP)''(SSP)-[1/2]-(FCP)...continue

There are only **two** rebounds between the (FSP) and the (SSP) by the other arm (exactly as in exercise #8). The secret to doing this combination is letting the fist move to the side in a smooth motion. Notice the underlined **(FCP)** by the larger left fist (**L**). Let this fist continue out to the side as the right fist (**R*) does the (FSP). (They are both going in the same direction and the body position is correct). Now it's ready to enter for the (SSP) after two rebounds.

Several of the practice exercises have the (SSP) following a (FCP) after three rebounds... (#9 & #14). Since these two combine on an odd bounce, we can use only one rebound inbetween and create the next technique....The Side Double Punch.

THE SIDE DOUBLE PUNCH   (SDP)

The Side Double Punch, indicated by (SDP), creates a double accented beat just like every other double strike. It is the first technique that will combine *two different sides of the bag within the same technique*. It is performed by throwing an opposite arm (FCP)-(SSP) combination, with one bounce inbetween **(FIG 9D)**. The Front Circle Punch is angled more to the side and uses a slight shoulder motion to move the elbow sideways. The fist crosses more "eye-to-eye" than straight out from the nose.

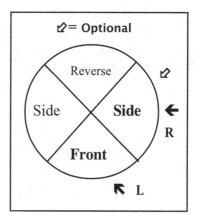

Fig 9D Fist entry of a "L-R" SDP

Fig 9E Side Double Punch

The second fist, which enters from the side of the bag, must have already drifted to the side position **(FIG 9E)**. The swing motion is made from the elbows, extending one fist out while pulling the other one in. As an example, for a left lead (SDP), the left fist will execute a Front Circle Punch, the bag will rebound to the back of the board once and be struck from the right side by the right fist. Both fists are thrown as one movement, like the Front Double Punch.

The following practice sequences will develop this skill.

#1 Side Double Punch, exit to Side Single Punch

$$\begin{array}{cccccc} L & L & L & \textbf{L-R} & \textbf{R} & R \\ \text{(FCP)'''} & \text{(FCP)'''} & \text{(FCP)'''} & \textbf{(SDP)'''} & \text{(SSP)'''} & \text{(SSP)}.... \\ \textit{1-2-3} & \textit{1-2-3} & \textit{1-2-3} & \textit{1-1-2-3} & \textit{1-2-3} & \textit{1-2-3} \end{array}$$

We see the (SSP) Punch (**R**) follows smoothly in a triplet rhythm because it came from the same side as the right fist in the Side Double Punch. Naturally we will not always follow the (SDP) with a same side punch. As we have seen, any technique following from the front will use *two rebounds*, as the next few practice patterns will demonstrate.

Sideways Striking Techniques

#2 Side Double Punch, second fist [1/2] to Front Circle Punch   * Exact Techniques only

   L   L-R   r   R   R   R-L   l   L
(FCP)'''(SDP)-[1/2]-(FCP)'''(FCP)'''(SDP)-[1/2]-(FCP)....repeat
   1-2-3   1-1-2   1-2-3 1-2-3   1-1-2   1-2-3

                                                      L   L-R   R
                                              * (FCP)'''(SDP)''(FCP)

#3 Side Double Punch, lead fist [1/2], to Side Single Punch, on opposite side   * Techniques only

                                                      ..to other side
                                                      ┌──────┐
   L   L   L-R   l   L   L
(FCP)'''(FCP)'''(SDP)-[1/2]-(SSP)'''(SSP)....Change lead
   1-2-3   1-2-3   1-1-2   1-2-3 1-2-3

                                              * (FCP)'''(SDP)''(SSP)
                                                      L   L-R   L

The last pattern is performed by allowing the lead fist of the Side Double Punch (**L**) to extend out to the side other and circle back "in" for the Side Single Punch. The swinging motion already aims the left fist in that direction, and creates a quick "side-side split fist". In fact, after a Side Double Punch, the fists are in the perfect position to repeat a Side Double Punch in the opposite direction.

#4 Side Double Punch, both fist [1/2] to opposite Side Double Punch

   R   R   R-L   *B*   L-R   R   r   R
(FCP)'''(FCP)'''(SDP)-[1/2]-(SDP)'''(SSP)-[1/2]-(FCP)...Change lead
   1-2-3   1-2-3   1-1-2   1-1-2-3 1-2-3 1-2

In the last sequence, notice how the second fist (**L**) smoothly becomes the "lead" fist for the next Side Double Punch. *The **(SDP)-[1/2]-(SDP)** combination can also be written as **(SDP)''(SDP)** or as (SDP)-[8]. We will see this in the Figure-8 pass through linking exercises shortly.

The Side Double Punch is easily followed by a Front Double Punch. Instead of extending the lead fist out to the side for another (SDP), keep it close to the chin. The second fist of the (SDP) will hit the side and circle back to lead the Front Double Punch. This combination uses two rebounds in-between.

#5 Side Double Punch, second fist [1/2] to Front Double Punch   * Exact Techniques only

   R   R   *R-L   l   L-*R   R
(FCP)'''(FCP)'''(SDP)-[1/2]-(FDP)'''(FCP)...Change lead
   1-2-3   1-2-3   1-1-2   1-1-2-3 1-2-3

                                              R   *R-L   L-*R
                                          * (FCP)'''(SDP)''(FDP)

Notice the left (**L**) fist in the (SDP) links from the side to the front to lead the (FDP).
The right fist (***R**) has not changed sides. It leads the Side Double Punch from the front, and follows in the Front Double Punch from the front. Techniques only (*) are shown to the right.

The Side Double Punch can also follow a Front Double Punch. To do this, let the lead (first) fist of the (FDP) continue moving to the side. This puts it in perfect position for the following (SDP). *This combination occurs with the triplet rhythm and has three rebounds inbetween.*

81

#6 Front Double Punch, to Side Double Punch, second fist return to front

   R   *R*   *R*   **R-*L*** ***L*-R**   **r**   *R*
(FCP)'''(FCP)'''(FCP)'''(FDP)'''(SDP)-[1/2]-(FCP)…repeat, change lead
  1-2-3 *1*-2-3 *1*-2-3 *1*-*1*-2-3 *1*-*1*-2   *1*-2-3

Notice the (SDP) follows the (FDP) after three rebounds because the left fist (*L*) hits twice in a row from the front of the bag - which must occur on an odd count. The right fist (**R**) which leads the (FDP) simply extends out to re-enter from the side. We can now begin using the (SDP) in the Basic Rhythm.

#7 From Basic Rhythm, Side Double Punch, second fist [1/2] to front

       R   **R-L** **l**   *L*
Basic LLRR…(FSP)'''**(SDP)**-[1/2]-(FCP)…Repeat

#8 Side Double Punch, Alternating lead hand

       R   **R-L** **l** *L*   *L*   ***L*-R** **r**   *R*
Basic LLRR…(FSP)'''**(SDP)**-[1/2]-(FCP)'''(FCP)'''**(SDP)**-[1/2]-(FCP)…Change lead

   Now we can combine the Side Double Punch with other techniques from the front. Linking fists will be **underlined bold**.

#9 Side Double Punch to Outward-Double Elbow Strike

         L   ***L*-R** **r**   *R*
Basic LLRR…(FSP)'''**(SDP)**-[1/2]-(O-DES)…Repeat, change lead
            e-f

> * Techniques only
>
>   ***L*-R**   *R*
>   **(SDP)** '' (O-DES)
>   e-f

   A tip to make this combination easier is to pull the right fist (**R**) underneath the left ear after the **(SDP)**. Twist from the waist with the movement. The key is to get the *right elbow* just under the nose.

#10 Side Double Punch to Outward-Triple Elbow Strike

     R **R-L** **l** **L-*L*\R** *R*   *L* ***L*-R** **r** **R-*R*\L** *L*
Basic LLRR…(FSP)'''**(SDP)**-[1/2]-(O-TES)'''(FCP)'''(FSP)'''**(SDP)**-[1/2]-(O-TES)'''(FCP)…repeat
          e-f \ f   e-f \ f

#11 Side Double Punch to Front-Fist Roll

     L   ***L*-R** **r** R-L-R-L-R *R*
Basic LLRR…(FSP)'''**(SDP)**-[1/2]-(F-Roll)'''(FCP)….repeat, change lead.

SIDE DOUBLE PUNCH & FIGURE-8 LINKING

Let's advance to include full Figure-8 linking. We can do a figure-[8] pass through with either one or both fists. This will create some special situations because each fist has a different "original position" with the lead fist in front and the second fist on the side. Performing the skills is not terribly difficult but writing practice exercises is more challenging. The side techniques force us to constantly change sides of the bag with either or both fists. I have always used the linking symbol [1/2] because it signals changing sides of the bag. However, sometimes it is easier to understand by showing every technique in the sequence with two rebounds ('') inbetween, and not use a linking symbol. This method is more precise in reflecting exactly what the fists are doing. Linking fist(s) will be **underlined bold**.

Single Fist Figure-8 Linking from the Side

#12 Side Double Punch, Lead (first) fist Figure [8] pass through   (exact techniques only at right)

$$L \quad\quad L\text{-}R \quad\quad l \quad\quad L \quad\quad\quad\quad\quad L \quad\quad L\text{-}\boldsymbol{R}^* \quad {}^*L \quad\quad L$$

Basic LLRR…(FSP)'''**(SDP)**-[8]-(FCP)…Basic   or   (FSP)'''(SDP)''(SSP)''(FCP)

The lead fist in the last exercise is the left (L) and its "original" position is in front. It strikes the bag, passes through to the side, hits and returns to the front. It makes a Figure-8 from "eye-to-eye". *There is an unwritten SSP that occurs. Because of this unwritten punch, I will not use the* [8] *symbol in the written exercise*. Also, notice a quick side-to-side split fist action between the right (larger $\boldsymbol{R}^*$ ${}^*L$) of the SDP and the L of the SSP.

#13 Side Double Punch, last (second) fist figure-[8] pass through

$$L \quad\quad L\text{-}\mathbf{R} \quad\quad \mathbf{R} \quad\quad R$$

Basic LLRR…(FSP)'''(SDP)''(FCP)''(SSP)

In the last sequence, the right fist links off the (SDP). Since it begins from the side the [8] gets it back to the original side position. To smoothly return to the front it must return [1/2] to the front. This is demonstrated below. (Linking fist is **underlined**.)

#14 Side Double Punch, last fist Figure - [8] and return to front   (exact techniques only)

$$L \quad\quad L\text{-}\mathbf{R} \quad\quad \mathbf{R} \quad\quad \mathbf{R} \quad\quad r \quad\quad R \quad\quad\quad L \quad\quad L\text{-}\mathbf{R} \quad\quad \mathbf{R} \quad\quad \mathbf{R} \quad\quad R$$

Basic LLRR…(FSP)'''**(SDP)**''(FCP)''(SSP)''-[1/2]-(FCP)   or   (FSP)'''**(SDP)**''(FCP)''(SSP)''(FCP)

It may be helpful to remember that in the [8], the fist hits the bag only twice. The above combination has the right fist making three continuous strikes. The exact same sequence is again shown on the right.

Double Fists Figure-8 Linking from the Side

Double fist Figure-8 linking from side-to-side draws an imaginary "8" with the fists from ear-to-ear, rather than out from the nose **[FIG 9F-1&2]**. The **lead** fist will travel "front-to-side" and return to the front while the **second** fist will travel from "side-to-front" and return to the side. The key feature is that **both** fists return to their original position. *The secret is keeping the elbows high....parallel or above.*

#15 Side Double Punch, Both fists [8]   (exact techniques only at right)

$$\begin{array}{ccccc} L & \text{L-R} & \text{B} & L & \\ \end{array}$$

Basic LLRR...(FSP)'''**(SDP)-[8]-(FCP)**...Basic   or   (FSP)'''**(SDP)''(SDP)''(FCP)**
$$\qquad\qquad\qquad\qquad \{\text{R-L}\}$$

with right column heads:
$$\begin{array}{cccc} L & \text{L-R} & \text{R-L} & L \end{array}$$

In the last combination, the bottom line {R-L} shows the fist order of **the unwritten (SDP)** that occurs when writing both fists [8] side-to-side. Again, **because of the unwritten punch this symbol will not be used in exercises** - but the movement is the same. This is a great looking combination.

> **Important:**
>
> **SDP '' SDP** is a key combination for both bag and fist control. Joined with the FDP''RDP combinations, your fists are flying all around the speed bag!

Fig 9F-1 Ex #15 **Double Fist figure [8] linking, Side-to-Side** * also, see page 116

In practice sequence #15, we followed the double fist [8] with a Front Circle Punch. We can use several other front techniques leading with the left arm.

#16   Side Double Punch, Both fists [8] to Front Double Punch   (Exact techniques only)

$$\begin{array}{ccccc} L & \text{L-R} & \text{R-L} & \text{L-R} & R \end{array}$$

Basic LLRR...((FSP)'''**(SDP)''(SDP)''(FDP)**'''(FCP)

Fig 9F-2 Ex #15 **Side-to-Side Figure 8 Linking from a different angle**

Combining the (SDP) with the (FDP) creates some of the fastest sounding speed bag combinations. A few interesting variations are offered below. These written patterns are the longest and most advanced we have had so far. The linking fists will be **underlined bold**. I have written most practice exercise with only the exact techniques and rebounds. *Be sure to notice the number of rebounds*. Try and completely understand the movements of each exercise. This is where the real action begins in "ultimate" speed bag control. Your hands and the bag are changing directions a lot, so take them slow at first and try not to get your fists tied in a knot!

#17 Alternating Side Double Punches to Front Double Punches   (exact techniques only)

              R   **R-L**   **L-R**   *R-L*   *L-R*   **R-L**   **L-R**   *R-L*   *L*
Basic LLRR…(FSP)'''**(SDP)''(SDP)''**(FDP)'''(FDP)'''**(SDP)''(SDP)''**(FDP)'''(FCP))…Repeat

#18 Continuous Side Double-to-Front Double Punches   (*exact techniques)

              R   **R-L**   l   *L-R*   *R-L*   **L-R**   r   *R-L*   *L*
Basic LLRR…(FSP)'''**(SDP)-[1/2]-**(FDP)'''(FDP)'''**(SDP)-[1/2]-**(FDP)'''(FCP)…Repeat

              R   **R-L**   *L-R*   *R-L*   **L-R**   *R-L*   *L*
  *   (FSP)'''**(SDP)''**(FDP)'''(FDP)'''**(SDP)''**(FDP)'''(FCP)…Repeat

#19 Front Double Punch, last (second) fist [8] pass to reverse, then to Side Double Punch

$$R \quad *R\text{-}L \quad L \quad L\text{-}R* \quad R\text{-}L \quad L \quad L\text{-}R \quad R$$

Basic LLRR…(FSP)'''(FDP)''(RSP)''**(SDP)**''(FDP)''(RSP)''**(SDP)**''(FCP)…Basic. Change lead

Exercise #19 looks great because the left fist appears to be passing front-to back while the right fist passes in and out from the side. A key feature is letting the right fist (*R) drift to the side to re-enter in the SDP. It also makes a fascinating rhythm which we will explore in the chapter of "Echo Rhythms".

#20 Front Double Punch, both fist [8] front-to-reverse, to Side Double Punch
  (*This is a very quick combination and demands fist control.*)

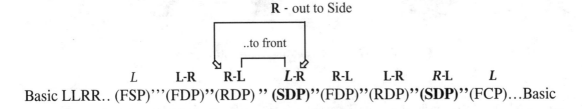

R - out to Side

..to front

$$L \quad L\text{-}R \quad R\text{-}L \quad L\text{-}R \quad R\text{-}L \quad L\text{-}R \quad R\text{-}L \quad L$$

Basic LLRR.. (FSP)'''(FDP)''(RDP) **''** **(SDP)**''(FDP)''(RDP)''**(SDP)**''(FCP)…Basic

In the last exercise, we have an interesting (RDP) '' **(SDP)** combination, which occurs with two rebounds inbetween. *The secret to performing* (RDP)''(SDP) *is knowing that the lead* (first) *fist (* R *) of the RDP will have to straighten* **out to the side** [brackets] *as the second fist connects in the RDP.* (See FIG on page 115).   This is a new movement and the fists are going in different directions at the same time. Also, notice that the second fist of the RDP (larger **L**) leads the SDP. It just passes from the back to the front [bracket]. We can go from a Side Double Punch to a Reverse Double Punch. This requires **three** rebounds to complete.

#21 Side Double Punch to Reverse Double Punch   (* exact techniques)

$$L \quad *L\text{-}R \quad R\text{-}L \quad B \quad L\text{-}R \quad R$$

Basic LLRR…(FSP)'''**(SDP)** ''' (RDP)-[1/2]-(FDP)'''(FCP)…repeat. change lead

Both - go behind for RDP

$$L \quad *L\text{-}R \quad R\text{-}L \quad L\text{-}R \quad R$$

* (FSP)'''**(SDP)** ''' (RDP)''(FDP)'''(FCP)…repeat, change lead

note 3 rebounds

Side-to-Reverse combinations are a little more difficult because both arms have to extend behind the bag - which is moving sideways. *The secret is to dip them both lower under the bag with the lead (first) fist of the SDP* [...left (*L) in #21...] *lower than the second fist*. Also, notice it requires three rebounds. These combinations will be further developed in the chapter of advanced skills.

When the single fist [8] and double fist [8] patterns are mixed together between front and side double punching, the result is an awesome display of blurring fists and sound.

THE SIDE-TRIPLE ELBOW STRIKE   (S-TES)

The Side-Triple Elbow Strike, represented by (S-TES), is performed almost exactly like the Outward-Triple Elbow Strike, except the third, or last, fist enters from the side. You can visualize it as (O-DES) + (SSP) = (S-TES) or as (O-SES) + (SDP) = (S-TES) When this skill is performed, the bag is struck by the point of the "outward" moving elbow, then fist and then the sideway fist...on the large knuckle of the index finger...all with one bounce inbetween **[FIG 9G-1,2&3]**.

Fig 9G-1 **Side-Triple Elbow Strike**

As usual, this Elbow-Fist\Fist sequence is shown in the bottom line. It produces three accented beats, exactly like the other triple elbow strikes. The number of rebounds before the next strike depends on its direction, but like the Side Double Punch, we will be constantly linking to different areas of the bag. Fortunately, linking will be exactly the same as with the Side Double Punch, for the fist movements are the same...we are only adding an elbow at the beginning. Practice sequences will again be written both with and without the linking symbols. The linking fist(s) will be **underlined bold**.

#1 From Basic, Side-Triple Elbow Strike, same lead arm   (*exact techniques)

　　　　　　　　L　　　*L-L*\R　　r　　R
Basic LLRR…(FSP)'''**(S-TES)**-[1/2]-(FCP)…repeat. Change lead
　　　　　　　　　　e-f \ f

　　　　　　　　L　　　*L-L*\R　　　R
*　(FSP)'''**(S-TES)''**(FCP)…repeat. Change lead
　　　　　　　e-f \ f

#2 From Basic, Side-Triple Elbow Strike, alternating lead arm (*exact techniques)

　　　　　　　L　　*L-L*\R　　r　　R　　　L　　　L　　　R　　*R-R*\L　　l　　L
Basic LLRR…(FSP)'''**(S-TES)**-[1/2]-(FCP)'''(FSP)'''(FCP)'''(FSP)'''**(S-TES)**-[1/2]-(FCP)…Basic
　　　　　　e-f \ f　　　　　　　　　　　　　　　　　**e-f \ f**

　　　　　　　L　　*L-L*\R　　　R　　　L　　　L　　　R　　*R-R*\L　　　L
*　　(FSP)'''**(S-TES)''**(FCP)'''(FSP)'''(FCP)'''(FSP)'''**(S-TES)''**(FCP)…Basic
　　　　　e-f \ f　　　　　　　　　　　　　　　**e-f \ f**

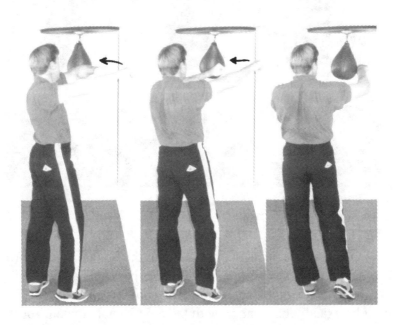

Fig 9G-2 **Side-Triple Elbow Strike, From Behind**

#3 Continuous, alternating Side-Triple Elbow Strikes (exact techniques only)
   * ***This is a very quick sequence and you must keep the elbows up***

$$L \qquad L\text{-}L\backslash R \qquad R\text{-}R\backslash L \qquad L\text{-}L\backslash R \qquad R\text{-}R\backslash L \qquad L$$
Basic LLRR…(FSP)''' **(S-TES)''(S-TES)''(S-TES)''(S-TES)''** (FCP)…Basic
$$\text{e-f}\backslash\text{f} \qquad \text{e-f}\backslash\text{f} \qquad \text{e-f}\backslash\text{f} \qquad \text{e-f}\backslash\text{f}$$

[There are several ways to write the last exercise using the linking symbols, so to avoid confusion I have just shown the techniques.]

The Side-Triple Elbow Strike can smoothly blend in with the other sideways techniques. A few practice patterns are given to learn these combinations.

#4 Side-Triple Elbow Strike, to same Side Single Punch. (same side as last fist in the triple strike)

$$L \qquad L\text{-}L\backslash R \qquad R \qquad r \qquad R$$
Basic LLRR…(FSP)''' **(S-TES)** '''(SSP)-[1/2]-(FCP)…Basic.
$$\text{e-f}\backslash\text{f}$$

$$L \qquad L\text{-}L\backslash R \qquad R \qquad R$$
*   (FSP)''' **(S-TES)** '''(SSP)''(FCP)…Basic.
$$\text{e-f}\backslash\text{f}$$

Fig 9G-3   Side-Triple Elbow Strike, different angle

Notice how the last fist of the (S-TES), the right (**R**), just keeps circling "in" from the same side. In the next combination, the lead, or first fist of the triple will re-circle in from the opposite side.

#5 Side-Triple Elbow Strike, to opposite Side Single Punch (* exact techniques)

L   L-**L**\R   1   L   L   1   L

Basic LLRR…(FSP)'''**(S-TES)**-[1/2]-(SSP)'''(SSP)-[1/2]-(FCP)…Basic. Change lead

e- **f** \ f

L   L-**L**\R   L   L   L

*   (FSP)'''**(S-TES)**''(SSP)'''(SSP)''(FCP)…Basic. Change lead

e-**f** \ f

#6 Side-Triple Elbow Strike, to opposite Side double Punch   (*exact techniques)

L   L-**L**\R **B** R-L   L   1   L

Basic LLRR…(FSP)'''**(S-TES)**-[1/2]-(SDP)'''(SSP)-[1/2]-(FCP)…

e- **f** \ **f**

L   L-**L**\R R-L   L   L

*   (FSP)'''**(S-TES)**''(SDP)''(SSP)''(FCP)…Basic.

e-**f** \ **f**

> **Remember**:
>
> The S-TES is just a SDP with an elbow in the front!
>
> *all* the fist linking options for the S-TES are *exactly* the same as the SDP

#7 Side Double Punch, to Side-Triple Elbow Strike (* exact)

R   R-L **B** L-**L**\R **r** R

Basic LLRR…(FSP)'''(SDP)-[1/2]-**(S-TES)**-[1/2]-(FCP)…Basic. Change lead

e-f \ **f**

R   R-L L-**L**\R   R

* (FSP)'''(SDP)''**(S-TES)**''(FCP)…Basic. Change lead

e-f \ **f**

The next few exercises will focus on either the lead (first) fist or second fist linking Figure-8 pass through off of the Side-Triple Elbow Strike.   The linking fist will be **underlined bold**.

#8   Side-Triple Elbow Strike, last (second) fist figure [8] pass through, to Side Single Punch

2nd fist passes front-to-side

L *L-L***R**   **R** R **R** R

Basic LLRR…(FSP)'''**(S-TES)**''(FCP)''(SSP)'''(SSP)''(FCP)….repeat. Change lead

e-f \ **f**

#9   Side-Triple Elbow Strike, last fist multiple figure [8] pass through linking

2nd fist, continuous linking

L *L-L***R**   **R**   **R**   **R**   **R** R

Basic LLRR…(FSP)'''**(S-TES)**''(FCP)''(SSP)''(FCP)''(SSP)''(FCP)…repeat. Change lead

e-f \ **f**

#10 Side-Triple Elbow Strike, lead (first) fist figure [8] pass through (note rebounds)

lead fist goes to side

L *L-L***R**   **L** L R *R-R***L**   **R** R

Basic LLRR… (FSP)'''**(S-TES)**''(SSP)''(FCP)'''(FSP)'''**(S-TES)**''(SSP)''(FCP)…repeat

e-**f** \ f   e-**f** \ f

lead fist goes to side

#11 Side-Triple Elbow Strike, alternating Side Double Punches
     Swing movement is the same. Just turn more to stick the elbow in front to lead the SDP.

L *L-L***R**   **R-L**   **L-R**   *R-R***L** L

Basic LLRR…(FSP)'''**(S-TES)**''(SDP)''(SDP)''**(S-TES)**''(FCP)

e-**f** \ f   e-**f** \ f

(In the last pattern, the fists are continually changing sides. There are several ways to write this using the linking symbols so to avoid confusion just the techniques are written.)

The past eleven practice patterns have used the Side-Triple Elbow Strike with other side techniques or the basic rhythm. It can also be used with any of the other techniques. The next few practice exercises will use the Side-Triple Elbow Strike with several other front techniques. Notice how the last fist of the (S-TES), which is coming from the side, leads the next technique.

#12 Side-Triple Elbow Strike and the Front Double Punch   (* exact techniques)

```
            L       L-L\R    r    R-L      L-R      R-R\L     l      L
Basic LLRR…(FSP)''' (S-TES)-[1/2]-(FDP)'''(FDP)'''(S-TES)-[1/2]-(FCP)…Basic
            e-f\ f                          e-f\ f
```

```
          L        L-L\R     R-L      L-R     R-R\L      L
      * (FSP)'''(S-TES)''(FDP)'''(FDP)'''(S-TES)''(FCP)…Basic
          e-f\ f                       e-f\ f
```

#13 Side-Triple Elbow Strike and the Outward-Triple Elbow Strike   (* exact techniques)

```
            L       L-L\R    r    R-R\L     L-R      R-R\L     l    L-L\R      R
Basic LLRR…(FSP)''' (S-TES)-[1/2]-(O-TES)'''(FDP)'''(S-TES)-[1/2]-(O-TES)'''(FCP)
            e-f\ f           e-f\ f                  e-f\ f          e-f\ f
```

```
          L      L-L\R     R-R\L      L-R     R-R\L     L-L\R      R
      * (FSP)'''(S-TES)''(O-TES)'''(FDP)'''(S-TES)''(O-TES)'''(FCP)
          e-f\ f          e-f\ f              e-f\ f           e-f\ f
```

#14 Side-Triple Elbow Strike and the Downward-Triple Elbow Strike   (* exact techniques)
** *Remove eyeglasses before doing Downward Elbow Strikes*

```
            L       L-L\R    r    R\L-L     L-R      R-R\L     l    L\R-R      R
Basic LLRR…(FSP)''' (S-TES)-[1/2]-(D-TES)'''(FDP)'''(S-TES)-[1/2]-(D-TES)'''(FCP)
            e-f\ f           f\ e-f                 e-f\ f           f\ e-f
```

```
          L      L-L\R     R\L-L      L-R     R-R\L     L\R-R      R
      * (FSP)'''(S-TES)''(D-TES)'''(FDP)'''(S-TES)''(D-TES)'''(FCP)
          e-f\ f          f\ e-f              e-f\ f           f\ e-f
```

Exercises #13 and #14 have *two* triple elbow strikes occurring with only two rebounds inbetween. I call this a "double triple". The next two exercises will have *three* continuous triple elbow strikes with only two rebounds inbetween. I call these a "triple triple".

#15 Several Side-Triple Elbow Strikes to an Outward-Triple Elbow Strike

$$L \qquad L\text{-}L\backslash\mathbf{R} \qquad R\text{-}R\backslash\mathbf{L} \qquad L\text{-}L\backslash\mathbf{R} \qquad R$$
Basic LLRR…(FSP)'''(S-TES)''(S-TES)''(O-TES)'''(FCP)….repeat. change lead
$$\qquad\qquad\qquad e\text{-}f\backslash f \qquad e\text{-}f\backslash f \qquad e\text{-}f\backslash f$$

#16 Several Side-Triple Elbow Strikes to a Downward-Triple Elbow Strike

$$L \qquad L\text{-}L\backslash\mathbf{R} \qquad R\text{-}R\backslash\mathbf{L} \qquad L\backslash R\text{-}R \qquad R$$
Basic LLRR… (FSP)'''(S-TES)''(S-TES)''(D-TES)'''(FCP)….repeat. change lead
$$\qquad\qquad\qquad e\text{-}f\backslash f \qquad e\text{-}f\backslash f \qquad f\backslash e\text{-}f$$

The "triple triple" combinations are fairly difficult because there is only two rebounds inbetween and there is a lot of arm movements. *The secret is to keep the elbows up at least parallel.*

#17 Side-Triple Elbow Strike and the Out & Down-4way Elbow Strike

$$L \qquad L\text{-}L\backslash\mathbf{R} \qquad R\text{-}R\backslash L\text{-}L \qquad L\text{-}R \qquad R\text{-}R\backslash\mathbf{L} \qquad L\text{-}L\backslash R\text{-}R \qquad R$$
Basic LLRR… (FSP)'''(S-TES)''(O-D 4way)'''(FDP)'''(S-TES)''(O-D 4way)'''(FCP)
$$\qquad\qquad\qquad e\text{-}f\backslash f \qquad e\text{-}f\backslash e\text{-}f \qquad\qquad\qquad e\text{-}f\backslash f \qquad e\text{-}f\backslash e\text{-}f$$

The next sequence will combine the Side-Triple Elbow Strike with the Reverse Double Punch Remember, there are three rebounds inbetween.

18 Side-Triple Elbow Strike to Reverse Double Punch

$$L \qquad L\text{-}L\backslash\mathbf{R} \qquad \mathbf{R\text{-}L} \qquad L\text{-}R \qquad R\text{-}R\backslash L \qquad \mathbf{L\text{-}R} \qquad R$$
Basic LLRR… (FSP)'''(S-TES)'''(RDP)''(FDP)'''(S-TES)'''(RDP)''(FCP)
$$\qquad\qquad\qquad e\text{-}f\backslash f \qquad\qquad\qquad\qquad\qquad \mathbf{e\text{-}f\backslash f}$$

HOOK PUNCH (HP)

The Hook Punch, symbolized by (HP), is a great punch to practice on the speed bag. Most other techniques have a relatively fixed motion into the bag, but the Hook Punch offers some personal variation. It can be tricky to combine it smoothly with the other striking techniques because of the way the punch connects the bag and the body movement used.

Basically, the front of the fist will contact the side of the bag… like a Front Straight Punch angled from the side **[Fig 9H]**. It is important that the bag contacts the large knuckles of the fist-not the small finger joints. The punching motion comes from the shoulder and chest pulling the arm in toward the chest. To execute it, we must emphasize the body turning into the bag. This body motion, along with the footwork and weight shift, may vary allowing for some individual differences in how we can use the Hook Punch with other techniques.

Right Fist   Left Fist

Fig 9H Hook Punch

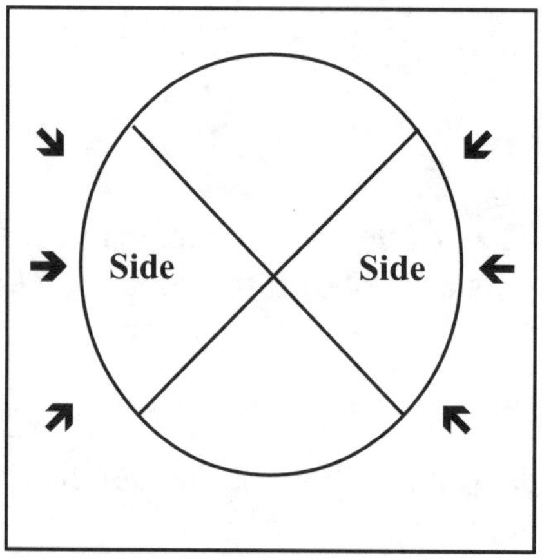

Fig 9-i Hook entry variations

The foot and leg action actually set up this technique. You can swivel on the ball of the foot, (pointing the heel out slightly) and adding a strong pivot in from the hip. This creates a very powerful punch, slamming the bag sideways. Another way to move the lower body is to keep the feet still and swivel only from the hips. As the arm performing the Hook contacts the bag the weight should be on the same side leg (right arm Hook, weight on right leg) and the knee almost straight.

The fist may contact the bag directly from the side but it *could* enter more from the "rear-side" angle **[FIG 9-i]** or contact the "front-side", depending on your body motion, so the rebounding angles can vary. As a result the next technique may occur after an even or odd number of rebounds. We will explore some of these differences as we progress through the exercises.

Along with the body motion, the fist position as it connects the bag can vary and you may have the thumb and little finger almost parallel, with the palm facing the floor when it connects **[FIG 9J]**. Or you may have the thumb slightly higher then the little finger and the palm facing more towards the stomach. It may vary with the combination you are using with it.

Because of the larger motions made in this technique, and the power delivered to the bag, the number of rebounds used in combinations with the Hook Punch may increase to either four or five. This will be identified as they occur.

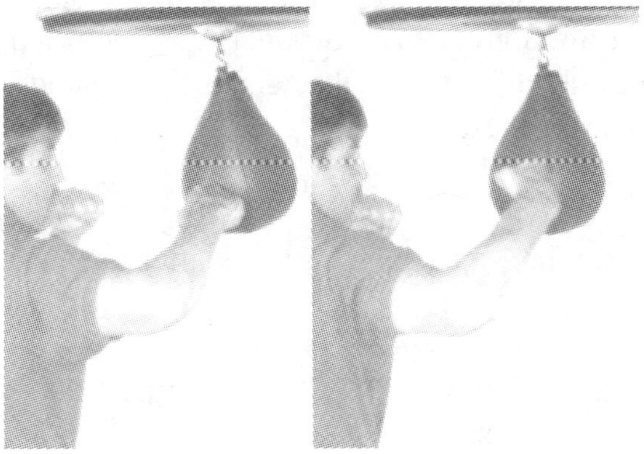

Several practice exercises include:

Fig 9J **Hook Fist on bag**

#1 Continuous Hook Punching, Same Side (note **five '''''' rebounds**)

$$R \qquad R \qquad R$$
(HP)'''''(HP)'''''(HP).....Change hands
Count   *1*-2-3-4-5 *1*-2-3-4-5

This combination is written with five rebounds. It is very difficult to complete the full motion on three rebounds. To perform this, we must continuously swivel the shoulder in toward the chest, bringing the front of the fist into the side of the bag. (The fist may actually contact more of the "rear-side"). This is easier if you let the thumb of the fist be slightly higher than your little finger.

#2 Alternate Hook punching

$$R \qquad R \quad L \qquad L$$
(HP)'''''(HP)''''(HP)'''''(HP)....continue
Count   *1*-2-3-4-**5** *1*-2-3-**4**

Notice 4 rebounds (**4**) between the opposite side Hooks (R and L) and five between the same side

#3 Continuous Alternating Hook punches (note the **4 rebounds** between)

$$R \quad L \quad R \quad L$$
(HP)''''(HP)''''(HP)''''(HP)
Count   *1*-2-3-4 *1*-2-3-4

This last sequence creates a very comfortable motion, swiveling back and forth.

To use the Hook with other techniques we need to learn how to "enter" (lead into) and "exit" Hook Punching in the basic rhythm. Here is where some personal differences may come in, depending on your method of execution. The key variations will be when we "exit" the Hook. The practice exercises below will highlight each method.

We can enter the Hook Punch with the opposite arm (from the last punch) by letting it follow the "inward" motion of a Front Straight Punch or by letting it follow the "outward" motion of a Front Circle Punch. The only difference is the number of rebounds between the techniques. The next practice patterns will demonstrate these.

4 Basic Rhythm, opposite arm Hook after FSP, same side arm exits after 3 rebounds.

L   **R**   *R*

Basic LLRR…(FSP)''''(**HP**)'''(FCP)…..repeat

Above we see the left (*L*) Front Straight Punch is followed by the (**R**) right Hook Punch. This is best done after four rebounds. Also, we exited the Hook by letting the hooking (right) fist perform a Front Circle Punch (FCP) after **3 rebounds**. Three rebounds work well when we do a Hook and *keep the weight on the same leg and hold the "hook" body posture.* In the above example, as the right fist connects in the Hook, your weight should be on the right leg. The right shoulder is also "in" closer to the bag than the left. Simply maintaining this position (or turning slightly further to face the side of the rebound board) will leave you in perfect position for the right fist to re-circle and perform the Front Circle Punch after three rebounds **[FIG 9K]**.

I call this "Hook and Hold" because your body is facing the left side of the board, directly into the rebounding bag and the first and third rebound after the hook will come from that side. (You could also use five rebounds if three is too fast.)

We can also let the right fist perform the (FCP) after four rebounds by flowing with the swing movement to change our body posture (by swiveling the hips) and facing the right side of the board. Then the bag will make a **fourth** rebound on the right side of the board before the right fist connects the Front Circle Punch. We will see this below:

#5 Basic Rhythm, opposite arm Hook after FSP, same side arm exits after 4 rebounds.

L   *R*   *R*

Basic LLRR…(FSP)''''(HP)''''(FCP)…..repeat

I call this the "Hook and Rotate" because you will swivel and rotate to face the *other* (right) side of the board for the next technique **[FIG 9L]**. This pattern gives you a little more time (one extra rebound) to position yourself and set up the (FCP). I like the two repeating "4-bounce" rhythms together.

Fig 9K Hook and Hold Combination

Because of swiveling with the bag motion as we did in #5, there is another variation we can do. As we shift to face the right side of the board, the right shoulder is moving "out" from under the board and the left shoulder is moving "in". Because of this move, we can also follow the right Hook with a left Front Straight Punch after 4 rebounds. We will see this in the next exercise.

Fig 9L Hook and Rotate Combination

#6 Basic Rhythm, opposite arm Hook after FSP, opposite side arm follows after 4 rebounds.

$$\qquad\qquad L \qquad\quad R \qquad\quad L$$
Basic LLRR…(FSP)''''(HP)''''(**FSP**)…..repeat

Notice here that the right fist (*R*) performs a Hook and the opposite arm (*L*) follows with a (FSP). This motion feels a lot like doing a right hook - left hook combination and the main difference is the angle of the left fist hitting the *front* of the bag, rather than moving to hit from the side. (For variety you can also use a left Front Circle Punch instead of the Front Straight Punch.)

In exercises number four, five and six we "entered" the Hook Punch after the Front Straight Punch. We can also enter the Hook after a Front Circle Punch. We will do this by following a (FCP) with the (HP) by the opposite arm. Because of the different punching angles in this combination, we must use an odd number of rebounds between the techniques. The following exercise will use **five** rebounds.

#7 Basic Rhythm, opposite arm Hook after FCP, same side arm exits after 3 rebounds (Hook & Hold)

$$\qquad\qquad L \qquad\quad R \qquad\quad R \qquad\quad L$$
Basic LLRR…(FCP)'''''(**HP**)'''(FCP)'''(FSP)…Repeat

Here we see the left Front Circle Punch (*L*) followed by the opposite arm right Hook Punch (*R*) after five rebounds. You can use three rebounds with practice. Both techniques enter smoothly on the same body motion. Simply emphasize the right hip swiveling "in" as the right arm follows the left. Also, the exiting technique (the FCP after three rebounds), is the same one we did in exercise #4. We could also use the exiting examples from exercises five or six.

We can perform the Hook Punch with the same arm that performs the last technique. Once again the key is the number of rebounds.

#8 Basic Rhythm, same arm enters Hook after FSP, same arm exits after 3 rebounds

$$\qquad\qquad L \qquad\quad R \qquad\quad R \qquad R \qquad L$$
Basic LLRR…(FCP)'''(FSP)'''''(**HP**)'''(FCP)'''(FSP)…repeat

Above we see the right fist (R) performs a (FSP) and then the same fist does a Hook after five rebounds. With practice it can be completed on three rebounds but it is not the smoothest combination and feels a little unnatural. Once again the same fist (Right) that did the Hook exited the Hook after three rebounds, (hook and hold) exactly like exercise #7.

Since we can enter Hook Punching after the "inward" moving FSP, we can also combine the Hook with several techniques that include this FSP motion within them. Below we'll see several exercises that display these combinations.

#9 Basic Rhythm, opposite arm Hook after FDP, same side arm exits after 3 rebounds.

              R   *R*-**L**   *R*   *L*   **R***   **R**   *L*   *L*

Basic LLRR…(FSP)'''**(FDP)**''''**(HP)**''''**(HP)**''''**(HP)**'''(FCP)'''(FSP)'''(FCP)….repeat.

In this last combination, we see the second fist (**L**) of the **FDP** connecting the bag as a Front Straight Punch would. The right fist, which leads the FDP, can naturally follow this motion and return as a Hook Punch. I have also included several alternate Hook Punches, and notice the same right (larger **R***) fist exits the (HP) to a (FCP) after three rebounds. Another technique that contains this FSP connection is the Outward-Triple Elbow Strike, and a Hook Punch can easily follow it also.

#10 Basic Rhythm, opposite arm Hook after O-TES, same side arm exits   (Hook & Hold)

              R   *R*-*R*\L   **R**   *L*   **R**   **R**   *L*   *L*

Basic LLRR…(FSP)'''**(O-TES)**''''**(HP)**''''**(HP)**''''**(HP)**'''(FCP)'''(FSP)'''(FCP)….repeat.
                e-f \ f

The Hook Punch can also follow any of the Sideway techniques. The Side Double Punch and the Side-Triple Elbow Strike are shown.

#11 Basic Rhythm, opposite arm Hook after SDP, same side arm exits after 3 rebounds.

              R   *R*-*L*   **R**   *L*   **R**   **R**   *L*   *L*

Basic LLRR…(FSP)'''**(SDP)**''''**(HP)**''''**(HP)**''''**(HP)**'''(FCP)'''(FSP)'''(FCP)….repeat.

Here we have the first fist (right) of the SDP passing to the other side as the left fist
(L) connects. Then the right fist re-enters as HP after 4 rebounds. We will see the same thing below after the Side-Triple Elbow Strike.

#12 From Basic Rhythm, opposite arm Hook after S-TES, same side arm exits

              R   *R*-*R*\L   *R*   *L*   **R**   **R**   *L*   *L*

Basic LLRR…(FSP)'''**(S-TES)**''''**(HP)**''''**(HP)**''''**(HP)**'''(FCP)'''(FSP)'''(FCP)….repeat.
                e-f \ f

Hook Punch and Linking

The fist performing a Hook Punch is constantly linking between areas of the speed bag. If it links side-to-front, it may occur on three rebounds-(Exercise #4), or four rebounds (Exercise #5 and #6). We can also perform the Hook Punch after a fists links to another side and returns. We will learn this in the next exercises. (I will write these using only the exact technique abbreviations and rebounds.

#13 Basic Rhythm, Single fist link [8], Opposite fist performs Hook (* exact techniques only)

L   *L*   R   *L*   **R**   R   *L*

Basic LLRR...**(FCP)**''**(RSP)**''**(HP)**''''(HP)''''(HP)'''(FCP)'''(FSP)....repeat, change lead

In this sequence we see the left fist (L) passes through and the opposite right fist (R) Hooks. I included several Hooks to make it flow easier. Notice the right fist (**larger R**) exits the hook to a (FCP) after three rebounds. The same move works well after the outward-elbow strikes, as the next two exercises will demonstrate.

#14 Basic Rhythm, Outward-Double Elbow Strike, last fist links [8], opposite fist Hook Punch

L   **L**   *L*   **R**   *R*

Basic LLRR...(FSP)''' **(O-DES)**''**(RSP)**''**(HP)**'''(FCP).....repeat, change lead
               e-**f**

In the last pattern the left fist (*L*) passes through [8] and returns. The right fist (*R*) connects with a (HP) after two rebounds. (You can use four if two is too fast). Again, we exited the (HP) to a (FCP) with the same arm after 3 rebounds. We will see a similiar pattern when we perform a Hook Punch after the Outward-Triple Elbow Strike.

#15 Basic Rhythm, Outward-Triple Elbow Strike, last fist links [8], opposite fist Hook Punch

2nd fist goes behind

R   *R-R****L**   *L*   **R**   *R*   *L*   *L*

Basic LLRR..... (FSP)'''**(O-TES)**''**(RSP)**''**(HP)**'''(FCP)'''(FSP)'''(FCP)....repeat, change lead
               e-f \ **f**

Here we see the **second** fist (L) of the (O-TES) links behind and returns. The key to doing this combination is to let the right fist immediately move to the side as the left is passing through to the Reverse Single Punch. You can also let the first fist pass through and follow with a Hook Punch, as exercise #16 will demonstrate.

#16 Basic Rhythm, Outward-Triple Elbow Strike, first fist links [8], opposite fist Hook Punch

Lead fist goes behind

L   L-**L****R**   L   **R**   R

Basic LLRR.....(FSP)'''(**O-TES**)''(**RSP**)''(**HP**)'''(FCP)....repeat, change lead

e-**f** \ f

A Hook Punch can also follow a *double fist Figure-8* pass through, as demonstrated below:

#17 Basic Rhythm, Both fists link [8] pass through, to Hook Punch.

L   **L**-**R**   **R**-L   **R**   R

Basic LLRR.....(FSP)'''(**FDP**)''(**RDP**)''(**HP**)'''(FCP)....repeat, change lead

In this last sequence we see that the first (lead) fist of the Reverse Double Punch (**R**) performs the Hook Punch. It must be moving out to the side as the left fist connects behind the bag and passes to the front. (In fact, Exercises #13–17 are the same, because the *right* fist performed a Hook Punch after a *left* Reverse Single Punch. Only the preceding technique and linking fists were changed.)

We can also follow a Hook Punch with a Reverse technique. The next exercise will use the Reverse Single Punch.

#18 Basic Rhythm, opposite arm Hook after FCP, same side arm exits to RSP after 3 rebounds.

L   **R**   **R**   **R**   r   **R**   L

Basic LLRR...(FCP)'''''(**HP**)''(RSP)'''(RSP)-[1/2]-(FCP)'''(FSP)...Repeat

Here we see the left Front Circle Punch (*L*) followed by the opposite arm right Hook Punch (*R*) after five rebounds. The right fist than re-circles to a RSP after 3 rebounds.

This combination is possible because of the fist contact points and the *angle of rebound* of the bag. A Reverse Double Punch or Reverse Fist Roll, lead by the right fist, could also be used.

The Hook Punch is a very versatile technique that gives some interesting variations to speed bag combinations. The previous exercises only teach the basics of using the Hook Punch.

There are many more possible combinations. For instance, we have only exited the Hook to a Front Circle Punch or a Front Straight Punch. Practice entering and exiting the Hook from all the previous techniques we have covered. I have offered a few challenging examples below. The basic rhythm is not shown but it can precede each. Be sure to count the rebounds to notice if you have to "hook and hold" (three rebounds) or "hook and rotate" (4 rebounds).

R	**L**	**R**	*R*	**R**	*R-L*	**R**	*R*

(FSP)''''(**HP**)''''(**HP**)''''(O-DES)''(RSP)''(SDP)''''(**HP**)'''(FCP).....basic
　　　　　　　　　　e-**f**

The underlined combination (**HP**)''''(O-DES), which is a Right Hook exiting to an Outward-Double Elbow Strike is a variation of the "hook and rotate". You do not have to rotate to face the right side of the board, because the finishing position of the (**HP**) puts your right elbow under the chin.... perfect position for the outward elbow technique. Just turn your head to the right and spot the bag.

L	*L-L\R*	*L*	**R**	*L*ᵏ	*L-R**	**R**

(FSP)''(S-TES)''(SSP)''''(**HP**)''''(**HP**)''''(SDP)''(FCP).....basic
　　　e-**f** \ f

This pattern has the lead fist (**L**) of the (S-TES) passing to a (SSP). The right fist (**R**) then does a Hook Punch (**HP**) from the other side after *four* rebounds. Notice the right fist enters next from the *same side* (**R***) in the (SDP). The key to getting it in position for this is to let it extend out to the right side of the bag *as the left fist* (*L*ᵏ) *does the Hook*. They will both be going in the same direction.

> **The last two side techniques are fairly difficult because we will be blind to the fist contact points on the bag. They demand excellent fist control and the ability to link smoothly between *all* four areas, (or sides) of the bag. You must also be aware of the fists' "angle of entry", and how it can effect the number of rebounds and combinations.**

Reverse-Side Double Punch (R-SDP)

The next technique from the side is the Reverse-Side Double Punch, symbolized by (R-SDP). This is the fourth double punch technique. It is possible because of the rebounding angle after a Reverse Single Punch, which *usually* enters straight from the back and a Side Single Punch, which *usually* enters from a *rear*-side angle The fist entries for a "**Left-Right**" Reverse-Side Double Punch are shown in **[FIG 9M]**. Since both are "rear" oriented, we can combine them after only one rebound. I emphasized usually, because it is tricky and you will need to experiment a little to find the most comfortable angle. (This technique looks similiar to the Reverse Double Punch, with only a slight difference in the angle of the second fist striking the bag.)

Fig 9N Reverse-Side Double Punch

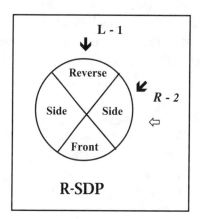

Fig 9M Fist angles of "L-R" Reverse-Side Double Punch

This technique really shows the adaptability of the Side Single Punch, and how it combines after one rebound to create double punches. But this is a more difficult technique than the (SDP) because we do not see the contact points for the fists. We must depend on the angle of entry to pull this one off. The bag will strike the large knuckle of the index finger in the Reverse Single Punch (RSP), rebound once and strike the same area of the fist coming from the side **[FIG 9N]**.

Ex #1 Reverse Single Punch, to Reverse-Side Double Punch -to- Side Single Punch

    L   *L*   **L-R**   **R***   *R*
(RSP)'''(RSP)'''**(R-SDP)'''**(SSP)'''(SSP)…Change hands

To complete this technique, the right fist (**R**) must be in the side position. We can move it there as the left fist completes the (RSP) and is re-circling to lead the (R-SDP). Also, we see the following Right (**R***) Side Single Punch takes three rebounds, because it follows from the same side.

Ex #2 Reverse Single Punch, to Reverse-Side Double Punch -to- Front Circle Punch (* exact techniques)

    L   *L*   **L**-R   r   **R**   *L*   *L*   **L**-R   **R**

(RSP)'''(RSP)'''**(R-SDP)**-[1/2]-(FCP)   or   *   (RSP)'''(RSP)'''**(R-SDP)**''(FCP)

Ex #3 Reverse Double Punch, -to- Reverse-Side Double Punch -to- (FCP) (* exact techniques)

   L-R   R-***L***   ***L***-R   r   *R   *L*-R   R-***L***   ***L***-R   *R

(RDP)'''(RDP)'''**(R-SDP)**-[1/2]-(FCP)   or   *   (RDP)'''(RDP)'''**(R-SDP)**''(FCP)

       Exercise #3 is a little more difficult because the lead fist (R) of the RDP must move to the side as the left is re-circling behind the bag. Notice the Reverse-Side Double Punch follows the Reverse Double Punch after three rebounds because the lead fist (larger *L*) of the R-SDP comes from the same side as the last fist of the previous reverse technique. Note also that we followed the (R-SDP) with a right (*R) Front Circle Punch after two rebounds.

Ex #4 Reverse Fist Roll -to- Reverse-Side Double Punch (linking symbol not used)

L-R-L-R-L   **L**-**R**   R
(R-ROLL)'''**(R-SDP)**''(FCP)

In this combination, notice how the next to last fist in the R-Roll (R) re-enters from the side. After it contacts the bag in the roll, let it extend to the side as the last fist (L*) connects in the Roll.

       The first four exercises have the **R-SDP** following a reverse technique. This technique combines with front techniques by passing a fist behind to set it up.

       Both fists will begin changing sides continually and using the linking symbols for *each* change can get confusing. Therefore, I will just use it for the setup technique. I will also write each exercise again with just the exact techniques. The fist linking behind will be in **underlined bold**. Let's begin with the Basic Rhythm

Ex #5 Basic Rhythm -to- Reverse-Side Double Punch, same leading fist (* exact techniques)

     L   **L**   l   ***L*-R**   R

Basic LLRR...(FSP)'''(FCP)-[1/2]-**(R-SDP)**''(FCP)'''...Repeat

     L   **L**   ***L*-R**   R

*   (FSP)'''(FCP)''**(R-SDP)**''(FCP)'''...Repeat

Ex #6 Basic Rhythm to Reverse-Side Double Punch, alternating lead fist   (* exact techniques)

$$L \qquad L \qquad l \quad *L\text{-}R \qquad R \qquad r \quad R\text{-}L \qquad L$$
Basic LLRR…(FSP)''’(FCP)-[1/2]-(R-SDP)''(FCP)-[1/2]-(R-SDP)''(FCP)…continue

|‾‾‾‾‾‾‾‾‾‾‾‾‾‾‾‾| lead fist goes to side

$$L \qquad L \quad *L\text{-}R \qquad R \quad R\text{-}L \qquad L$$
*   (FSP)''’(FCP)''(R-SDP)''(FCP)''(R-SDP)''(FCP)…continue

This pattern is the most difficult yet, but *the secret is to let the leading fist of the R-SDP (*L)* *contact the back of the bag and move to the other side as the right (R) fist is going* (FCP)-[1/2].

Ex #7 Basic Rhythm to continuous alternating Reverse-Side Double Punches (* exact techniques)

$$L \qquad L \qquad l \quad L\text{-}R^* \quad *R\text{-}L \quad L\text{-}R \quad R\text{-}L \qquad L$$
Basic LLRR…(FSP)'''(FCP)-[1/2]-(R-SDP)'''(R-SDP)'''(R-SDP)'''(R-SDP)''(FCP)

$$L \qquad L \quad L\text{-}R^* \quad *R\text{-}L \quad L\text{-}R \quad R\text{-}L \qquad L$$
*   (FSP)'''(FCP)''(R-SDP)'''(R-SDP)'''(R-SDP)'''(R-SDP)''(FCP)

The key to this last exercise is noticing that the *second* fist of each R-SDP (*R & L*) hits the side of the bag, then re-enters from the back to lead the next R-SDP. This requires three rebounds.

The Reverse-Side Double Punch can also be completed after a FDP by linking either fist behind for the reverse punch. It is easier to use the second fist.

Ex #8 Front Double Punch to Reverse-Side Double Punch, same leading arm (* exact techniques)

$$R\text{-}L \quad B \quad L\text{-}R^* \quad R\text{-}L \quad B \quad L\text{-}R^*$$
Basic LLRR…(FDP)-[1/2]-(R-SDP)''(FDP)-[1/2]-(R-SDP)…..repeat

2nd fist goes behind
|‾‾‾‾‾|

$$R\text{-}L \quad L\text{-}R^* \quad R\text{-}L \quad L\text{-}R^*$$
*   (FDP)''(R-SDP)''(FDP)''(R-SDP)…..repeat

In this combination, both fists hit the front of the bag in FDP, then both change sides. The (R) fist leads the FDP then floats to the side, while **the second fist** (L) hits and links behind [brackets]. This is done by simply extend the left arm out, then flex them both back in with the left hitting the bag first. It happens quickly. Passing the *second* fist of the FDP through in this combination causes the same fist to lead the R-SDP's. Also, notice that only the right fist (R*) enters from the side.

We can also combine these two techniques by passing the first fist through to lead the R-SDP. This will alternate the lead fist of the R-SDP.

Ex #9   Front Double Punch to Reverse-Side Double Punch, alternating lead arm   (* exact techniques)

$$\textbf{R}\text{-}L \quad \text{B} \quad \textbf{R}\text{-}L \quad L\text{-}R \quad \text{B} \quad \textbf{L}\text{-}R$$
Basic LLRR…(FDP)-[1/2]-**(R-SDP)**''(FDP)-[1/2]-**(R-SDP)**

Lead Fist goes behind

$$\textbf{R}\text{-}L \quad \textbf{R}\text{-}L \quad L\text{-}R \quad \textbf{L}\text{-}R$$
*   (FDP)''**(R-SDP)**''(FDP)''**(R-SDP)**

This pattern is a little more difficult because the second fist of the FDP is not naturally moving out to the side, and the motion is slightly awkward. Notice the leading fists of both the FDP's and the R-SDP's alternate.

The Reverse-Side Double Punch can be used after any elbow strike that ends with a fist, as the next three patterns will demonstrate.

Ex #10   Outward-Double Elbow Strike to Reverse-Side Double Punch   (* exact techniques)

$$L \quad \textbf{L} \quad 1 \quad \textbf{L}\text{-}R \qquad\qquad L \quad \textbf{L} \quad \textbf{L}\text{-}R$$
Basic LLRR…(FSP)'''(O-DES)-[1/2]-**(R-SDP)**   **or**   *   (FSP)'''(O-DES)''**(R-SDP)**
e-f   e-f

The key to this combination is having the right fist out to the side of the speed bag, ready to enter. Extend it as the left fist comes under the right ear (for the O-DES.) This is the same position as the set up for the S-TES, (except the side fist doesn't enter until the left fist connects *behind* the bag.)

Ex #11   Downward-Triple Elbow Strike to Reverse-Side Double Punch

$$R \quad R\backslash L\text{-}\textbf{L} \quad 1 \quad \textbf{L}\text{-}R \qquad\qquad R \quad R\backslash L\text{-}\textbf{L} \quad \textbf{L}\text{-}R$$
Basic LLRR…(FSP)'''(D-TES)-[1/2]-**(R-SDP)**   or   *   (FSP)'''(D-TES)''**(R-SDP)**
f \ e-f   f \ e-f

In Exercise #11, the second fist (**L**) passes through, but the first fist (R) could also. This next combination will have a side fist moving to lead the R-SDP. This changes the combination entirely.

Ex #12 Side-Triple Elbow Strike -to- Reverse-Side Double Punch (note three ''' rebounds)

$$L \qquad L\text{-}L\backslash \mathbf{R} \qquad \mathbf{R}\text{-}L$$
Basic LLRR…(FSP)'''(S-TES)'''(R-SDP)
$$\text{e-f}\backslash \mathbf{f}$$

Since the last fist (**R**) of the S-TES comes from the *side,* (just like the R-SDP in exercise #7) the bag must rebound three times for it to lead a reverse technique. The left fist simply extends to the side to be in position for the R-SDP.

Let's turn our attention to some techniques that can follow the Reverse-Side Double Punch. We have already followed it with the a SSP (from the same side), FCP, and the FDP, but it will combine with **any** technique, as the following examples demonstrate. (The *Basic Rhythm* will not be written.)

Ex #13 Reverse-Side Double Punch -to- opposite-Side Single Punch

$$\mathbf{L}\text{-}R \qquad L \qquad \mathbf{L}\text{-}R \qquad L$$
(R-SDP)''(SSP)'''**(R-SDP)**''(SSP)….. This happens very quickly

Here we see the lead fist (**L**) quickly passing to the other side, creating a quick side-to-side split fist.

Ex #14 Reverse-Side Double Punch -to- Side Double Punch

$$\mathbf{R}\text{-}L \qquad L\text{-}R \qquad \mathbf{R}\text{-}L \qquad L\text{-}R$$
(R-SDP)''(SDP)'''**(R-SDP)**''(SDP)

Notice that the right fist moves from behind the bag to the right side. Let it join the motion of the left fist as it flexes in to the chest and extend it out to the side in a non-stop motion.

Ex #15 Reverse-Side Double Punch -to- Downward-Triple Elbow Strike (**underlined tech's are Ex #11**)

$$\mathbf{R}\text{-}L \qquad L\backslash \mathbf{R}\text{-}R \qquad \mathbf{R}\text{-}L \qquad L\backslash \mathbf{R}\text{-}R$$
(R-SDP)''(D-TES)''**(R-SDP)**''(D-TES)…..repeat, change leading fist
$$\text{f}\backslash \mathbf{e}\text{-f} \qquad\qquad \text{f}\backslash \text{e-f}$$

The secret to this combination is letting the right arm (**R**) lead the R-SDP and raise up into the downward-elbow strike position in one non-stop motion. This will position the right elbow just above the left fist after it enters from the side and passes to the front. Also, try to keep the right forearm as parallel as possible after the elbow connects (**e** of bottom line .)

Ex #16   Reverse-Side Double Punch to Side-Triple Elbow Strike   **(underlined are Ex #12)**

R-L   *L-L\R*   *R-L*   *L-L\R*
(R-SDP)''(S-TES)'''**(R-SDP)**''(S-TES)…repeat, change leading fist
       e-f\ f   e-f\ f

We can now begin to mix the four double punches together in continuous combinations. The next four practice sequences will demonstrate several examples. *Because both fists may change to different sides of the bag at the same time only the exact techniques will be used, without the linking symbols*. To make it easier, the technique before each R-SDP is underlined.

Ex #17 Continuous double punching in double bounce rhythm   (2nd fist links to lead the R-SDP)

L-R   *R-L*   *L-R*   *R-**L***   *L-R*   *R-L*   *L-R*   *R-L*
(FDP)''(R-SDP)''(SDP)''(FDP)''(R-SDP)''(FDP)''(RDP)''(SDP)''…repeat

In this last pattern, we see the second fist of the (FDP) { larger, **bold** } passes through to lead the next (R-SDP). In the next sequence, the first fist will pass through.

Ex #18 Continuous double punching in double bounce rhythm   (1st fist links to lead the R-SDP)

***L**-R*   ***L**-R*   *R-L*   ***L**-R*   *L-R*   ***R**-L*   *R-L*   *L-R*   *R-L*
(FDP)''(R-SDP)''(SDP)''(FDP)''(R-SDP)''(FDP)''(R-SDP)''(SDP)''(SDP)''…repeat

Ex #19 Continuous double punching in double & triplet rhythm

                                      L stays behind bag

L-R   *R-L*   *L-**R***   *R-L*   *L-R*   *R-**L***   *L-R*   *R-L*
(FDP)'''(SDP)''(FDP)''(R-SDP)''(SDP)'''(RDP)'''(R-SDP)''(SDP)''…repeat

Ex #20 Mixed double punching and triple elbow striking in double & triplet rhythm

*L-**R***   *R-L*   *L\R-R*   *R-L*   *L-L**R***   *R-L*   *L-R*   *R-**R**\L*   *R-L*
(FDP)''(R-SDP)''(D-TES)''(RDP)''(S-TES)'''(R-SDP)''(SDP)''(O-TES)''(R-SDP)''…repeat
          f\ e-f   e-f\ f   e-**f**\ f

This last exercise is a little tricky and more difficult because it uses three triple elbow strikes. You must keep the elbows up to pull it off. The key is noticing that the *second* fist passes through to lead the first two R-SDP's (…and notice the *three* rebounds after the S-TES.) The *first* fist of the O-TES passes through to lead the last R-SDP.

The last twenty practice exercises are not all the possible combinations for using the Reverse-Side Double Punch, but they will give you a good base for using it in your non-stop, continuous combinations. It will take some time and patience to master.

Side-Reverse Double Punch   (S-RDP)

This last technique again features the uniqueness of the Side Single Punch. We saw the rear-side fist angle allows it to combine with the Reverse Single Punch, but this time we will reverse the fist order. The Side-Reverse Double Punch is symbolized by (S-RDP). This is probably the most difficult technique because *it is the only one that has the lead, or first fist, from the side* **[FIG 9-O].** Also, the second fist must be behind the bag, which is going sideways! The bag will strike the large knuckle of the index finger in the (SSP), rebound once and strike the same area of the fist coming from the rear **[FIG 9-P].**

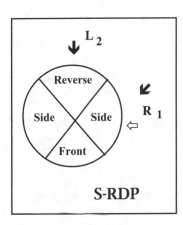

Fig 9-O Fist angles of "L-R" Side-Reverse Double Punch

Fig 9-P   Side-Reverse Double Punch

As we see in this picture, the right arm leads the S-RDP from the side, which will put the first rebound on the *left* side of the board. But the *left arm* must be positioned to follow from behind the bag after one rebound. This is one of the few times when it's advantageous to let the arm doing a (RSP) to angle slightly down at the elbow. This allows the bag to pass to the side of the rebound board which would normally be blocked by the "reverse" technique arm. You may also find it helpful (when you anticipate going to a S-RDP) to keep the *reverse arm* slightly lower by allowing the elbow to drop.

The following exercises will help familiarize you with this technique. *At this level, both fists are changing sides with every technique, so the linking symbols will not be used*. The exact fist movements are the most important key. The first few exercises demonstrate ways to "enter" the S-RDP, and then we will look at different way to "exit" the technique. (Have patience on this one, because sometimes you get it…and sometimes you don't. I think it is the single most difficult technique.)

Ex # 1 Side Single Punch, to Side-Reverse Double Punch, to Reverse Single Punch.

R	*R*	**R-L**	*L*	*L*
(SSP)'''	(SSP)'''	**(S-RDP)**'''	(RSP)'''	(RSP)

This first pattern enters (and exits) the S-RDP in the simplest way because it is a constant triplet rhythm. The next two examples will show that this works with *any* side technique, because the last fist comes from the side

Ex # 2 Side Double Punch, to Side-Reverse Double Punch, to Reverse Single Punch.

*L-**R***   **R-L**   *L*   *L*
(SDP)**'''**(**S-RDP**)'''(RSP)'''(RSP)

Ex # 3 Side-Triple Elbow Strike, to Side-Reverse Double Punch, to Reverse Single Punch.

            L   *L-L**R**   **R-L**   *L*   *L*
Basic LLRR…(FSP)'''(**S-TES**)**'''**(**S-RDP**)'''(RSP)'''(RSP)
                e-f \ **f**

The last three practice sequences set up the S-RDP from the a same side technique. We can also enter the S-RDP from an *opposite* side technique, by linking the first fist through to the other side. The next exercise will demonstrate.

Ex #4 Side Double Punch, to opposite side Side-Reverse Double Punch, to Reverse Single Punch

            R   **R-**L   **R-L**   *L*   *L*
Basic LLRR…(FSP)'''(SDP)''(**S-RDP**)'''(RSP)'''(RSP)

Here we see the right fist (*R*), which leads the SDP crossing to the *other side* to lead the S-RDP. Of course this needs only two rebounds and occurs pretty quickly. You cannot hesitate after the left fist connects in the SDP. This creates a side-to-side split fist, which can be unstable (due to fist angle), so there is a secret to making this work. ***The key is the left (L) fist***. When you anticipate going to the S-RDP from the opposite side, use the swing alteration we learned earlier in the chapter for side-to-side split fist combinations (page 76.) *Drag* the fist more directly into the side (not rear-side) of the bag by letting the left shoulder move the arm across, and not flex the elbow completely. Angle (bend) the fist *toward your little finger,* which creates a flatter surface for the bag over the thumb. The beauty of this "trick" is it also gets the left arm in better position for the fist to pass behind the bag (for the second fist of the (S-RDP.) Call it cheating the angles…but at this level, every little bit helps.

We can enter this technique after a front technique by passing a fist through and leading from the side, as the next several exercises will demonstrate.

Ex #5 Basic rhythm, Front Circle Punch, to Side-Reverse Double Punch, to Reverse Single Punch

           L   ***L***   *R-L   *L*   *L*
Basic LLRR…(FCP)'''(FCP)'''(S-RDP)'''(RSP)'''(RSP)…

Here we see the left fist (***L***) doing a FCP and linking behind to re-enter as the second fist in the S-RDP. A tip is to hold it lower, so the bag won't hit the left arm after the right fist (*R) connects. Also, the right fist must be ready to lead in from the side.

We can also combine the Side-Reverse Double Punch after a Front Double Punch. Here we can choose which fist will go to the **side** to lead the S-RDP,….the *lead* (first) fist, or *second* fist. (Of course, the other fist must pass through for the reverse punch.)

Ex #6 Front Double Punch (*lead* fist -**R**- goes to side), to Side-Reverse Double Punch, to Reverse
Single Punch.

Lead fist to Side

R   **R**-L   **R**-L   L   L

Basic LLRR…(FSP)'''(FDP)**'''(S-RDP)**'''(RSP)'''(RSP)

This is a new movement, and the first time a lead fist has gone directly to the side.

Ex #7 Front Double Punch (*second fist* - **L** - goes to side), to Side-Reverse Double Punch, to Reverse
Single Punch.

R   *R*-**L**   **L**-*R*   R   R

Basic LLRR…(FSP)'''(FDP)**'''(S-RDP)**'''(RSP)'''(RSP)

These last two exercises differ in the order of how the fists contact the bag In exercise #6, notice that *both* the double punches are done "**R**-L"…or, they both have the same leading fist. In #7 though, we have "*R*-**L**" and "**L**-*R*", or, the left fist hits twice in a row. In either case, just have the fist you want to lead with extend out to the *side* of the bag.

We have this same option with *any* technique from the front that has two fist, such as the Outward or Downward Triple Elbow Strikes, or the Out & Down 4way Elbow Strike. The next example will demonstrate using the Downward-Triple Elbow Strike.

Ex #8 Downward-Triple Elbow Strike (*lead* fist -**L**- goes to side), to Side-Reverse Double Punch, to Reverse Single Punch.

L   **L**\R-R   **L**-R   R   R

Basic LLRR…(FSP)'''(D-TES)**'''(S-RDP)**'''(RSP)'''(RSP)

f \ e-f

Ex #9 Downward-Triple Elbow Strike (*second* fist -**R**- goes to side), to Side-Reverse Double Punch, to Reverse Single Punch.

L   L\R-**R**   **R**-L   L   L

Basic LLRR…(FSP)'''(D-TES)**'''(S-RDP)**'''(RSP)'''(RSP)

f \ e-**f**

In the past nine exercises, we have followed the S-RDP with a Reverse Single Punch, (RSP) after three rebounds. This is the easiest since the last fist of the S-RDP comes from the reverse position. However, we can have the reverse fist pass to the front to lead the next technique. The next few exercises will demonstrate. [The first (*lead*) fist of the Front Double Punch, will go to the side to lead the S-RDP, (just like exercise #6). It will be the right fist (*R).]

Ex #10 Side-Reverse Double Punch, reverse fist links to the Front Circle Punch.

$$*R\text{-}L \qquad R\text{-}L \qquad L \qquad R$$

Basic LLRR…(FDP)'''(S-RDP)''(FCP)'''(FSP)'''…..repeat

Ex #11 Side-Reverse Double Punch, reverse fist links to the lead Front Double Punch.

$$*R\text{-}L \qquad R\text{-}L \qquad L\text{-}R$$

Basic LLRR…(FDP)'''(S-RDP)''(FDP)'''…repeat.

Ex #12 Side-Reverse Double Punch, reverse fist links to the lead Outward-Triple Elbow Strike.

$$*R\text{-}L \qquad R\text{-}L \qquad L\text{-}L\backslash R$$

Basic LLRR…(FDP)'''(S-RDP)''(O-TES)'''…repeat. Change lead
e-f \ f

Ex #13 Side-Reverse Double Punch, reverse fist links to the lead Side-Triple Elbow Strike.

$$*R\text{-}L \qquad R\text{-}L \qquad L\text{-}L\backslash R^{\nwarrow}$$

Basic LLRR…(FDP)'''(S-RDP)''(S-TES)''….repeat. Change lead
e-f \ **f**

Exercises #12 and #13 are almost exactly the same except for the entrance of the last right (**R** $^{\nwarrow}$) fist, which comes from the *side* in exercise #13. These two combinations are difficult because of the rotation needed to set up the left elbow. It is easier to go to the Downward-Triple Elbow Strike, as seen next.

Ex #14 Side-Reverse Double Punch, reverse fist links to the lead Outward-Triple Elbow Strike.

$$*R\text{-}L \qquad R\text{-}L \qquad L\text{-}L\backslash R$$

Basic LLRR…(FDP)'''(S-RDP)''(D-TES)'''…….repeat. change lead
f \ e- f

The most challenging combinations come when combining the Side-Reverse Double Punch and the Reverse-Side Double Punch together. These combinations may use two or three rebounds, depending on the order that we throw them and which fist we want to lead the next technique. The next two exercises will go from the S-RDP to the R-SDP.

Ex # 15 Side-Reverse Double Punch, *second fist* leads the following Reverse-Side Double Punch

$$*R\text{-}L \qquad R\text{-}L \qquad L\text{-}R \qquad\qquad (\text{Key:} \quad L \text{ - stays behind the bag})$$

Basic LLRR…(FDP)'''(S-RDP)'''(R-SDP)''…repeat. Change lead

The key feature to note here is the second, or last fist of the S-RDP (**L**) leads the R-SDP after three rebounds, because it is hitting the back of the bag twice in a row. It may help to let the left fist drop under the bag after the S-RDP and wait until it rebounds three times.

Then circle it up to lead the R-SDP. Also, the right fist must re-enter from the side of the bag again. Let it drift out to the right side as the left fist circles up to lead the last R-SDP. It may feel wierd.

In the next example, we will have the *first* fist of the S-RDP lead the next technique.

Ex # 16 Side-Reverse Double Punch, *first fist* leads the following Reverse-Side Double Punch

R-L   R-L   R-L   (Key: **R** - hits side, then goes behind)

Basic LLRR...(FDP)''''(S-RDP)''''(R-SDP)''...repeat. Change lead

Again, this takes three rebounds because both the (**L** & **R**) fists come from behind the bag.

The next two combinations will be from the R-SDP to the S-RDP. First, we will have the *second fist* of the FDP, pass through to lead the R-SDP.

Ex # 17 Reverse-Side Double Punch, *second fist* leads the following Side-Reverse Double Punch

R-L   L-R   R-**L***   L-R

Basic LLRR...(FDP)''(R-SDP)'''(S-RDP)''(FDP)'''...repeat. or change lead

In this combination, we need three rebounds between the R-SDP and S-RDP because the second fist of the R-SDP (R) hits twice in a row from the right side of the bag. This can cause a problem for the left fist (**L***) in the S-RDP, because the bag will rebound twice on the *left side* of the board, and the left arm must be out of the way. Let it drop down underneath, then re-circle up as the right leads.

Finally, we can have the *lead fist* of the R-SDP move to the side to lead the S-RDP. This will be a little more difficult.

Ex # 18 Reverse-Side Double Punch, *first fist* leads the following Side-Reverse Double Punch

R-**L***   L-R   L-R

Basic LLRR...(FDP)''(R-SDP)''(S-RDP)''...repeat. or change lead

This combination happens very fast and needs great fist control. Notice that the left fist (**L**) leads both techniques. The key is noting the right fist (**R**) hits the *side* of the bag and then the left (**L**) hits the *other side*. Also, neither fist connects the bag from the same area twice. The right fist goes from the front, to the side and to the back. The left fist goes from the front to the back to the side. When you start moving your fists continually around the bag, then you have exceptional fist control. For me, one of the most difficult speed bag combinations is two back-to-back S-RDP's, alternating the lead.

Ex # 19 Several Side-Reverse Double Punches, alternating the lead

*R-L   R-L   L-R   R-L   *L-R   L-R   R-L   L-R

Basic LLRR...(SDP)''(**S-RDP**)'''(S-RDP)''(FDP)'''(SDP)''(**S-RDP**)'''(**S-RDP**)''(FDP)'''repeat

This last pattern has the lead fist of a SDP (*) extending out to lead the **S-RDP**. Notice how the lead of the S-RDP alternates. The underlined techniques are the same combinations leading with the opposite fist. This is one of those combinations where sometimes you get it and sometimes you don't. It all depend on the angles of fist entry, and angles of bag rebound. These can change slightly.

The Side-Reverse Double Punch is the fifth double punch technique. The final few exercise patterns will mix these all together in various combinations. As a quick review, the general fist angle's of entry for all of the double punches, with a **L - R** fist order, are shown in **[FIG 9-Q]**.

Left - Right Fist order for all Double Punches   1 = lead Fist   2 = second fist

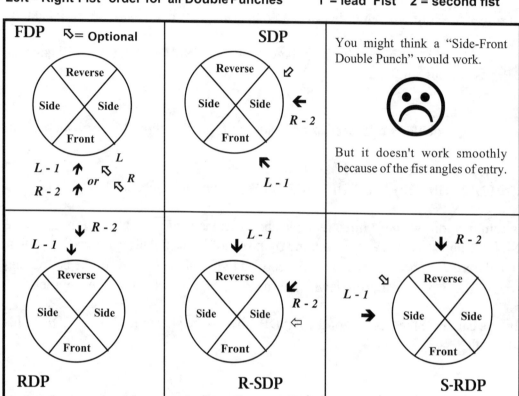

Fig 9-Q Fist angles & Bag areas for five "*L-R*" Double Punch techniques

In the following exercises, be sure to notice the number of rebounds inbetween and how the last fist of a technique usually leads the next technique.

Ex # 20 Continuous FDP - RDP - SDP - SDP   * (**See Fig. demonstration, page 115**)

L-R   R-L   L-R   R-L   L-R   R-L   L-R   R-L
(FDP)''(RDP)''(SDP)''(SDP)''(FDP)''(RDP)''(SDP)''(SDP)…repeat

Ex # 21 Various combinations of double punch techniques

L-R   R-L   L-R   L-R   L-R   R-L   L-R   R-L
(FDP)''(RDP)''(SDP)''(S-RDP)'''(R-SDP)''(SDP)'''(R-SDP)'''(RDP)''…repeat

22 Various combinations of double punch techniques

L-R   **R**-L   L-R   L-R   R-L   L-R   R L   L-R   R-L
(FDP)''(R-SDP)''(SDP)''(S-RDP)'''(RDP)''(SDP)'''(R-SDP)''(FDP)'''(SDP)''…repeat

Exercises #20 , #21 and #22 are written so you can go from one to the other, because the (FDP) is the same in all patterns.

The six techniques using the side area of the bag completes 24 techniques and their basic use for continuous, non-stop speed bag striking. If you understand how they fit together and can execute all the practice exercises, than you are well on your way to ultimate speed bag control, and far superior to almost anyone on the bag. However…(there's always a "however"), we have only touched the basics, or the tip of the iceberg, and there is much more to learn. Believe it or not, the next chapter will fine tune these skills and open up ways to *double and triple the combination possibilities.*

There are several "secrets" to this combination.

First, for FDP '' RDP, [frames 1 - 8] simply extend both fists straight out and back through the bag.

Next, getting into the SDP set position in frame 9. The key is frame #7 (circled), where the second (**L**) fist of the RDP connects the bag. The lead (**R**) fist *must be going out to the side* as this fist connects. You only have two rebounds to get it there. By the time the left fist is in frame #8, the right fist must be in the frame #9 position.

Frames #9 - 16 are the SDP'' SDP combo. As the left fist hits in frame #15, circled, keep the right fist by the chin, to repeat frame #1

Exercise 20, page 114   FDP - RDP - SDP - SDP combinations. See Text Box.

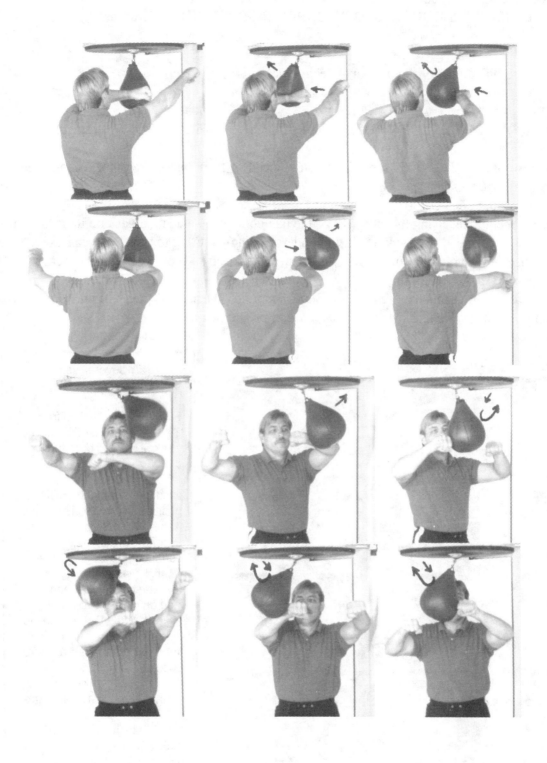

Multiple Views of Continuous SDP''SDP figure -[8] Combinations

CHAPTER 10

ADVANCED SKILLS & COMBINATIONS

The previous chapters have covered twenty four individual techniques for smooth and continuous speed bag striking. This chapter will focus on advanced mechanics of using those skills, or multiple ways to create combinations. It is strongly encouraged to thoroughly understand all previous techniques, rhythmic variations and the method used to write combinations. They will *all* be used and expanded upon. Also, the practice exercises usually began with-and exited into-the Basic Rhythm. That will not be necessary here, for we will be examining fist movements within techniques and combinations in much closer detail. Only the specific combinations will be shown in most of the exercises, except when the entry setup is helpful. Actually we will be focusing more and more on combinations outside of the basic three bounce "triplet" rhythm, and using the much faster double bounce rhythm, and eventually one rebound between techniques. Advanced skills will find us continually linking combinations from all sides in a nonstop blitz. If you want to "master" the speed bag, then this chapter is for you.

For this chapter I am assuming a certain level of ability on your part. By now you should be familiar with the speed, sound, rhythm and movements of the bag. You should be able to visualize it in front of you, mimic the technique movements and hear the rhythms they produce. Hopefully, you are comfortable with the technique abbreviations and symbols for written combinations. Be careful to examine each exercise thoroughly, noting exactly where *one rebound* ('), *two rebounds* ('') or *three rebounds* (''') occur,- or if a technique is "outward" or "downward". It makes a great deal of difference! These are punching skills that will occur in a small area very quickly. I also strongly encourage covering this chapter in the order it is presented. Topics will sequentially build, each expanding from the previous one, and many of the exercises are not easy. To make the fastest progress at this point, I would suggest learning all exercise sequences first **without** the bag. When you take some of the exercises to the bag, you may initially have a lot of "breakdowns". Do not become discouraged by it. The combinations in this chapter will become more and more complex. Many of the topics will be covering precise fist movements that you must understand before trying them on the bag. Even if you are not able to perform every single practice exercise immediately, strive to understand the concept of what is being discussed. Much of the material is easy to understand in theory, but the physical skills will take more time and concentration.

When in doubt **always** slow down and emphasize proper position. Your efforts and journey through this chapter will reward you with complete understanding of techniques along with absolute control of your fists, elbows and the bag.

SWING MOVEMENT AND COMBINATIONS

Through all the techniques and practice exercises, body movement has always been a smooth transition of leaning into the bag with each strike. The natural follow through of one technique leads to the setup for the next technique. When we look at this more closely, we find that all movement sets up techniques going "out" from the center of the body or "in" to the center of the body. All possible technique combinations are dictated by this "out-in" arm and body movement. For example, it is very awkward to follow a right Front Straight Punch (FSP) with a left Inward-Single Elbow Strike (I-SES). Also, it is near impossible to follow a right Front Straight Punch with a left Outward-Single Elbow Strike. In the first example, two "in" movements by opposite arms do not work well. In the second example, an "in" movement (FSP) of one arm and the "out" motion (O-SES) of the other is awkward.

The Basic Rhythm is a perfect example of this.

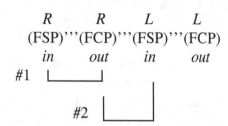

> **SECRET:** The *Angle of Fist entry* and the *Angle of Bag Rebound* are the keys to all combinations, from the simple Basic Rhythm to the most advanced combinations. Subtle changes make for many variations.

In #1, the Right (FSP) "in" motion is followed by the Right (FCP) "out" motion. This shows that the "in" motion is best followed by the "out" motion of the **same** arm. To complete the sequence with #2, the Right (FCP) "out" motion is followed by the Left (FSP) "in" motion. This shows the "out" motion of one arm is naturally followed by the "in" motion of the **opposite** arm.

This in-to-out (same arm), out-to-in (opposite arm) is exactly how all of the techniques are structured. In the (FDP) for example, the lead fist is moving "out" from the center of the body and the second fist is moving "in" toward it. Another example is the Outward-Triple Elbow Strike, (O-TES). The lead arm (elbow-fist) is moving "out" and the following arm (fist) is moving "in". All the two arm techniques follow this rule.

This can greatly broaden your awareness in understanding all the combination possibilities that can exist when flowing from one technique to another. Let's examine #1, the "In-to-out" movements of the same arm. Twelve techniques can follow the "inward" (FSP) in the triplet rhythm.

EXAMPLE 1

	L	*L*	*L-R*	*L-R*	*L-Lead*	*L*	*L*
Basic LLRR…**(FSP)'''**	1-(FCP)	2-(FDP)	3-(SDP)	4-(F-Roll)	5-(O-SES)	6-(O-DES)	
							e-f

L-L\R	*L-L\R*	*L\R-R*	*L-L\R-R*	*L-L\R-R*	*L\R-R*
7-(O-TES)	8-(S-TES)	9-(D-TES)	10-(O-D 4way)	11-(O-I 4way)	12-(I-TES)
e-f \ f	e-f \ f	f \ e-f	e-f \ e-f	e-f \ f-e	f \ e-f

Every one of the twelve possible techniques begins with the left arm making an "outward" motion from the center of the body. It does not matter if you hit the elbow or the fist, as long as the same arm moves from "in" to "out".

When looking at #2, the "out-to-in" motion of opposite arms, we find six techniques that can smoothly follow the "outward" (FCP) after three rebounds.

EXAMPLE 2

	L	*R*	*R*	*R*	*R*	*R*	*R*
Basic LLRR...**(FCP)'''**	1-(FSP)	2-(SSP)	3-(I-SES)	4-(D-SES)	5-(I-DES)	6-(D-DES)	
					f-e	e-f	

Notice that after the "outward" (FCP) with the left arm, the opposite (right) arm follows with an "inward" motion. There are actually more than these six techniques however, for we can usually follow an outward technique with another outward technique if we lead with the same arm. We'll identify this as #3 "Out-to-Out" movements. For example....

EXAMPLE 3

	L	*L*	*L-R*	*L-R*	*L-lead*	*L*	*L*	*L-L\R*
(FCP)'''	1-(FCP)	2-(FDP)	3-(SDP)	4-(F-Roll)	5-(O-SES)	6-(O-DES)	7-(O-TES)	
						e-f	e-f\f	

	L\R-R	*L-L\R*	*L-L\R-R*	*L-L\R-R*	*L\R-R*
	8-(D-TES)	9-(S-TES)	10-(O-D 4way)	11-(O-I 4way)	12-(I-TES)
	f\e-f	e-f\f	e-f\e-f	e-f\f-e	f\e-f

Because of the arm and body movements most of these combinations would occur automatically without much concentration. However it is easy to figure out all the possible combinations that can follow *any* technique by examining how the technique ends. Consider these five techniques:
1-**(D-DES)** 2-**(D-TES)** 3-**(O-TES)** 4-**(S-TES)** 5-**(SDP)**. Each one ends with an "inward" fist.
   e-f   f\e-f   e-f\f   e-f\f

Any of the twelve techniques identified earlier in example #1 (following the "in" motion) can be used to follow these techniques. We can do the same for techniques ending with an "outward" fist movement:
1-**(F-Roll)** 2-**(O-SES)** 3-**(O-DES)**
                                      e-f

Any of the six techniques identified in example #2 can follow these. But here we can also add the twelve combinations of #3 ("out-to-out" movements), making a total of 18 different techniques that can naturally follow these, or any techniques that ends with an *outward* fist. Also, notice they all occur in the basic triplet rhythm, because each technique comes from the same side as the previous one.

The possible technique combinations that can follow a single or double fist pass through are also greater than you might think. When performing a single fist [8] from the front, the fist passes through to the back and returns to its original position in the front. The last strike is the (RSP) that occurs behind the bag, so the next technique from the front (opposite side) will occur after two rebounds. Once the fist returns to the front-any of the twelve techniques identified in #1, following the "IN" (FSP), are possible as the next example demonstrates.

EXAMPLE 4   Figure-[8] pass through, same arm follows with "outward" moving technique

L	*L*		*L*	*L-R*	*L-R*	*L-Lead*	*L*	*L*	*L-L\R*
(FCP)"	**(RSP)"**		**1-(FCP)**	**2-(FDP)**	**3-(SDP)**	**4-(F-Roll)**	**5-(O-SES)**	**6-(O-DES)**	**7-(O-TES)**
└─ [8] ─┘								e-f	e-f \ f

L-L\R	*L\R-R*	*L-L\R-R*	*L-L\R-R*	*L\R-R*
8-(S-TES)	**9-(D-TES)**	**10-(O-D 4way)**	**11-(O-I 4way)**	**12-(I-TES)**
e-f \ f	f \ e-f	e-f \ e-f	e-f \ f-e	f \ e-f

The same is true when both fists pass through after a Front Double Punch, as in the next example:

EXAMPLE 5   Double fist Figure-[8] last fist follows with "outward" movement.

L-R	**R-L**	
(FDP)"	**(RDP)"**	ANY of the above twelve techniques leading with the left arm.
└─ [8] ─┘		

The last fist to return is the "L" (left). You will almost always follow this movement with an "outward" technique leading with the (left) arm. Of course if the order was {L-R}, you would lead outward with the right arm.

Lastly, we do not have to lead back with the same arm (or last arm) that passed through. We can follow with the opposite arm with any "inward" moving technique.

EXAMPLE 6   Figure-[8] pass through, opposite arm follows with "inward" moving technique

L	*L*		*R*	*R*	*R*	*R-Lead*	*R*	*R*
(FCP)"	**(RSP)"...**		**1-(FSP)**	**2-(I-SES)**	**3-(I-DES)**	**4-(F-Roll)**	**5-(D-SES)**	**6-(D-DES)**
					f-e			e-f

The point is to make you aware of all the possible combinations available from any one technique to another. This can help you avoid getting into "combination ruts", where one certain technique always follows another. At the very least there are at six possible combinations to any technique and often eleven or more. As we progress through this chapter, we will learn to master many advanced combinations and begin learning several exceptions to the normal rules of speed bag rhythm.

ADVANCED PUNCHING

Continuous punching from the same bag area, either front or reverse, has always occurred with an *odd* number of rebounds in-between. We normally use *three* (triplet rhythm), but the bag is in the correct position to be hit *from the same side* after **one** rebound. That is how the "double punches" are created, by allowing the "other fist" to follow and hit the bag after only one rebound. But we do not have to follow

with the *other* fist after one rebound. We can follow with the *same* fist after one rebound.
 I have heard this called "fast punching" or "rhythm punching". This works with almost every technique. This is tricky, because we can not do this when swinging in a small circle. There is not enough time to complete the movement. Instead, swing in a very short straight line into the bag and back. This is a compact movement and the fist stays in a relatively fixed position. It only moves about an inch or so back and forth. This method of swinging creates a feeling of tension in your forearms and feel like you are "chopping" the bag. The next few practice exercises will using the Front Circle Punch (FCP).

Normal triplet Rhythm = 3 rebounds   Advanced Punching combination = 1 rebound

```
      R         R         R                    R        *R        *R         R
#1  (FCP)'''(FCP)'''(FCP)                   (FCP)'''(FCP) ' (FCP)'''(FCP)
```

On the right we see two FCP's (*R) with only one rebound in-between. It sounds just like a Front Double Punch (FDP). This single fist can also return after *another* technique

Normal triplet Rhythm   Advanced Punching combination

```
     L-R       R         L-L\ R      R              L-R       *R          L-L\ R       *R
#2  (FDP)'''(FCP)  &  (O-TES)'''(FCP)           (FDP) ' (FCP)   &   (O-TES) ' (FCP)
              e-f\f                                          e-f\f
```

Returning after another technique takes some anticipation, and if you just hold the fist up, the bag will rebound into it. Again, It is a choppy motion. However, the FCP (*R) Right fist could also be the *lead fist of another FDP*. We will see this below.

Normal triplet Rhythm   Advanced Punching combination

```
     L-R       R-L       L-L\ R      R-L            L-R       *R-L        L-L\ R       *R-L
#3  (FDP)'''(FDP)  &  (O-TES)'''(FDP)           (FDP) ' (FDP)   &   (O-TES) ' (FDP)
              e-f\f                                          e-f\f
```

These advanced combinations happen very quickly and I find it best to do one or two and go back to the triplet rhythm. And it seems to work best with the (FCP) and (FDP). *It is very difficult to follow any technique with an elbow strike after only one rebound.* There is not enough time to position the elbow. Below are a few practice exercises using advanced punching combinations from the front. (advanced punch combinations are underlined).

```
      R       R       R      R-L    L-R      R      R-L     L-R     R-L     L-R-L-R..
#4  (FSP)'''(FCP) ' (FCP)'''(FDP)'''(FDP) ' (FCP)'''(FDP)'''(FDP) ' (FDP)'''(F-ROLL)
```

```
      R       R-R\L     L        L      L-L\R    R-L    L-R    R-L-R-L    L-L\R    R-L
#5  (FCP)'''(O-TES) ' (FCP)'''(FCP)'''(O-TES) ' (FDP) ' (FDP)'''(F-ROLL)'''(O-TES) ' (FDP)'''
              e-f\f                      e-f\f                                 e-f\f
```

As mentioned in Chapter 5, all fist movements done from the front of the bag can also be done from the back of the bag, and we can do Advanced Punching combinations with the reverse punches. It is a little more difficult because it is an awkward movment from behind, and we can not see the contact points. **The next few practice exercises show the advanced combinations with the Reverse Single Punch (RSP) and Reverse Double Punch (RDP).**

Normal triplet Rhythm = 3 rebounds   Advanced Punching combinations = 1 Rebound

    R   *R*   *R*   *R*   **R*   **R*   *R*
#6 (RSP)'''(RSP)'''(RSP)   (RSP)'''(RSP) ' (RSP)'''(RSP)

    L-R   *R*   *L-R*   **R*
#7 (RDP)'''(RSP)   (RDP) ' (RSP)

    L-R   *R-L*   *L-R*   **R-L*
#8 (RDP)'''(RDP)   (RDP) ' (RDP)

We can also mix the Front and Reverse advanced combinations together, having the fist(s) pass through after the "repeated", or second, punch. To do this, simply let it continue through the bag after the short "chopping" motion of the punch. It works with either *one or both fists*. (Two rebounds during the [1/2]). The advanced combination is also shown at the right without the linking symbol.

#9 Single Fist (FCP) to (RSP)   * Exact Techniques at right.

    R   R   R   **r**   R   R   R   R   R   R
(FCP)'''(FCP) ' (FCP)-[1/2]-(RSP) ' (RSP)   * (FCP) ' (FCP)''(RSP) ' (RSP)

#10 Double punches, (FDP) to (RDP) (this happens quick!)

   R-L   **L-R**   **R-L**   B   **L-R**   **R-L**   **L-R**   **R-L**   **L-R**   **R-L**
(FDP)'''(FDP) ' (FDP)-[1/2]-(RDP) ' (RDP)   * (FDP) ' (FDP)''(RDP) ' (RDP)

These are difficult to do, especially on a 9" x 6" or smaller bag. *The secret is to anticipate the change, knowing when to stop the circular motion of the fists and start making the short back and forth movement.* It also must happen automatically. If you try to control each single movement, it will be difficult. Also, you must keep the fists high. Mix these in occassionally with your front and reverse combinations.

The most important thing to remember about these "advanced punching" combinations is that the next technique came from the *same side* of the bag. (We will do this from *different* sides of the bag at the end of the chapter.)

ADVANCED FRONT FIST ROLLING

We just saw that techniques from the same side can follow after *one* rebound. Fist Rolling can be tied to any technique that ends with a fist in the same way, as demonstrated in the next sequences:

```
        L       L-R     L-R-L-R...
   1   (FSP)'''(FDP) ' (F-Roll)...
```

In the first example the (F-Roll) "immediately" follows the (FDP). As soon as the right fist connects immediately follow with the left into the fist roll. This combination is relative easy because the elbows are already in the proper position

```
        L       L-L\R ------ L-R-L-R...
   2   (FSP)'''(O-TES) ' (F-Roll)....
             e-f\f
```

> The *last* fist of a Front Technique can also act as the *first* Fist of a Front Fist Roll

In the second example, the right (**R**) is the last fist of the (O-TES). As soon as the right fist connects, immediately follow with the left into the fist roll. *One secret is to keep the elbows almost parallel-particularly the lead elbow*, [the left in this example]. The lead elbow in the Outward Elbow Strikes tends to finish in a lower position. It must be kept even with the fist to complete the "immediate" fist roll, for it is very difficult to fist roll with the elbows lower than the fist. *Another secret to "advanced fist rolling" is the last fist in the technique before the Fist Roll.* Since we usually emphasize the first fist contact in a fist roll it is easier to view the *last fist* of the technique, (**R**) also as the *first fist* of the Fist Roll. That also helps overcome any momentary hesitation in beginning the roll. The (O-TES) is the easiest elbow technique to join with the Front Fist Roll. The most difficult techniques to combine this way are the Downward Elbow Strikes. Example three and four below are slightly more difficult.

```
        L       L\R-R ------ L-R-L-R...                    L       L-L\R-R ------ L-R-L-R...
   3   (FSP)'''(D-TES) ' (F-Roll)...        And      4   (FSP)'''(O-D 4way) ' (F-Roll)...
             f\e-f                                             e-f\e-f
```

In example three, the right elbow strikes down into the bag followed by the right fist. The right elbow ends up in a low and "inside" position when the last fist connects. The same is true in example four, which shows this combination from the Out-and-Down 4way strike. Three rebounds allows enough time to correct the elbow position but for an immediate Fist Roll it must return to "out and parallel" very fast. There are a couple of ways to doing this smoothly. One is to *emphasize "under and over" rolling motion of the last fist* (**R**). This will get your right fist even with the elbow underneath the left fist. Another method is *to snap the right elbow "out" to parallel while the fist connects*. This method is a little more difficult and takes more control, but either method will work. An excellent way to develop control for this is to practice immediate Fist Rolling from the Downward-Double Elbow Strike as written below:

```
        L          R -------- L-R-L-R
    (FCP)'''(D-DES) ' (F-Roll)......
             e-f
```

Fist Rolling creates the fastest accented rhythmic tempo and puts the bag and fists in a blur of motion. I like to create combinations which steadily increase fist and bag motions, as well as build tension in the rhythm, and climax it with an immediate Fist-Roll, as in the following example....

L	L-R	R-L	L-L\R	R-R\L	L-L\R-R	R-R\L-L	L-L\R-**R** --------**L**-R-L-R
(FSP)'''(FDP)'''(FDP)'''(O-TES)'''(O-TES)'''(O-D 4way)'''(O-D 4way)'''(O-D 4way) ' (F-Roll)
	e-f \ f	e-f \ f	e-f \ e-f	e-f \ e-f	e-f \ e-**f**

The last example is shortened due to space. To get the true feel of this, perform four (FDP), then four (O-TES). Or, reverse the order, doing the Four Way strikes first, then the Outward-Elbow Strikes and follow the Front Double Punches with the immediate Fist Roll. Mix them all together in different combinations. It is a great sound and visual display!

ADVANCED ELBOW STRIKING

Of all the techniques on the bag those using the elbows seem to fascinate people the most. Mastery of them is a foundation for "ultimate speed bag" diversity. In truth, these techniques are fairly easy to execute and most people learn to use them pretty quickly. Virtually every fist linking combination can follow or setup elbow techniques...and the only "secret" to performing them is...keeping the elbows up (some secret, huh?) The advanced part comes in learning how to use the one unique factor they offer....shoulder rotation and positional relief.

From the first chapter I have emphasized the "basic striking position" with the elbows high, simply because it is the only way to keep them ready to enter smoothly. With bag control this position becomes more natural and your hands will always seem ready to enter. You should have fewer and fewer "late" hits. Because elbow techniques emphasize shoulder rotation, which allow the elbows to momentarily drop-they can relieve the burning and let the shoulders rest. This may sound like a contradiction, because we have always kept the arms up in the ready position....now we are allowing them to drop lower on purpose to rest. Actually, this is one of the my best secrets to advanced speed bag. The fist or elbow does NOT always have to stay "up" in the ready position, but only be in the correct position just prior to re-entering. There is a big difference between letting an arm rest and then repositioning, versus swinging from the waist. Your "breakdowns" will immediately tell when you do not make it. Only practice can reinforce this concept, and all the techniques are much easier to learn with the arms held up.

When performing complex multiple fist combinations, the arms will get tired and tend to drop. Oddly enough, the elbow techniques are super for relaxing the arms. Here's how. After a "hot" sequence of multiple fist linking, peppered with fist rolls, the shoulders really start burning. Now break into some elbow striking techniques. Here are few examples of shoulder resting elbow combinations.

$$L\text{-}L\backslash R \qquad R\text{-}R\backslash L \qquad\qquad L\text{-}L\backslash R \qquad R\backslash L\text{-}L$$
#1   (O-TES)'''(O-TES)   #2   (O-TES)'''(D-TES)....repeat x 2 or 3, then change lead
$$e\text{-}\mathbf{f}\backslash f \qquad e\text{-}f\backslash\mathbf{f} \qquad\qquad\quad e\text{-}f\backslash\mathbf{f} \qquad \mathbf{f}\backslash e\text{-}f$$

In these examples, the larger swinging motion of the techniques allows the arms to relax. But there is also a "hidden" feature within the combinations. In example #1, we see the left elbow leads. After it strikes, let it stay down slightly lower than normal. It will get to rest as the right fist strikes the bag then returns to lead the Right (O-TES). It actually does not have to move until the right fist connects (...*Right fist* '''*Right elbow - Right fist*). Then only the left fist (**L**) needs to come up into the bag, allowing even a few more moments of rest. However, the fist is NOT swinging in from the waist. You will let it reposition at the chin just prior to entering. You can do the same thing for the right fist. Repeating exercise #1 in this way several times will let both shoulders relax.

In #2, we see the same thing, but here only one shoulder, the right (**R**), is getting the rest. After the right fist connects in the O-TES, the elbow can stay lower for only the fist needs to raise up to lead the next D-TES. Since this combination naturally repeats itself, the right arm gets time to rest. After two or three repetitions, simply change the lead by performing either two O-TES in a row or two D-TES.

You do not have to change the speed of your swinging motion for this to work because the triplet rhythm of these combinations naturally slows your movements, but I will generally slow it down slightly, creating a noticeable speed change and allowing the arms to make slightly larger rotations (and giving them more time in the "down" position).

Another method for elbow techniques to relieve your shoulders is to let one arm break off into a solo, performing several independent techniques, such as:

$$L \qquad\qquad L \qquad\qquad L\text{-}L\backslash\mathbf{R}$$
#3   (O-DES)'''(O-DES)'''(O-TES)...repeat with a right lead
$$e\text{-}f \qquad\qquad e\text{-}f \qquad\qquad e\text{-}f\backslash\mathbf{f}$$

Here we have the left arm performing two Outward-Double Elbow Strikes while the right arm gets to stay down and rest for 10 rebounds before entering (**R**) during the (O-TES). A slightly more difficult one arm resting combination is written below.

$$L \qquad\qquad R \qquad\qquad R \qquad\qquad L$$
#4   (O-DES)'''(D-DES)'''(O-DES)'''(D-DES)...repeat several times
$$e\text{-}f \qquad\qquad e\text{-}f \qquad\qquad e\text{-}f \qquad\qquad e\text{-}f$$

Here we find each arm performing several double elbow strikes during which the other can rest. Notice the left arm can rest for 11 rebounds after the first (O-DES).

These four combinations relieve my shoulders, allowing a recharge before blasting off into the multiple fist linking combinations soon to be covered. This momentary recharge is vital. Rather than "stop" entirely, grab some quick relief with these last 4 exercises, or discover other combinations that work for you. Armed with this "hidden" rest stop, You can work out for 20 minutes NON-STOP, and extend your fatigue factor for several hours.

ADVANCED REVERSE PUNCHING & LINKING

Linking different sides of the bag offers the greatest amount of rhythmic creativity and combination variety. To extend this ability we need to develop more control from the reverse punching position. Chapter five focused on using reverse punches as a quick pass through, and ended with showing how the RDP offered the same linking opportunities as the FDP.

I will expand on that here. We will start using the reverse area as a *point of origin*, leaving our fists behind the bag rather than in the usual chin position. To do this both arms must already be extended. The key is to keep the elbows high and slightly bent, leaving the fists in more or less of a side-reverse position, giving just enough room for the bag to clear when rebounding. The following exercises will develop control from this position. The linking fist will appear larger in **underlined bold**.

Quick Review: One half-figure 8, **[1/2]**, takes the fist to another side of the bag and *stays there*. The full figure-8 movement takes the fist to another side of the bag and then *returns to the original position*. For clarity, The following exercises are written with just *exact techniques* and no linking symbols.

Single fist figure-8 pass through to Reverse Double Punch

     L   *L*   **L**   **L**   *L-R*   *R*   **R**   **R**   *R-L*   *L*
1. (RSP)'''(RSP)'''(RSP)''(FCP)''(RDP)'''(RSP)'''(RSP)''(FCP)''(RDP)'''(RSP)…repeat

Reverse Double Punch, Figure-8 with second fist to Reverse Double Punch

     L   *L*   *L-***R**   **R**   *R-L*   *L*
2.   (RSP)'''(RSP)'''(RDP)''(FCP)''(RDP)'''(RSP)…repeat, change leading arm

Reverse Double Punch, Figure-8 with lead fist, to Reverse Double Punch, as done in Chapter 5.

     L   *L-R*   **R**-*L*   **R**   *R-L*   *L-R*   *R-L*   **L**-*R*   **L**   *L-R*
3. (RSP)'''(RDP)'''(RDP)''(FCP)''(RDP)'''(RDP)'''(RDP)'''(RDP)''(FCP)''(RDP)…continue

Notice that with a second fist figure-8, as in exercise #2, the (RDP) alternates the lead fist after the figure-8, and in #3, the lead fist figure-8, it does not. This next exercise will use both the lead and the second fist figure-8 pass through from a (RDP).

Reverse Double Punch, lead and second fist figure-8 pass through, to Reverse Double Punch

     L   *L-R*   **R**-*L*   **R**   *R-L*   *L-R*   *R-***L**   **L**   *L-R*
4. (RSP)'''(RDP)'''(RDP)''(FCP)''(RDP)'''(RDP)'''(RDP)''(FCP)''(RDP)..change lead

Now we will speed things up a bit by letting the fists *continually* Figure-8 pass through.

Reverse Double Punch, Continuous Figure-8 pass through with lead fist.

```
                       ┌──────┐ Lead Fist
     R      R-L    R    R-L    R    R-L    R    R-L
 5.  (RSP)'''(RDP)''(FCP)''(RDP)''(FCP) (RDP)''(FCP)''(RDP) ......Change lead
```

Reverse Double Punch, Continuous Figure-8 pass pass thourgh with second fist

This is a very quick changing combination and will take some concentration for the fists will be moving in different directions at the same time. The lead fist will be dropping down and extending out as the second fist is flexing in toward your face. Begin SLOWLY.

```
                       ┌──────┐ 2nd Fist
     R     R-L    L    L-R    R    R-L    L    L-R    R    R-L
 6.  (RSP)'''(RDP)''(FCP)''(RDP)''(FCP)''(RDP)''(FCP)''(RDP)''(FCP)''(RDP) ...
```

Notice how the second fist immediately passes through and returns to lead the next RDP

Reverse Double Punch, continuous Figure-8 pass through with Both fists

```
     R      R-L    L-R    R-L    L-R    R-L    R-L
 7.  (RSP)'''(RDP)''(FDP)''(RDP)''(FDP)''(RDP)''(FDP)''...continue, change lead
```

These last three patterns again show the options of linking the lead, second or both fist from either FDP or RDP - First seen in Chapter 5. They also demonstrate one of the "secrets" of the speed bag. Repetitive punching (especially *double* punching) from opposite sides will chop off the third beat of the "triplet rhythm". At least every other rebound is accented and the rhythm naturally sounds faster. This perception of faster rhythm is **not** directly related to the hands moving faster. They are still moving at a constant speed with controlled force. Of course, this will increase with real hand speed, and the key is building enough fist control to be able to do it as fast as you want. That is the advanced part! Once you can link from any combination with either hand, then your rhythms sound much faster and you are not working harder.

Let's continue with [1/2] Link. These next exercises will be slightly more difficult because they will create "split-fist" combinations, with the hands on different sides of the bag. They will be going in opposite directions and continually changing positions. The linking fist will be larger in **underlined bold**.and the linking [1/2] symbol will be used to show when (and which) fist changes sides.

Reverse Double Punch, One-Half Figure 8 by *lead* fist, to Front Straight Punch (* note **two** '')

```
     R      R-L    r    R    L    R    r    R-L    L        and split fists combo's
 8.  (RSP)'''(RDP)-[1/2]-(FSP)''(RSP)''(FSP)-[1/2]-(RDP)'''(RSP)
                    split  fists  combo
```

```
     R      R-L    r    R    L    R    L    l    L-R    R
 9.  (RSP)'''(RDP)-[1/2]-(FSP)''(RSP)''(FSP)''(RSP)-[1/2]-(FDP)'''(FCP)
                    split  fists  combo
```

127

Having the hands split, one in front and one in reverse position-which creates the (FSP)''(RSP) is very impressive at high speed. Although it is relatively easy to do, it looks complicated and offers a great amount of variety for advanced combinations, as we will cover in an upcoming section.

From this split hand position either fist can [1/2] through to the other side. In exercise eight both fists ended up in the reverse position and in number nine (#9) they ended up in the front position. Now we will One-half link with both fists *just before* the split fist combination.

$$L \quad \textbf{L-R} \quad \textbf{B} \quad \textit{R-L} \quad \textbf{L} \quad \textbf{l} \quad \textit{L} \quad \textit{R} \quad \textbf{L} \quad \textbf{l} \quad \textit{L-R}$$
10. (RSP)'''(RDP)-**[1/2]**-(FDP)'''(FCP)-**[1/2]**-(RSP)''(FSP)''(RSP)-**[1/2]**-(FDP)…
split fists combo

$$L \quad \textbf{L-R} \quad \textbf{B} \quad \textit{R}\textbf{-L} \quad \textbf{l} \quad \textit{L} \quad \textit{R} \quad \textbf{L} \quad \textbf{l} \quad \textit{L-R}$$
11. (RSP)'''(RDP)-**[1/2]**-(FDP)-**[1/2]**-(RSP)''(FSP)''(RSP)-**[1/2]**-(FDP)…
split fists combo

$$R \quad \textbf{R-L} \quad \textbf{r} \quad \textit{R} \quad \textbf{L} \quad \textbf{l} \quad \textit{L-R} \quad \textbf{l} \quad \textit{L} \quad \textbf{R} \quad \textbf{r} \quad \textit{R-L}$$
12. (RSP)'''(RDP)-**[1/2]**-(FSP)''(RSP)''(FDP)-**[1/2]**-(RSP)''(FSP)-**[1/2]**-(RDP)…

Exercise twelve is a little tricky, but the lead fist links off the double punches.
Now we can mix multiple fist linking together. (Remember, the fist may exit and stay on the opposite side from where it started for one or two punches). * Be sure to note which fist links, the first or second.

$$R \quad \textbf{R-L} \quad \textbf{B} \quad \textbf{L-R} \quad \textit{L} \quad \textit{L} \quad \textit{L} \quad \textit{R} \quad \textbf{L} \quad \textit{L} \quad \textit{L} \quad \textit{L-R}$$
13. (RSP)'''(RDP)-**[1/2]**-(FDP)''(RSP)''(FCP)''(RSP)''(FSP)''(RSP)''(FCP)''(RSP)''(FDP)
split fists combo

$$R \quad \textbf{R-L} \quad \textbf{R} \quad \textbf{R} \quad \textit{R} \quad \textit{R} \quad \textbf{R} \quad \textbf{R} \quad \textbf{R} \quad \textit{R-L} \quad \textit{L}$$
14. (RSP)'''(RDP)''(FCP)''(RSP)''(FCP)'''(FCP)'''(FCP)''(RSP)''(FCP)''**(RDP)**'''(RSP)..

The last 14 exercises all started from the reverse position behind the bag, and are only a few that can help build fist control. There is an endless total and I encourage you to create your own.

LINK [1/2] & WAIT

With more linking skill and control from behind the bag, we can begin using it in several ways. The last few exercises utilized one method….letting one fist [1/2] link to the opposite side and wait for several strikes before re-entering. In exercise 13, the right hand had to stay close to the chin while the left hand linked. In exercise 14, the left arm had to stay extended as the right fist passed through. In this next example, the fist in question, not the linking fist, will be larger in **underlined bold**.

$$L \quad \textbf{L-}\textit{R} \quad \textit{B} \quad \textit{R} \quad \textit{R} \quad \textit{R}\textbf{-L} \quad \textit{B} \quad \textbf{L-}\textit{R}$$
1.   (FSP)'''(FDP)-[1/2]-(RSP)'''(RSP)'''(RDP)-[1/2]-(FDP)…

After the (FDP), both arms are extending out to pass under the bag. Just extend your left arm (large **L**) out and leave it during the two Reverse Single Punches by the right fist. It then re-enters as the second fist of the Reverse Double Punch. This method is very efficient to use if you are only going to wait for one or two strikes before re-entering.

DRIFT [1/2] and RE-ENTER

But if we want to perform some complex linking maneuvers with one fist and then re-enter with the other, we need to use another way, which I call the "drift" method. To do this, simply let the resting fist "drift" quickly to the other side of the bag just before it will re-enter, as done in the next exercise.

$$L \quad \ \ *\textbf{L}\text{-}R \quad \ R \qquad R \qquad R \qquad R \quad \ \ * \ R\text{-}\textbf{L} \quad B \quad \ L\text{-}R$$
1. (FSP)'''(FDP)''(RSP)''(FCP)''(RSP)'''(RSP)'''(RDP)-[1/2]-(FDP)...

After the first (FDP), the left fist (*L) is held in the front ready position as the right fist performs several linking punches. Just before you perform the (RDP) the left fist "drifts" behind the bag to re-enter. Let it "drift" just after the second (RSP), noted by the *. This is easy to perform here, for as the right fist strikes the bag from behind it will drop down and extend out. Let the left arm drop slightly (to chest level) as this (RSP) is performed and join the right-at its lowest point. Then they simply extend out together in position for the (RDP). Use this when you feel like performing a lengthy one arm solo. Leaving the arm extended is tiring (try it that way.) It also commits that arm to re-enter from the reverse position.

Each technique for re-entering, either the "[1/2] and wait" or the "drift [1/2]" are very useful and will be used in the following sections. Practice both methods.

ADVANCED REVERSE FIST ROLLING & LINKING

As we gain control from behind the bag, we can begin using reverse rolls with our front techniques. There are two areas to develop. First is linking into the reverse roll and then linking out of the reverse roll. Let's begin with entering the roll.

Reverse Fist Rolling is one of the more awkward techniques. We have to lean back slightly to perform it and the fists are moving very fast to a blind part of the bag. To enter the Reverse Fist Roll after a front technique, both fists link [1/2] after *most* techniques that use both fists. This includes the Front Double Punch, the Out-or-Down Triple Elbow Strikes and the Out-&-Down four-way technique, (but not the Inward Elbow Strikes.) Fortunately, linking from them to a reverse roll is done the same way in each case. The following sequence shows how. (The fist in question is larger and **underlined bold**. For clarity, under each One-half link I've placed the order of the fists passing through.)

$$L \qquad \textbf{L}\text{-}R \quad B \quad \ \textbf{L}\text{-}R\text{-}L\text{-}R \qquad R$$
1. (FSP)'''(FDP)-[1/2]-(R-Roll)'''(RSP)
     {L-R}

Notice that after the (FDP), both fists pass through to the other side [1/2]. They pass through in the same order as they connect, left (**L**) then right fist. The first fist to pass through can smoothly flow into the reverse roll by circling "up" into the back of the bag. This method will work regardless of the front technique used, as the next examples will demonstrate.

     L   *L*-**L***R*   B *L-R-L-R...*   *L*   *L**R*-**R**   B *L-R-L....*

2. (FSP)'''(O-TES)-[1/2]-(R-Roll) and (FSP)'''(D-TES)-[1/2]-(R-Roll)

          e-**f**\\f {L-R}   **f**\\e-f {L-R}

In both cases, the first fist to pass through begins the roll. Of course, you can execute the fist roll by leading with the other (second) fist. **Actually, most people will tend to lead back with their *dominant* hand, regardless of whether it is first or second**. I believe it is better to eliminate this "handedness" and become equally proficient with both fists from any position. These practice exercises are for developing this control and smoothness in the combination.

To exit a Reverse Fist Roll to a front technique, we must [1/2] link to the front with both fists. It is easiest to have the last (*second fist* passing through to the front) lead the next technique.

    *L-R-L-R-***L**   B   **L**-*R*   *L-R-L-R-***L**   **L**-*R*

3. (R-Roll) -[1/2]-(FDP)   Exact Techniques only   (R-Roll) " (FDP)

         {R-L}

In this sequence, the last two punches of the roll are...R-L. The "R" leads the fists under the bag in the order of R-L. Since the left fist is the last to pass through, it leads the Front Double Punch. We must anticipate when we will exit and pull the fists back to the front. This is not terribly difficult but we must maintain control to keep a constant hand speed. If you rush the [1/2] link to the front you will hit the bag harder, changing its speed and forcing a late punch in the front. You can practice this easily without a bag by slowly rolling the fists in the reverse direction and flex your arms to pull your fists to the chin position. Do not pull both fists together at the same time, but let one follow the other.

Once you can enter or exit the Reverse Fist Roll smoothly there are an numerous possibilities for its use. Some example combinations are: * Exact Techniques only.

    L   *L*-**L***R* B *L-R-L-R-***L** B *L**R*-**R**   *L*-**L***R*   *L-R-L-R-***L**   *L**R*-**R**

4. (FSP)'''(O-TES)-[1/2]-(R-Roll)-[1/2]-(D-TES)'''...   * (O-TES) " (R-Roll) " (D-TES)'''

         e-**f**\\f {L-R}   {R-L} **f**\\e-f   e-**f**\\f   f\\e-f

    L   *L*-**L***R*-**R**   B *L-R-L-R-***L** B *****L**   *L*-**L***R*-**R**   *L-R-L-R-***L**   *****L**

5. (FSP)'''(O-D 4way)-[1/2]-(R-Roll)-[1/2]-(O-DES)'''...   * (O-D 4way) " (R-Roll) " (O-DES)'''

        e-**f**\\e-f {L-R}   {R-L} e-**f**   e-**f**\\e-f   e-**f**

In the last sequence, we exited the Reverse Roll to the (O-DES). Anytime we combine (R-Roll) to an Outward Elbow technique we must lead back with the last arm to pass under, which in this example is the left (***L**). There are times when we can exit the R-Roll and lead back with the first fist, such as the Front Fist Roll. An example is:

      L   *L-R*   B *L-R-L-**R**-L*   B **R**-*L-R-L-R*

6.   (FSP)'''(FDP)-[1/2]-(R-Roll) -[1/2]-(F-Roll)....

               {L-R}   {**R**-L}

After the (FDP), the first fist to pass through (left) leads in the Reverse Roll, and after the (R-Roll), the first fist [**R**] to pass through leads into the Front Roll. Another example is:

    *L-R-L-**R**-L* B   **R**   *R-L*   *L-R*   B *L-R-L-**R**-L* B   **R**

7.   (R-Roll) -[1/2]-(FSP)'''(FDP)'''(FDP)-[1/2]-(R-Roll) -[1/2]-(D-DES)....

         {**R**-*L*}   {L-R}   {**R**-*L*} e-f

In this example we see the left fist is the last fist to hit in the (R-Roll), but the "other" [**R**] fist follows with an "inward" technique (FSP & D-DES) from the front.

This last example will use everything discussed in this section on Reverse Fist Rolling

     L   *L-L\R*   B *L-R-L-R-**L***   B   **L**-*R*   B *L-R-L-**R**-L* B   **R**   *R*

8. (FSP)'''(O-TES)-[1/2]-(R-Roll) -[1/2]-(FDP)-[1/2]-(R-Roll)-[1/2]-(FSP)'''(FCP)...repeat

       e-f \ f {L-R}   {**R**-L}   {L-R}   {**R**-L}

ADVANCED REVERSE DOUBLE PUNCH & LINKING COMBINATIONS

The Reverse Double Punch offers a great deal of variety in linking. We have already seen that either the "lead" fist, 'second' fist , or both fists can link through the bag. But there is an advanced option when we pass both fists through. I call it "rotating the fists." This occurs two ways: first, when linking to the RDP from another technique, and second when linking from the RDP to another technique. Let's examine these separately.

ROTATING THE FISTS

When linking to the RDP from a front technique, we have always passed the fists straight through and begun the RDP with the last fist under. (In the next examples, for clarity I will *not* use the linking symbols, and only use the exact techniques and rebounds inbetween. The fist under discussion will be larger in **underlined bold**.) This would be written as:

    L-**R**   **R**-*L*   *L*-**R**

1. (FDP)''(RDP)''(FDP)

Notice the RDP has a right lead ("**R**-L"). The right fist was the last fist to pass under after the FDP. Let's begin to *"rotate"* the fists and change the lead of the RDP.

      L-*R*   **L**-*R*   *R-L*
2. (FDP)''(RDP)''(FDP)

This *"rotating"* of the fists within the RDP smoothly changes the lead and makes the combination *look* entirely different. We can do this easily by having the first fist of the FDP (the "**L**") pass under the bag and circle up and over the second fist as it passes through. This is a very subtle motion and at speed it is almost impossible to pick out, but….the hands have changed position. This will work after almost any technique with both fists in it, and this rotation becomes quite striking when used with the elbow strikes, as seen below.

     L-L\R   *R-L*   *L-***L***R*   ***L**-*R*   *R-R\L*
3. (O-TES)''(RDP)''(O-TES)''(RDP)''(O-TES)..repeat or change to the D-TES
    e-**f** \ f   e-**f** \ f   e-**f** \ f

This combination has three (O-TES) in it. The leading arm of the first two (O-TES) is the left, and the last fist of the elbow strike leads the first RDP. When the fist order RDP was rotated (*) **after the second (O-TES)** - *which is really nothing more than a FDP with an elbow in the front*, this changed the leading elbow of the next O-TES. This could not be done if the fists were not rotated. It also adds visual variety to the combination. But, the sound has not changed, for the "beat" of the bag is exactly the same.

We saw in chapter 9 *Side Techniques* that going to a Reverse Double Punch from a side technique happens in the triplet rhythm, or three rebounds.

    L   *L*-**R**   **R**
4. (FSP)'''(SDP)'''(RSP)…change leading fist

Here we see the second fist (**R**) of the SDP going to a RSP after three rebounds. We also see the reverse technique being led by the last fist of the SDP, as shown below.

    L   *L*-**R**   **R**-*L*
5. (FSP)'''(SDP)'''(RDP)….change lead

But we can also "rotate" this RDP fist order after the SDP. It still requires three rebounds.

    L   *L*-**R**   **L**-*R*
6. (FSP)'''(SDP)'''(RDP)….change lead

You will find this rotation more difficult, because the bag stays on the left side of the board for two rebounds and the left arm must extend under it to lead the RDP.

When going from a Reverse Double Punch to any other technique we will usually lead the next technique with the last fist to pass under. The following sequence demonstrates this with several techniques.

    R-L   *L*-**R**   **R**   *L*   *L*-**R**   *R-***L**   **L**-*L\R*   *R-L*
7. (RDP)'''(RDP)''(O-DES)'''(FSP)'''(FDP)''(RDP)''(O-TES)''(RDP)…repeat. Change lead.
           e-f   e-f \ f

Notice how each technique following the (RDP) begins with the *last* fist to contact the bag and pass under to the front position. Of course, reverse punches follow themselves on a triplet rhythm but when going from a Reverse Double Punch to **most** other techniques, it occurs on two rebounds. We see that in exercise #7 and again in the following exercise using double punches.

    L-R   *R-L*   *L-R*   *R-L*   *L-R*

8. **(RDP)**''(FDP)''**(RDP)**''(SDP)''''**(RDP)**.....Repeat.   (Note 3 rebounds between SDP and RDP)

There are several exceptions to this when going from a Reverse Double Punch-to-Side Single Punch. We will cover them in "advanced side techniques" and "super advanced punching" combinations.

We can also rotate the fists going from a Reverse Double Punch to a Front Double Punch. Again, this changes the normal lead, as we will see below. (Just *exact techniques* shown)

    L-*R*   **L-R*   *R-L*

9. (RDP)''(FDP)''(RDP)

Here we see the ***L-*R*** fist order of the FDP was rotated. It is easily accomplished by circling the lead fist of the RDP (**L**) up and into the bag while the second fist drops under and falls in behind it. The next few sequences will help you practice rotating the fists with RDP, FDP and elbow strikes. The techniques with the fist order rotated are underlined. Be sure and notice the number of rebounds between techniques. We will also use this maneuver in the "echoing" chapter, so control here is important.

    L-R   **L**-*R*   *R-L*   *L-R*   *R-L*   **R**-*L*   *L-R*   **L**-*R*   **L**-*R*

10. (FDP)''(RDP)''(FDP)'''(FDP)''(RDP)''(FDP)'''(FDP)''(RDP)''(FDP)

    L-R   **L**-*R*   *R-R\L*   *L-R*   *R-L*   **R**-*L*   *L-L\R*   **L**-*R*   **L**-*R*

11. (FDP)''(RDP)''(O-TES)''''(SDP)'''(RDP)''(FDP)'''(O-TES)''(RDP)''(FDP)

                  e-f\f   e-f\f

    L-L\R   **L**-*R*   *R-L*   **R**-*L*   *L\R-R*   **L**-*R*   *R-R\L*   *L-L\R-R*   **L**-*R*   **L**-*R*

12. (O-TES)''(RDP)''(FDP)''(RDP)''(D-TES)''(RDP)''(S-TES)''(O-D 4way)''(RDP)''(FDP)

    e-f\f   f\e-f   e-f\f   e-f\e-f

It is interesting to notice the last two double punches in #10, #11 and #12. To *continually* rotate the fists we can simply lead with the same fist (**L**) each time.

ADVANCED SPLIT FISTS & LINKING COMBINATIONS

Several times during this chapter we have had the fists "split" between the front and the back of the bag and performed alternate punching. This occurs after one fist moves [1/2] to the other side. We can use the skills of "Link 1/2 and wait" and "drift 1/2 then re-enter" to split the fists. Here we will examine several advanced "mechanics" of splitting the fists apart all around the bag.

So far we have only split the fists from single or double punch combinations. We can do this after Outward or Downward Triple Elbow Strikes and the O-D 4way. This offers some new possibilities.

Lead Fist [1/2]

As mentioned earlier, during a technique using both fists either the first or second fist to hit the bag can [1/2] to the other side. The mechanics of the combination change depending on which fist passes through. When you [1/2] the first (leading) fist, it will **not** perform a (RSP) until the other fist has made contact in the technique. Let's examine the next sequences:

```
      L      L-R    l    L      R
1.   (FSP)'''(FDP)-[1/2]-(RSP)''(FSP)…
```

In the above combination, the left fist "**L**" leads the (FDP) and makes first contact. It then passes to the back of the bag and can not do the (RSP) until after the right fist has completed the second strike of the (FDP). This happens without conscious effort and is very natural. Notice how the punching order maintains a constant *left-right* fist order. The same holds true in the next combinations.

```
      L      L-L\R    l    L      R                           L      L\R-R    l    L      R
2.   (FSP)'''(O-TES)-[1/2]-(RSP)''(FSP)…      and    3.   (FSP)'''(D-TES)-[1/2]-(RSP)''(FSP)…
      e-f\ f                                                   f \ e-f
     |_____|  to Reverse                              |_____|  to Reverse
```

Because of the elbow-fist\fist order of the (O-TES), the first fist (left) passes to the back while the right fist makes contact, then re-enters (exactly as in a Front Double Punch). But after the (D-TES), the left fist must wait on the right elbow and then the right fist before re-entering in (RSP). However, in either example the left fist had to wait on the other fist, and the *left-right* fist punching order is maintained.

Second Fist [1/2]

This is not true when we link with the last fist within the technique, as this next example illustrates.

```
      L      L-R*    r    R*      L
4.   (FSP)'''(FDP)-[1/2]-(RSP)''(FSP)…
```

Above we see that when the last fist (**R***) links [1/2], that it *immediately* re-enters as (RSP). It hits twice in a row. The same holds true for Triple Elbow Strike combinations, as seen here.

```
      L      L-L\R    r    R      L                           L      L\R-R    r    R      L
5.   (FSP)'''(O-TES)-[1/2]-(RSP)''(FSP)…      and    6.   (FSP)'''(D-TES)-[1/2]-(RSP)''(FSP)…
      e-f\ f                                                   f \ e-f
```

Notice that in both examples the last fist links and immediately does the (RSP). Although this occurs automatically, the first fist will have a momentary pause in front of the bag as the technique is completed and the link is executed. This pause is noticeable in the (D-TES) combination, for the first fist (left) will hit the bag and then wait for the right elbow-and-fist to make contact, link [1/2] and then wait for the (RSP). This pause can often find your front fist low and out of position.

Splitting the Fists after Fist Rolling

Splitting the fists after a fist roll is a very quick and exciting combination. We can do this from either a Front or Reverse Roll. There are two methods to do this from a Front Fist Roll. The smoothest way is to determine which fist to keep in **front**, then change the fist position to strike the bag in a *Front Straight Punch* position (on the front of the fist). As this occurs, the other fist passes [1/2] to the back and re-enters. With this method the *left-right* order of the fists striking the bag never changes.

As in example #7 below, the right fist hits the front of the bag during the (F-Roll), (then passes under to the back) then the left fist hits the front in (FSP) position, then the right fist enters as the (RSP). It is important to make the "L" of the FSP strike as an extension of the F-Roll, without hesitation.

        *R-L-R-L-***R**   **r**   **L**   *R*   *R-L-R-L-***R**   **L**   *R*

7. (F-Roll)-[1/2]-(FSP)''(RSP)...   this could also be written as: (F-Roll) ' (FSP)''(RSP)...

Example #8 demonstrates the second way to do this. Note that the right fist (**R**) strikes the front of the bag during the (F-Roll), then passes [1/2] to the rear and immediately re-enters as the (RSP).

        *R-L-R-L-***R**   **r**   **R**   *L*   *R-L-R-L-***R**   **L**   *R*

8. (F-Roll)-[1/2]-(RSP)''(FSP).....   (F-Roll) ' (FSP)''(RSP)...

In this method, the constant Left-Right striking of the fists is altered, because the right fist hits the bag twice in a row, once in the front, then behind. This causes the left fist to pause momentarily, then start again. Neither #7 or #8 is wrong, but I believe #7 is a easier, particularly on a small, fast bag.

When splitting the fists from a Reverse Fist Roll, The same two options exist, as seen below:

        *R-L-R-L-***R**   **r**   ***L**   *R*   *R-L-R-L-***R**   **r**   **R**   *L*   *R*

9. (R-Roll)-[1/2]-(RSP)''(FSP)...   10. (R-Roll)-[1/2]-(**FCP**)''(RSP)''(FSP).....

Once again, in #9, the continuity of *left-right* hitting is maintained. After the right fist hits the bag in the (R-Roll), it passes to the front. Then the left fist hits the back of the bag as (RSP) and the right follows after two rebounds as the (FSP). [Even though the left fist (***L**) is written as (RSP), it is done from- and is a continuation of- the fist roll. The right fist has exited the roll by going to the front, leaving only the left behind the bag. By itself, a fist striking alone behind the bag is a (RSP)]. In example #10 again we see the right fist striking twice in succession, first behind in (R-Roll) and then again as (**FCP**). (It is easier to go to FCP here, for it is difficult to get the fist into FSP position.) As with the Front Fist Roll, either method will work but I find #9 much easier at high speed.

Double Fist Splitting

Throughout this section we have moved one fist [1/2] to the front or back of the bag and left the other in its original position. Because we can move either fist to the other side, we can also advance this to move each fist to the other side at the **same** time. This may sound complicated but in practice it is pretty simple, although it takes concentration. Like all of the other split fist techniques, there are several methods to do this. (The following sequence begins from the split fist position with the left fist behind and the right fist in front.)

```
              to front           to back
                 |              ↗        ↘
   L      R      L    l    R    r   R     L      R
11 (RSP)''(FSP)''(RSP)-[1/2]- (FSP)-[1/2]-(RSP)''(FSP)'''(RSP)
```

In the above sequence the left fist begins behind the bag and the right fist is in front. The left fist performs (RSP)-[1/2] {underlined} and then the right fist immediately does **(FSP)-[1/2]-(RSP)** {Bold}. This actually happens separately, for the left fist will move to the front and pause a split second before the right fist goes behind-but it happens so fast it appears as if the fists change at the same time. *The secret to this is to concentrate on the **front** fist, because it will actually strike the bag twice, once in front and once behind.* (the two **"R"** fists). It may be easier to let the fist moving to the front (left) to drop a little as it passes through and make a little larger circle, which will keep it moving and avoid a quick pause in front while the other fist hits twice, but the pause in front is barely noticed.

In the second method, we will change the order of the fist that strikes the bag twice. Instead of it being "Front-[1/2]-Reverse" it will be "Reverse-[1/2]-Front", as shown below:

```
   R      L     *R    r    L    l    L    *R    L
12 (FSP)''(RSP)''(FSP)-[1/2]- (RSP)-[1/2]-(FCP)''(RSP)''(FSP)…
```

This method will work but it is awkward because the Right Fist {*R}, must [1/2] to the back of the bag and pause there fully extended while the left strikes behind and then comes to the front. I would rather use method in exercise #11 because if a fist pauses it will be in the front and not as obvious. Whichever method you use, it looks great. It is the "ultimate" in splitting the fists. When done quickly, it is almost an optical illusion!

In both exercises eleven and twelve one of the fists strikes the bag twice in a row, but the continuous double bounce rhythm is never changed. There is a third way to complete the double fist split. This way will maintain a continuous right-left fist sequence but the double bounce rhythm will be interrupted by one triplet rebound because the bag will be struck twice in a row from the same side. We will see this below.

```
    L      R      L    l    R    r    L      R    L
13a (RSP)''(FSP)''(RSP)-[1/2]-''(FSP)-[1/2]- '''(FCP)''(RSP)''(FSP)…
```

Notice here that the fist sequence never changes but **three** rebounds are seen between the **(FSP)-[1/2]-'''(FCP)** because they *both* connect in front of the bag. Here is what happens. The left fist (**L**) in the (RSP)-[1/2]- passes to the front. Then the right fist (**R**) connects in the **(FSP)-1/2** and passes to the back. Since the left fist is already in front the left **(FCP)** must follow the right after three rebounds.

In 13a the bag is struck twice in a row from the front. We can put the triplet rhythm between two Reverse Single Punches, as the next example illustrates.

       R   *L*   **R**   r   **L***   *l*   *R*   *L*

13b   (FSP)''(RSP)''(FSP)-[1/2]-''**(RSP)**-[1/2]- '''**(RSP)**''(FSP)...

Here we see the right fist (**R**) doing a (FSP)-[1/2] and passing behind, then left fist (**L***) connects in (RSP),-and passes to the front- followed by a right (RSP). Both RSP's must follow each other on three rebounds.

Splitting the fists "front-to-back" for alternate punching is an exciting demonstration of bag control. The visual effect of the fists moving in opposite directions, couple with its fast double beat rhythm is an amazing display of sight and sound. I encourage you to perfect front-to-back split fist combinations until you master it. We can also split the fists on the sides of the bag, as we will see in the next section.

ADVANCED SIDE TECHNIQUES

Side techniques offer a great deal of variety because of how they blend with techniques from other areas. This is directly related to the fist's angle of entry and the angle of bag rebound. The key is learning how to smoothly flow from one "striking area" to any other area.

There are several new things to explore in linking to side techniques and linking from a side technique to any other. We have already seen that most front techniques link to the sides after three rebounds. Here we will learn the exceptions. Consider the following combination.

  L-**R**   **R**-*L*

(FDP)'''(SDP) Notice the second fist (**R**) of the FDP leads the SDP after three rebounds, because both of these connect the front of the bag, and "Rule of Rhythm #1" says if the next strike comes from the same side as the last one, it must be after an odd number of rebounds. We can use the first fist (L) to immediately perform the Side Single Punch (SSP) after only *two* rebounds. It works because of the *angle of rebound* and because the SSP enters mostly from the *rear-side*, creating:

  L-**R**   **L**   *L*-**R**   *l*   **L**

(FDP)''(SSP) or (FDP)-[1/2]-(SSP) We can do this by allowing the outward moving left fist, (**L**) which is leading the FDP, to simply extend further and re-circle in from the side. This is only a slight variation of letting it pass through to a RSP, for the fist will enter from the *rear-side* angle. Because of this fist angle we can follow it in several ways. (I will not use the [1/2] symbol in the sideways exercises because both fists are changing to different sides and it is confusing.)

EX #1 Front Double Punch-to-Side Single Punch, same fist returns for RSP

L-*R*   **L**   **L**
(FDP)''(SSP)'''(RSP)

The left fist can easily go to RSP here by adjusting the arm position to re-circle from behind the bag. But we can use this to perform a slightly advance split fist maneuver.

EX #2 Front Double Punch to Side Single Punching split fists

L-R   *L*   *R*
(FDP)''(SSP)''(SSP)…continue

This combination looks great, because the fists were moving "forward" then suddenly switched to "sideways". Lets really jazz this up by doing the same thing, but allowing the second fist (R), to pass through to the back and Perform RSP.

Ex #3 Front Double Punch-to Side Single Punch-to Reverse Single Punching by other fist

L-**R**   *L*   **R**   *R*
(FDP)''(SSP)''(RSP)'''(RSP).

This a little more complex, for after the right fist (**R**) hits the bag in the FDP it must pass to the reverse position. If you extend it straight, the bag will hit the right arm during the SSP. You can do this in several ways. One, by allowing the right fist to "1/2 and wait" extending through to the back but down lower than usual, so the bag willnot hit the arm. Second, pass it under as the left fist performs the SSP. I will conclude this by returning the left fist back to the front, creating a FSP-RSP split fist combination.

Ex #4 Front Double Punch-to Side Single Punch-to Reverse Single Punch-to split fists front and back.

L-*R*   **L**   *R*   *****L**   *R*
(FDP)''(SSP)''(RSP)''(FSP)''(RSP)..

Since the left fist (**L**) is moving "in" on the SSP, it easily comes to the front for the FSP (*****L**). This combination may tie your hands in a knot at first but it looks great. Also, notice the order of contacting the front, side, reverse then front of the bag, with only two rebounds between.

This maneuver will also work from the Outward and Downward-Triple Elbow strikes, as well as the Out-&-Down 4way Elbow Strike because all three of these techniques use both fists and all three end with a fist. The next exercise demonstrates this with the Downward-Triple Elbow Strike.

Ex #5 Downward-Triple Elbow Strike to Side Single Punching split fists

  L\ *R-R*   **L**   *R*
(D-TES)''(SSP)''(SSP)…continue
  f \ e-f

We can get *to* split fist side single punching several different ways. From reverse techniques, we can let the *lead* fist link to the front, then go to the side.

EX #6 Reverse Double Punch, lead fist links to Front Straight Punch-to side single punching split fists

***R**-*L*   ***R**   *L*   **R**
(RDP)''(FSP)''(SSP)''(SSP) …continue.

As the lead fist (***R**) moves into the FSP, let the left fist drift to the side. Another way is to let the lead fist go to the side.

EX #7 Reverse Double Punch, *lead* fist links to Side Single Punching split fists

***R**-*L*   ***R**   *L*
(RDP)''(SSP)''(SSP)…continue.

In this sequence, The right fist (***R**) leads the RDP. As it strikes the bag and drops down, angle it out from the elbow to the side. But also note that the second fist (L) does the same thing, almost instantaneously, creating the split fist combination.

This is completed off the Reverse Roll, by linking the next to last fist to the side.

Ex #8 Reverse Roll to Side Single Punching split fists

  R-L-**R**-L   **R**   *L*
(R-Roll)''(SSP)''(SSP)…continue

This combination takes a little pre-anticipation. Practice it slowly by moving the next to last fist of the Reverse Roll (**R**) to the side as the last fist in the roll (L) connects.

Going from a side technique to an other technique *usually* takes two rebounds (the "super advanced" section will highlight the exceptions). Here we can do several combinations. One I call a "triple-triple" (which we did initially on page 93, Ex. #15 & 16), which is combining three different triple elbow strikes in succession with only two rebounds in between. The following will use the Downward-Triple Elbow Strike and then the Outward-Triple Elbow Strike.

Ex #9 Three triple elbow strikes with two rebounds in-between…. "Triple-Triple" combinations

  L-L\R   *R-R*\L   *L*\R-R   *R-L*   *L-L*\R   *R-R*\L   *L-L*\R
(S-TES)''(S-TES)''(D-TES) '' (RDP) '' (S-TES)''(S-TES)''(O-TES)
  e-f \ f   e-f \ f   f \ e-f   e-f \ f   e-f \ f   e-f \ f

The key to this combination is keeping the elbows high. You can substitute either the Outward or Inward elbow strike for the (D-TES), for all can be done with a left arm lead.

Another advanced maneuver from a side technique is allowing the lead fist to extend **behind** the bag and wait for the other to link to a reverse technique. We will see this in the next combination.

Ex #10 Lead fist extend and hold after a Side Double Punch

    L-*R*   *R*   *R*-**L**   *L*-**L***R*   *R*   *R*-**L**

A (SDP)''(FCP)''(RDP)   **B** (S-TES)''(FCP)''(RDP)

                                    e-**f** \ f

In sequence 10A, the leading fist (**L**) of the SDP simply connects and extends, waiting behind the bag while the Right fist performs (FCP)-[1/2]. This brings the right fist behind the bag, where both join to perform RDP. *Although the linking symbol* **[1/2]** *was not shown, the principle of* "**1/2 & wait**" *is the same.* (You could also lead the RDP with the left fist). This works just as well from a Side-Triple Elbow Strike, as demonstrated in 10B. We can also enter front-reverse split fist combinations from the Side Double Punch.

Ex #11   Side Double Punch-to-Side Single Punch-to-Split Fists front and back

*****L**-*R*   *****L**   *R*   *****L**

(SDP)''(SSP)''(FSP)''(RSP)…continue.

Here the left fist leads the SDP then passes to the other side, then goes to the reverse position. This occurs very smoothly. The key is to let the left fist re-circle *under* the right fist as it positions for the FSP and let it pass under the bag as the right fist connects.

We can now mix all the methods of "splitting the Fists" together into multiple split fist combinations.

Ex #12   Combining the methods of entering split fist combinations

R-*L*   *R*   *L*   *L*-*R* *****L** *R*   *R*-*L*   *R*   *L*   *L*-*R*   *L*   *R*

(FDP)''(SSP)''(SSP) '' (SDP)''(SSP)''(*FSP*) '' (RDP)''(SSP)''(SSP) '' (FDP)''(RSP)''(FSP) ''…repeat

       Ex: #2   Ex: #11   Ex: #7   Pg. 134, Ex #1

This may look confusing, but the first three underlined techniques are the same as exercise #2 of this section. The second group of three (not underlined) are exercise #11 and the third underlined group is exercise #7. The last three (not underlined) is the very first advanced split fist combination covered (lead fist [1/2], page 134). This sequence just links them together. The only tricky part begins with the left fist (*****L**) over the SSP. It will drop under and go behind the bag with the next *FSP*. But the right fist (*R*) hits the bag and also passes through to the reverse position. That is how both fists get behind the bag to set up for the **R**-**L** (RDP). There are many different combinations like this, with your fists splitting continuously all around the bag. In the next example, notice how the lead fist of the SDP can end up doing either RSP, FSP or SSP in a split fist combination. The lead fist is **underlined Bold**. Actually, after a SDP, you can put it anywhere you want (…once you understand the rebounding angles of the bag.)

L-R	*L*	*R*	*L*	*L-R*	*L*	*R*	*L*	*L-R*	*L*	*R*	*L*

(SDP)''(RSP)''(FSP)''(RSP)''(SDP)''(FSP)''(RSP)''(FSP)'''(SDP)''(SSP)''(SSP)''(SSP)'' ..repeat

⌞_____⌟ to reverse   ⌞_____⌟ to front   ⌞_____⌟ to other side

Rotating the Fists after Side Double Punch

We have rotated the fists from front and reverse double punching. But we can also rotate the fists *after* the Side Double Punch. (On page 132, exercise seven, we did this to a RDP.) Now let's do this when going to the Front Double Punch. To this point we have always followed the Side Double Punch with a Front Double Punch by leading with the *last* fist to connect in the SDP, as shown in the next example.

L-**R**	r	**R**-*L*		*L*-**R**	**R**-*L*

1. (SDP)-[1/2]-(FDP)   or   (SDP)''(FDP)

Notice how the last fist of the SDP, the right fist (**R**) links from the side to lead the FDP. We can "rotate" the fists and change the lead of the FDP, as shown below:

L-*R**	r	**L**-*R*		*L*-*R**	**L**-*R*

2. (SDP)-[1/2]-(FDP)   or   (SDP)''(FDP)

This is slightly more difficult than the Front-Reverse rotating. *The secret is to let the fist coming from the side, the right (R*) in this example, duck under the lead fist and fall in behind it.* Combining all of the "rotating fists" possibilities takes some practice. It may be best to start out without a bag, and just mimic the movements of the fists.

3. Mixing Front, Side and Reverse Double Punch combinations and "rotating fists" options

L-R	*R-L*	*L-R*	**L-R**	**L-R**	**L-R**	*R-L*	**R-L**	*L-R*	**L-R**	*R-L*

(FDP)''(RDP)''(SDP)''(FDP)''(RDP)''(FDP)'''(SDP)'''(RDP)''(FDP)''(RDP)''(SDP)''repeat

The underlined techniques had the fists "rotated". Note the place where three rebounds is needed. These combinations are tricky and take some concentration. A little secret to make rotating the fists easier is knowing that the fist order does not change when we do this. As mentioned earlier, notice how all the rotated fist techniques have the same lead (left). Also, the fist order is the same (L-R). Knowing this, it is a lot easier to rotate the fists by concentrating on keeping the same fist order. Just remember you cannot rotate the fists to a Side Double Punch   (unless you go to the other side.)

Just like the O-TES, D-TES and O-D 4way E.S, we can also rotate the fists after the Side-Triple Elbow Strike (S-TES), for it is really a Side Double Punch with and elbow on the front. An example of this is shown below. rotated fists are **bold**

4. "Rotating the fists" after Side-Triple Elbow Strike (S-TES)   (note ''' rebounds)

L-L\R	*R-L*	*L-L\R*	**L-R**	*R-R\L*	*L-R*	*R-R\L*	**R-L**

(S-TES)''(FDP)'''(S-TES)''(FDP)''(S-TES)'''(RDP)''(S-TES)'''(RDP)''..... repeat

e-f \ f   e-f \ f   e-f \ f   e-f \ f

Rotating the Fists after Reverse-Side Double Punch

Because the last fist in the Reverse-Side Double Punch enters from the side, we can also rotate the fists after this technique (just like the Side Double Punch.) This can be performed to the FDP or RDP.

Ex #1 Reverse-Side Double Punch to Front Double Punch, rotating the fists of the FDP

L-*R**   *L-R*   **R**-*L**   **R**-*L*
(R-SDP)''(FDP)''**(R-SDP)**''(FDP)...

Normally, we would lead back with the last fist of the R-SDP, which came from the side. But here the first fist (**L** & **R**) circles back in front of the side entry fist to lead the FDP. It helps to purposefully duck the side fist (R* & L*) slightly down after contacting the side of the bag and circle it under the other fist. It then follows behind as the second fist of the FDP and links behind.

Ex #2 Reverse-Side Double Punch to Reverse Double Punch, rotating the fists of the RDP

L-*R**   *L-R*   **R**-*L**   **R**-*L*
(R-SDP)'''(RDP)'''**(R-SDP)**'''(RDP)...Here we see all the combinations occur in the triplet rhythm.

Now we can use four different double punch techniques and rotate the fists. In the next few exercises, the *second* fist of the FDP (larger *R* and *L*) passes through to lead the R-SDP, and the rotated fists techniques are underlined

Ex #3 Continuous double punching and rotating the fists in the double bounce rhythm.

L-R   *R-L*   *L-R*   **L-R**   *R-L*   **R-L**   *L-R*   **L-R**   **L-R**   *R-L*
(FDP)''(R-SDP)''(SDP)''(FDP)''(RDP)''(FDP)''(R-SDP)''(FDP)''(RDP)''(SDP)...repeat

Ex #4 Continuous double punching and rotating the fists in a mixed double and triplet rhythm.

L-R   **L-R**   *R-L*   **R-L**   *L-R*   *R-L*   *L-R*   **R-L**   *R-L* ↙
(FDP)''(RDP)'''(R-SDP)''(FDP)''(R-SDP)''(SDP)'''(R-SDP)'''(RDP)'''(R-SDP)''...repeat

Notice how the fist order of the last (R-SDP)↙ was also rotated. Practice exercises #3 and #4 are challenging and can tie your fists in a knot. Working these through will help build excellent fist control.

Splitting the Fists after Reverse-Side Double Punch

Splitting the fists after a Reverse-Side Double Punch is just like after a SDP, since the *last* (second) fist in this technique comes from the side. We have several options available. We can easily enter side-to-side split fist combination after two rebounds.

Ex #5 Splitting the Fists after Reverse-Side Double Punch: Side-to-Side

L-R　　*R-L　　*R　　L
(FDP)''(R-SDP)''(SSP)''(SSP)''…repeat

This happens pretty easy because the lead fist (*R), simply moves out to the other side of the bag to enter after two rebounds. But we can also enter a front-to-reverse split fist combination, as demonstrated in the next example.

Ex #6 Splitting the Fists after Reverse-Side Double Punch: Front-to-Reverse

L-R　　R-L　　*R　　L
(FDP)''(R-SDP)''(FSP)''(RSP)''…repeat

This is possible because a (FSP) can also follow the (L), which came from the side, after two rebounds. The left fist then goes behind the bag for the (RSP).

Rotating the Fists after Side-Reverse Double Punch

Because the last fist in the Side-Reverse Double Punch enters from the back of the bag (reverse position), the fists can rotate after this technique just like the Reverse Double Punch. This can be performed to the FDP or RDP.

Ex #1 Side-Reverse Double Punch to Front Double Punch, rotating the fists of the FDP

L-*R**　　*L-R*　　**L**-*R**　　*L-R*
(S-RDP)''(FDP)''**(S-RDP)**''(FDP)…

Normally, we would lead back with the last fist of the S-RDP, which came from behind. But here the first fist (L) circles back in front of the side entry fist to lead the FDP. It helps to purposefully duck the fist coming from the reverse position (R*) slightly down after contacting the back of the bag and circle it *under* the other fist. It then follows behind as the second fist of the FDP and extends to the side.

Ex #2 Side-Reverse Double Punch to Reverse Double Punch, rotating the fists of the RDP   (note ''')

L-*R*　　*L-R*　　*L-R*　　*L-R*
(S-RDP)'''(RDP)''**(S-RDP)**'''(RDP)…

We can now use all five double punches together in combinations, occasionally rotating the fists for variety. These last two exercises will offer some challenging possibilities..

Ex #3 Continuous double punching and rotating the fists in a mixed double and triplet rhythm.

L-R　**L-R**　*R-L*　**R-L**　R-L　*R-L*　**R-L**　**L-R**　*R-L*　*R-L*
(FDP)''(RDP)''(SDP)''(FDP)''(S-RDP)'''(R-SDP)''(FDP)''(R-SDP)''(FDP)''(RDP)…..repeat

Ex #4 Continuous double punching and rotating the fists in a double rhythm.

L-R   **L-R**   **L-R**   *R-L*   **R-L**   *R-L*   **R-L**   *R-L*   *L-R*
(FDP)''(RDP)''(FDP)''(R-SDP)''(FDP)''(S-RDP)''(FDP)''(R-SDP)''(SDP)''..rotate to FDP, repeat

Mastering the ability to rotate the fists freely, at will, not only gives you great control of your fists but also opens up a lot more varied combinations.

Splitting the Fists after Side-Reverse Double Punch

We have the *same possibilities available* for splitting the fists after a Side-Reverse Double Punch as we do the Reverse Double Punch. Since the last (second) fist in this technique comes from the *reverse* position (behind the bag), we can split the fists *either*: front-to-reverse or side-to-side, as the next couple of practice sequences demonstrate.

Ex #5 Splitting the Fists after Side-Reverse Double Punch: Front-to-Reverse

           ... to front   ... to front

L-R   L-**R**   L   R   *R-L*   R-**L**   R   L
(FDP)''(S-RDP)''(FSP)''(RSP)''(FDP)''(S-RDP)''(FSP)''(RSP)''....repeat

Ex #6 Splitting the Fists after Side-Reverse Double Punch: Side-to-Side

L-R   L-**R**   L   R   *R-L*   R-**L**   R   L
(FDP)''(S-RDP)''(SSP)''(SSP)''(FDP)''(S-RDP)''(SSP)''(SSP)''....repeat

Throughout this book, We have had numerous practice exercises "splitting the fists" to opposite sides of the bag. With practice, you should be able to split the fists between any sides of the bag you want, after any technique. This creates exciting combinations, and displays excellent fist and bag control.

SUPER ADVANCED PUNCHING COMBINATIONS

Now it is time to get "radical" and push the limits. Super Advanced Punching combinations are really the "ultimate" extension of the Side Single Punch. This punch opens the door to a whole new level of combinations, speed and control. Here we will break....or at least stretch the rules of rhythm, because the '*angles*' of fist entry and resultant bag rebound are the most important feature. This is also the time where actual *fist speed* will make a difference.

To be successful in this section you will need good control of all five double punches and passing your fists all around the bag. The previous practice exercises in this chapter were offered to develop that control. To continue, I must assume a certain amount of physical skill and understanding on your part, because the practice exercises and combinations written here are addressing as much theory as practice…and we are about to do some combinations much faster than before! We will also see that there are always several ways to write technique combinations.

Every time the bag is struck it rebounds in a particular direction, and the direction it travels help create the three "rules of rhythm" that generally apply. This, coupled with the fist angle of entry, is how all the double punches that use the Side Single Punch (SDP, R-SDP and S-RDP) are possible. But there is also a point in any rebound when the bag is straight in line with the swivel. At this point, it really does not matter how many *times* it has rebounded, or from what *angle* it got there — it can be struck by a fist from **any** direction. It works best with the Side Single Punch, (as seen in the R-SDP and S-RDP.) We can use this to create some "super advanced" punching combinations. I use the word "super" because in the previous section for "advanced punching", techniques had one rebound in-between but the next punch always came from the *same side*. Now we are going to put techniques together on *different sides* of the bag with only **one** rebound in-between. I will set this up with one preliminary combination

In the last section (advanced side techniques) we had the lead fist of a Front Double Punch come in from the side after *two* rebounds (page 137.) This is shown below.

L-*R*   **L**

(FDP)''(SSP)   This works because of the *angle* of rebound. The left fist (**L**) enters from the *rear*-side, and waits for the bag to make its second rebound off the front of the board. In the next example, when the bag is struck by the right fist, it will rebound once off the back left part of the board…and at the moment when it is in a straight line with the swivel, the left fist enters from the *side*. It looks like this:

Ex #1A Front Double Punch to Side Single Punch with *one* rebound in between

L-*R*   * **L**

(FDP) ' (SSP). This happens incredibly fast and we need fast hands to do it. You can not try to "see" the bag in a straight line with the swivel. The left must immediately follow the right. If your left fist (from the side * **L**) is slightly late, the bag will be angled to the front of the board, but the fist angle will still let this work. (For an instant the bag and fist are traveling in the *same* direction…toward your face. Not a good time to miss the bag!) This may be easier if you use the "alternate" method for side single punching discussed earlier on page 76. Also, note you now have a **choice**….to do a FDP-SSP combination with one **or** two rebounds in-between. There are many options available to follow this last SSP. A couple are offered below.

1B. follow from same side.   1C. Follow from *opposite* Side Double Punch

L-*R*   *L*   **L**   *L*-*R*   L   **L**-*R*   *R*-*L*   R   **R**-*L*
(FDP) ' (SSP)'''(SSP)…   (FDP) ' (SSP)''(**SDP**)''(FDP) ' (SSP)''(**SDP**)….repeat

In 1C, notice how the lead of the FDP is changed, so the SSP changes from side-to-side (L & R).

Here we can create a "super advanced double punch" combination, by following the SSP with a RSP from behind the bag after one rebound. Actually, we have already done this! *The SSP can be the lead fist of a Side-Reverse Double Punch (S-RDP).*

Ex #2A Front Double Punch to Side-Reverse Double Punch with *one* rebound in between.

L-*R*   *L*-**R**
(FDP) ' (S-RDP) *The secret to this combination is getting the right fist (R) behind for the reverse*

punch. Do not extend the fist straight through the bag, but rather quickly loop it underneath. The last fist is the right (*R*) behind the bag. We can follow this in many ways. A few are offered below.

2B. Follow with same fist RSP

   L-R   *L*-**R**   **R**   *R-L*   *R*-**L**   **L**
(FDP) ' (S-RDP)'''**(RSP)**''(FDP) ' (S-RDP)'''**(RSP)**''…repeat

2C. Repeat FDP ' SDP combination by alternating the lead. (this is faster than 2A.)

   L-R   *L*-**R**   **R**-*L*   *R-L*
(FDP) ' (S-RDP)''(FDP) ' (S-RDP)''…repeat

                        L-R   *L*-**R**
    The last fist of the (FDP) ' (S-RDP) is the right (*R*) behind the bag. In 2B & 2C, we followed with the same fist (right). We can easily follow this with the left fist behind the bag after one rebound.

2D. Follow with Opposite fist RSP

   L-R   *L*-**R** ------- *L*
(FDP) ' (S-RDP) ' (RSP). The last fist (**R**) of the **S-RDP** could also be the *first fist* of a RDP, created by the last two fists. (**R** --- *L*). There are several ways to write this combination, and I think it is easier to understand when written as shown in the next combination:

Ex #3A. Combining the Front Double Punch, Side Single Punch and Reverse Double Punch

   L-R   *L*   *R-L*
(FDP) ' (SSP) ' (RDP) Now we have two double punches separated by a Side Single Punch, all with only one rebound in-between. Notice the fist order of contact. The only other time we have had the fists connect the bag *five times in a row with only one rebound in-between* was in a fist roll…..but that was always repetitively from the *same side*. Here we are doing it from three different sides. (Maybe this should be super advanced fist rolling?) In fact, It is a fascinating combination to follow this with a Reverse Fist Roll (R-Roll) after one rebound.

  3B Combining the FDP, SSP, RDP and advanced Reverse Fist Roll, with one rebound in-between.

   L-R   *L*   ***R*-L**   *R-L-R...*
(FDP) ' (SSP) ' (RDP) ' (R-Roll). This creates an amazing visual image, because we hear this as a continuous fist roll, but the fists are moving in all different directions. It may be easier to imagine the fist roll beginning with the left (*L*) fist. (…As a matter of fact, we can also eliminate the RDP and follow the SSP with the R-Roll.) Another option after the RDP is to let the lead fist (**R*) return to the front and set up a Split Fist combination.

3C. Follow RDP (lead fist link [1/2] to front) with Split Fist combination

   L-R   *L*   ***R*-L**   **R**   *L*   *R*   *L ...*
(FDP) ' (SSP) ' (RDP)''(FSP)''(RSP)''(FSP)''(RSP)''…Repeat

We can also let *both* fists pass through to the front and repeat the sequence.

3D   Follow RDP (*Both* fists link to front) to Front Double Punch after 2 rebounds

$$L\text{-}R \quad\quad L \quad\quad \textbf{\textit{R-L}} \quad\quad L\text{-}R \quad\quad L \quad\quad R\text{-}L$$
(FDP) ' (SSP) ' (RDP) '' (FDP) ' (SSP) ' (RDP) ''…repeat

Exercise 3D repeats the exact sequence. We can change the fist order of the sequence in several ways. I will call them option 1, option 2, and option 3.

3E   Alternate the SSP to the other side, Option 1- Allow three rebounds between the FDP's.

$$L\text{-}R \quad\quad L \quad\quad R\text{-}L \quad\quad L\text{-}R \quad\quad \downarrow \quad R\text{-}L \quad\quad \textbf{R} \quad\quad L\text{-}R \quad\quad R\text{-}L$$
(FDP) ' (SSP) ' (RDP)'' (*FDP*) ''' (**FDP**) ' (SSP) ' (RDP)'' (*FDP*)'''…repeat

Here we see three rebounds between the (**FDP**)'s. This triplet rhythm gives a little break in the flurry of movement. It also interesting to note that, beginning with the SSP, this sequence has double punches following one, two and three rebounds. But we can also use the advanced technique of *rotating the fists* of the *FDP* after the RDP.

3F   Alternate the SSP to the other side, Option 2- ***Rotate The Fists*** to Front Double Punch (…**this is much faster than exercise 3E**)

$$\downarrow$$
$$L\text{-}R \quad\quad \textbf{L} \quad\quad R\text{-}L \quad\quad \textbf{R-L} \quad\quad \textbf{R} \quad\quad L\text{-}R$$
(FDP) ' (SSP) ' (RDP)'' (**FDP**) ' (SSP) ' (RDP)…repeat, (rotate fists to FDP)

Rotating the fists of the **FDP** moves the SSP to the other side. Also, no fist hits twice in a row. The side punch motion and the fist rotation happen very quickly and make this a pretty hairy exercise. It takes extremely advanced fist control. Allow yourself some room for error on this one. ☺

There is one more way to rotate the SSP to the other side, by following the RDP with a *Side Double Punch* (SDP) after two rebounds.

3G   Alternate the SSP to the other side, Option 3-Follow RDP with a SDP   [brackets underneath]

$$L\text{-}R \quad\quad L \quad\quad R\text{-}L \quad\quad \textbf{L-R} \quad\quad R\text{-}L \quad\quad \textbf{R} \quad\quad L\text{-}R \quad\quad \textbf{R-L}$$
(FDP) ' (SSP) ' (RDP)'' (**SDP**)'' (FDP) ' (SSP) ' (RDP)'' (**SDP**)''…repeat
$$\lfloor \quad\quad\quad \rfloor$$

$$L\text{-}R \quad\quad L \quad\quad R\text{-}L^{*}$$

Following from the side offers one more way to follow the (FDP) ' (SSP) ' (RDP). In 3G a SDP was used, but we could also use a Side Single Punch (SSP). Again, the key is the Side Single Punch, which I will use to write the next combination.

Ex #4A   Combining the Front Double Punch, Side Single Punching and Reverse Double Punch

*L-R   L   R-***L****-----***R***
(FDP) ' (SSP) ' (RDP) ' (SSP)   Now we are moving our fists from the front, to the left side, to behind, and to the right side all with *one rebound in-between*. The last fist in the RDP (**L***) could also be the *first* fist of a R-SDP. Again we see any fist combination possible from a FDP is possible from a RDP The fist movements must be *very* small circles.   Actually, It almost feels like a "chopping" in and out motion, and it is easy to get them tied in a knot. If this entire six punch sequence is a little too much (it happens real fast) than try doing just the underlined combination alone, or using three rebounds in-between.

The right fist (*R*) of the SSP can allow us to repeat the sequence just as if we had rotated the fists. It will lead the FDP after two rebounds.

Ex #4B   Continuous Front Double Punch, Side Single Punch and Reverse Double Punching

*L-R   L   R-L   **R**   R-*L   **R**   *L-R   L*
(FDP) ' (SSP) ' (RDP) ' (SSP) ' ' (**FDP**) ' (SSP) ' (RDP) ' (SSP)' '…repeat

Now it feels like the fists are rolling around the bag from the left, to the right and back again.

The Side Single Punch makes all this possible. But we are only half way done…..because a Side Single Punch is also the *second fist* of a **Side Double Punch**. Now we can start all over from the *side* of the bag. Consider this next super advanced combination.

*L-***R***----------***L***
(SDP) ' (RSP). The second fist of the SDP (**R**) is a Side Single Punch. This fist could also be the *first* or *lead fist* of a { **R**---**L**} S-RDP. We can follow this with the another Reverse Single Punch to create another "super advanced double punch" combination with one rebound in-between.

Ex #5A   Side Double Punch to Reverse Double Punch with one rebound in-between

L-R   L-R
(SDP) ' (RDP)… And we have already followed a RDP with a SSP, so we can add it on, as shown below.

Ex #5B   Side Double Punch, Reverse Double Punch, Side Single Punch with one rebound in-between

L-R   L-R   L
(SDP) ' (RDP) ' (SSP)…Here we go rolling our fists around the bag again. We can create some interesting variations with this. A few examples are offered below.

Ex #5C   Side Double Punch, Reverse Double Punch, Side Single Punch, same leading fist

L-R   L-R   L
(SDP) ' (RDP) ' (SSP)' '…repeat

Ex #5D   Side Double Punch, Reverse Double Punch, Side Single Punch, alternate leading fist by following with a SDP.

L-R	L-R	L	L-R	R-L	R-L	R	R-L

(SDP) ' (RDP) ' (SSP)''(SDP)''(SDP) ' (RDP) ' (SSP)''(SDP)''....repeat

The SDP alternates the lead of the combination and also moves the SSP to the other side (**L** & **R**).

Ex #5E Side Double Punch, Reverse Double Punch, Side Single Punch, alternate leading fist by going to a FDP.

L-R	L-R	L	L-R	R-L	R-L	R	R-L

(SDP) ' (RDP) ' (SSP)''(**FDP**)'''(SDP) ' (RDP) ' (SSP)''(**FDP**)'''.....repeat

This last sequence uses *three* rebounds between the Front and Side Double Punch. But if you have stayed with me this far, then you do not need three rebounds! At the point of the **FDP**, we can add Exercise #4. (...Hold onto your bag, because we're about to jump to warp speed.)

Ex #5F   Double Punching and Side Single Punching around the bag, *option 1*

L-R	L-R	L	L-R	L	R-L

(SDP) ' (RDP) ' (SSP)''(**FDP**) ' (SSP) ' (RDP)''.....repeat

Instead of repeating the same combination, let's follow the last RDP with Side Single Punch after one rebound and begin it all over from the front of the bag.

Ex #5G Double Punching and Side Single Punching around the bag, *option 2*

L-R	L-R	L	L-R	L	R-L	R	R-L	R	L-R	L

(SDP) ' (RDP) ' (SSP)''(FDP) ' (SSP) ' (RDP) ' (**SSP**)''(FDP) ' (SSP) ' (RDP) ' (SSP)''...repeat

The secret to understanding these "super advanced " punching combinations is knowing the options available to begin them starting from *either* the Side, Front or Reverse Double Punch. Generally, if it is started from the *side* of the bag (with a SDP), then the fists can make **five** single punches in a row with one rebound in-between. If you begin from behind the bag (with the RDP), then the fists can make **three** single punches around. If you begin from the *front of the bag* (with a FDP), then the fists can make **six** continuous punches around the bag with one rebound in-between. But, there is one last possibility which breaks even this rule. I call this the ultimate "super advanced" punching combination. I will start from a Front Double Punch (FDP).

Ex #5H The ultimate "Super Advanced" Punching Combination. Nine punches (Six Techniques) with only one rebound in-between.

L-R	L	R-L	R	L-R	L

(FDP) ' (SSP) ' (RDP) ' (SSP) ' (RDP) ' (SSP)''...repeat

Sure, it does not look like much, but this one can eat your lunch because the underlined techniques (RDP)'(SSP)'(RDP) are very difficult to complete in this order. This is a sequence where sometimes you get it and sometimes you do not. (The SDP cannot be used in this particular "one rebound only" sequence, because we can not get to a SDP without using two rebounds.) With control, you can repeat just the RDP-SSP techniques…at least in theory, but bag control is almost impossible.

Trying to create very long combinations like this is extremely difficult because the rebounding angle of the bag varies slightly, and breakdowns can be numerous. I use "super advanced" combinations sparingly, throwing a few in occasionally with my regular techniques. This creates a quick rush of fists flying around the bag, then out again. The previous exercises were offered to help you develop that skill, but a few interesting combinations are offered below. Be sure to notice either one, two or three rebounds.

```
          L      L-R      L      R-L     L-R      R      R-L      L     L-R-L-R....
Basic…(FSP)'''(FDP) ' (SSP) ' (RDP)''(FDP)''(RSP)''(FDP)''(RSP)''(F-Roll)….
```

```
        L-R-L-R-L    L-R      L    R-L-R-L-R   R-L      R      R-L     L-R      R      R ....
Basic…(F-Roll)'''(FDP) ' (SSP) ' (R-Roll)'''(RDP) ' (SSP)''(SDP)''(FDP)''(RSP)''(FCP)…
```

```
          R      R-L      L      L-R     L-R      L      L-L\R      R      R-L     R-L      L ....
Basic…(FCP)'''(FDP)''(RSP)''(SDP) ' (RDP) ' (SSP)''(O-TES)''(RSP)''(SDP) ' (RDP)''(FCP)..
                                                   e-f \ f
```

This last sequence features an Outward-Triple Elbow Strike. The last two parts of this technique are actually both fists (f \ f) connecting like a Front Double Punch. We can start the super advanced punching combinations from here, as the next exercise demonstrates

Ex # 6 Super Advanced Punching combinations after an Outward-Triple Elbow Strike.

```
 L-L\R      L      R-L      R      R-R\L      R      L-R      L
(O-TES) ' (SSP) ' (RDP) ' (SSP)''(O-TES) ' (SSP) ' (RDP) ' (SSP)''…Repeat
e-f \ f                          e-f \ f
```

The key here is noticing that the lead fist (**underlined**) breaks out to the side, just like the lead fist of a FDP. This is easier if you keep the elbow up in a parallel position for the SSP.

We can do these combinations after *almost* any Triple Elbow Strike (all except the Inward-Triple Elbow Strike), or the Out-&-Down 4way Elbow Strike. The following are several examples.

Ex # 7 Super Advanced Punching Combinations after an Downward-Triple Elbow Strike.

```
 R-L      L\R-R      L      R-L      R      R\L-L      R      L-R
(FDP)'''(D-TES) ' (SSP) ' (RDP) ' (SSP)''(D-TES) ' (SSP) ' (RDP)''… to front, Repeat
       f \ e-f                          f \ e-f
```

Notice that in Ex# 7 the lead fist of the D-TES goes to the side. It does not matter if the fists are separated by an elbow. I think the D-TES is easier to use then the Outward-Triple Elbow Strike because the elbow does not have to quickly get up in position to lead the technique. The elbow of the leading fist can stay down for a moment's rest.

Ex # 8 Super Advanced Punching combinations after an Side-Triple Elbow Strike.

```
R-L      L-L\R    L-R       L       L-R     R-R\L    R-L       R
(FDP)'''(S-TES) ' (RDP) ' (SSP)''(FDP)'''(S-TES) ' (RDP) ' (SSP)''...Repeat
        e-f \ f                           e-f \ f
```

This combination is exactly like starting from a SDP, since the fists are the same.

Finally, we can mix the Triple Elbow techniques together, as the next few sequences will demonstrate.

Ex # 9 Mixing Triple Elbow Strikes and Super Advanced Punching combinations.

```
R-L      L-L\R    L-R       L       L-R     R\L-L    R        L-R      L       L-L\R
(FDP)'''(S-TES) ' (RDP) ' (SSP)''(FDP)'''(D-TES) ' (SSP) ' (RDP) ' (SSP)''(O-TES)...repeat
        e-f \ f                           f \ e-f                            e-f \ f
```

Ex # 10 Mixing Triple and 4way Elbow Strikes with Super Advanced Punching combinations.

```
R-L       L-L\R-R      L       R-L      R       R-R\L    L-L\R    L-R
(FDP)'''(O-D 4way) ' (SSP) ' (RDP) ' (SSP)''(O-TES)'''(S-TES) ' (RDP)''...to front, repeat
        e-f \ e-f                           e-f \ f    e-f \ f
```

The last few patterns are just a few of the possibilities for *Super Advanced Punching* with elbow strikes. These types of combinations demand extremely good control of your fists, swing motion and feel for the bag. Mastering these will take some time.

PUTTING IT ALL TOGETHER

The "Super Advanced" combinations brings us to the final frontier...putting *all of this* together into action on the bag. By *all of this*, I mean **everything** that came before, ie...24 techniques (chapters four-nine), and all the advanced topics, such as advanced punching, advanced fist rolling, advanced elbow striking, advanced reverse punching & linking, advanced reverse fist rolling, rotating the fists, advanced split fists, advanced side combinations and super advanced punching combinations. It is not necessary to do all of these to be excellent on the speed bag. Nor is it necessary to mix all of the advanced topics together in a nonstop fashion. All the practice exercises were written to demonstrate the incredible variety of combinations available. The hardest part has been conveying it in a reliable fashion, so YOU can become more skillful and increase your understanding of the how the speed bag works. When I am hitting I am usually thinking about two or three techniques ahead and setting up for an advanced combination or two. I will pick several to work on for a few combinations—then go on to a few more. Any more than that gives me brain strain. I have a few that I really like and others I rarely do. Working too many "drills" can become monotonous. My own personal favorite type of workout is "echoing", and hitting to music. I have devoted a separate chapter to this. I will close this chapter by writing one long, continuous combination. Each line of techniques will end with a fist roll, and the next line will begin with the same roll.
In every line, I will highlight some key fist movements that might not be obvious, and list them *by line*

number after the combinations. Also, because the fists will be constantly linking to all sides of the bag, I will **not** use the linking symbols, but only the exact techniques. Be sure and count the rebounds.

              L   *L-R*   *R-L*   *L\R-R*   *R-L*   **R-L*   *L*   *L*   L-**R***   *L-R-L-R*
#1 RRLL....(FSP)'''(FDP)'''(SDP)''(D-TES)''(RDP)''(**FDP**)''(RSP)'''(RSP)'''(RDP)''(F-Roll)
                             f \ e-f

      L-R-L-*R**   *L*   *R*   **L**   **R**↙   *R*   *L*   *L-R*   *R-L*   *L-R*   **L-R**-*L-R*
#2 (**F-Roll**)''(RSP)''(FSP)''(**RSP**)'(**FSP**)''(RSP)''(FSP)''(RDP)'''(RDP)''(SDP)''(**F-Roll**)

      L-R-L-R-L   *L-L\R*   *R-R\L*   *L\R-R*   *L*   **R-L*   **R***   *L*   *L-L\R-R* ------ *L-R-L-R*
#3 (F-Roll)''''(**S-TES**)''(**S-TES**)''(**D-TES**) ' (SSP) ' (RDP)''(**FSP**)''(RSP)''(O-D 4way) ' (**F-Roll**)
           e-f \ f   e-f \ f   f \ e-f   e-f \ e-f

      L-R-L-**R**-*L*   *L*   *L*   **L-R**   *R*   *R*   *R-L*   *L*   *L-R*   *R*   *R-L-R-L*
#4 (F-Roll)''(RSP)'''(RSP)''(**FDP**)''(RSP)''(RSP)''(FDP)''(RSP)''(FDP)''(RSP)''(F-Roll)

      R-L-R-L   *L*   **L*\R-R   *L-R-L*-**R-L**   *L*-**R***   *L*   *R*   *R-L*   *R-L*   *L-R* ------ *L-R-L-R*
#5 (F-Roll)''(RSP)''(**D-TES**)''(R-Roll)''(FDP)''(SSP)''(RSP)''(SDP) ' (RDP)''(FDP) ' (F-Roll)
                       f \ e-**f**

      L-R-L   *L\R*-**R***   **R**   *R\L-L*   *L*   *L\R-R*   **R-L**   **L-R**   **R**   *R-L-R-L*
#6 (F-Roll)'''(D-TES)''(RSP)''(D-TES)''(RSP)''(**D-TES**)''(RDP)'''(**RDP**)''(FCP)''(**R-Roll**)
            f \ e-f   f \ e-f   f \e-f

      R-L-**R-L**   *L-R*   **R-L*   *R*   *L*   *R*   *R*   ****L**   *L-L\R* ------- *L-R-L*
#7 (R-Roll)''(SDP)''(SDP)''(Hook)''''(Hook)''''(**Hook**)''''(FCP)'''(D-DES)'''(O-TES) ' (F-Roll)
                                         e-f   e-f \f

      R-L-**R**-*L**   **L*   *R*   *R*   *L*   *L-L***R**   *R-L*   *L-R*   *R-L*   *L\R-R*
#8 (R-Roll)''(O-DES)'''(D-DES)''(O-DES)''(D-DES)'''(O-TES)''(RDP)''(SDP)''(SDP)''(**I-TES**)
            e-f   e-f   e-f   e-f   e-**f** \ **f**   **f** \ **f-e**

Line 1

        (FDP) = *fists rotated*

          ****R** = Right fist drift [1/2] & re-enter as **R*** (from **FDP** to RDP)

Line 2

        (F-ROLL) = **L**- *Left fist links behind*   **R*** = *use FSP fist position*

        (RSP)''(FSP)''(RSP)''(FSP) = *Double Fist Split,* Left (RSP) to front, Right (**R**↙) to behind

(SDP)''(**F-Roll**) = *fists rotated after SDP to start roll.*

Line 3

(**S-TES**)''(**S-TES**)''(**D-TES**) = *Triple-Triple (3 triple elbow strikes in a row)*

(**D-TES**) ' (SSP) ' (RDP) = *Super Advanced punching combination*

(**FSP**) = **R - Right fist of (RDP) splits to front of bag for* **FSP**

(O-D 4way) ' (**F-Roll**) = Advanced Front Fist Foll after O-D4way. (follows after one rebound.) Let the last fist of the elbow strike also begin the F-Roll.

Line 4

R (Top line over F-Roll) = *Right fist will wait at* **chin** *while left does RSP's. (* **L** *) does same thing after (***FDP**)

(FDP)''(RSP)''(FDP)''(RSP) = *second fist passes through for* RSP

Line 5

*L = left fist of D-TES passes through to lead R-Roll. *The right fist also links behind.*

R-L (top line, over R-Roll) = *Beginning with* **R**, *Both fists return to front.*

(FDP)''(SSP) = *Lead fist (* L *) of* FDP *goes to Side after two rebound.*

R* (top line, over FDP) = *Extend fist out to the "rear-side" of bag* [set up for next RSP]

(SDP) ' (RDP) = *Super advanced punching combination*

(FDP) ' (F-Roll = *Advanced Front-Fist Rolling. Let the last fist (R) of FDP start the F-Roll.*

Line 6

R* (top line) = *Second (Last) fist of* D-TES *links to* RSP. *This happens twice.*

D-TES = *Both fists of D-TES link to RDP*

RDP = *Second fist of RDP (* R *) links to* FCP, [left stays behind bag]. *Right fist immediately links behind to lead the* R-Roll, *which ends line 6.*

Line 7

R-L (top line) = *Right fist extends out to side for* SDP. *Left fist ends R-Roll and leads* SDP.

*R = Right fist stays close to shoulder after SDP *for* Hook Punch.

(Hook)''''(FCP)= *Hook and Rotate*

*L = Left arm must get in position for D-DES. *Raise it as you begin the previous* FCP

(**O-TES**) ' (F-Roll) = *Advanced Front Fist Roll. Last "R" fist in O-TES begins the F-Roll.*

Line 8

Line 7 ends with a (F-Roll). Notice the change to a (R-Roll) to start line 8.

R-L* = *(Top Line, over R-Roll) Both fists return to front, beginning with Right Fist* (**R**)

(O-DES)'''(D-DES)'''(O-DES)'''(D-DES) = double elbow striking sequence, beginning with the left elbow, just after the left fist (**L***) passed through.

L\R (top line over O-TES) = Both fists pass through to RDP.

(I-TES) = *Last technique of the combination.*

It may take some time to work through the whole eight line sequence. I suggest trying all the striking movements *without the bag* first, to lock in the fist and elbow movements. Try to hear the sound of the rebounds, or better yet, "voice" them by saying **Da da da**…etc. The faster you can visualize and hear the rhythms, the faster you will be able to learn the incredible variety of combinations that are possible. (We will explore *voicing* out the rhythm in the next chapter.)

Lastly, I suggest you forget about hitting the speed bag as hard and fast as you can, but rather hit at your most comfortable speed. Hitting as fast as you can is a super workout, but usually gets you all clenched up tight. Relax a little. A rigid stick is not as fast as a whip. Your punching speed will *increase as you relax*, and gain control. As you progress and become more comfortable with all the techniques, you can begin adding extra little body movements with your swinging. Things like head bobs, leaning left and right, picking up your feet….moving with the beat. These are hard to do when blasting away at maximum speed. Slow down and dance a little! We will explore some other workout options, and fun with rhythm in the chapter on echoing and hitting to music. Do not be afraid to add some personal flair and self-expression, because that is where the real fun comes in. Or what I call….Ultimate Speed Bag!

This chapter covered *advanced punching and combination movements* on the speed bag. For more *Advanced Fitness work-outs*, where you can increase cardiovascular fitness and expand your personal body coordination in a more physical and creative way, see the Appendix section.

A few of my faithful training partners waiting to workout. they love Speed Bag

…but they don't seem to take it too Seriously.

Chapter 11

Echo Rhythms & Training to Music

> **Echo Rhythms** *will use most of the advanced topics and skills covered in the previous chapters. The written practice exercises for "Echoing" will be some of the most difficult in this book, and complete understanding of all techniques and the written symbols is necessary. All the previous practice exercises have prepared you in both hitting ability and reading ability, for this chapter. It may take time and patience to work through these echo exercises. But don't give up! It's worth the effort.*

In this chapter, we will focus exclusively on the sound and rhythm of the bag. The first section will explore Echo rhythms and the second will discuss hitting the speed bag to music.

ECHO RHYTHMS

From the first techniques and practice exercises you may have noticed that certain techniques make the same sound and rhythm patterns. For example, (F-Roll) sounds the same as (R-Roll). Also, (FDP), (RDP), (SDP) make the same sound and "beat". In fact, all the single, double and triple strikes "echo" each other in sound and rhythm. Now we'll begin playing with the accented rhythms and "beat".

Deliberate echoing is a creative exercise in duplicating a specific rhythm with different techniques in a non-stop manner from all sides of the speed bag. You can use these "echo" rhythms to sharpen your understanding of how subtle differences in the fist order of linking can change the techniques used in combinations, yet make the same sound. Rhythm echo's can be any length but we will focus on short bursts of rhythms created by the double and triple strike techniques in the faster double bounce rhythm. For these exercises I will indicate the "sound" of the rhythm underneath, which is more important here than counting. The "**D**" represents the main accents of the bag striking the board directly off the fist or elbow. Afterbeats are not indicated. The loudest accents, which are usually the last fist in a technique, are underlined (**D**). These can be used for "voicing" out the rhythms. I will also separate the combination echo's with several dots inbetween. (On the bag they are not separated but have two rebounds between.)

In these exercises the both fists are constantly changing sides, so I will not use the linking symbols [8] or [1/2], because there would be too many "unwritten" techniques. Each rhythm pattern will have various "markings" (bold text, larger type, italics, underlining etc.) in the top (arm) line and middle (technique) line to highlight important factors which will be discussed. I may also use top brackets over the line. You **must** practice these slowly without the bag to see and feel the fist changes. Most importantly, try to "*hear the beat*" of the rhythm with your fists. Let's begin with an easy echo pattern.

Echo pattern #1-A

```
                    ┌──lead fist──┐
                    ┌──────┐
L-R     R-L     L-R     L           L-R     R-L     L-R      L
(FDP)''(RDP)''(FDP)''(RSP)…….(SDP)''(SDP)''(FDP)''(RSP)…..Repeat

DD      DD      DD      D…………….DD      DD      DD       D
```

The first pattern uses the FDP and RDP. The second uses the SDP and FDP. Notice in the second sequence the FDP smoothly follows the SDP in the double bounce rhythm. I will use this relatively simple echo to explore some subtle changes and how they effect the "look" of the combination.

Notice in the first pattern of #1A, the (FDP)''(RSP) - the Lead fist (L) passed through and returned. We can vary the lead arm by changing the linking fist, or passing the second fist through to the RSP. This would not change the accented beats or rhythm, but would look entirely different.

#1-B

```
                    ┌──second fist──┐
                    ┌──────┐
L-R     R-L     L-R     R           R-L     L-R     R-L      L
(FDP)''(RDP)''(FDP)''(RSP)…….(SDP)''(SDP)''(FDP)''(RSP)…..Repeat

DD      DD      DD      D…………….DD      DD      DD       D
```

Here, in the opening pattern we have the second fist (L) linking which changes the leading fist of the second pattern in comparison to #1-A. Passing the second fist seem to be the easiest and most natural method, since there is no hesitation. just let the last fist keep moving through bag. Passing the second fist also changes the lead of the next technique, (and using the first fist often does not.)

As we saw in the "advanced" chapter, we can also vary the fist order of the RDP by rotating the fists. The one (RDP) in this combination follows the beginning FDP. Reversing this fist order behind the bag would again change the "look" but have the same sound. We will see this below.

#1-C

```
        Fists Rotated        second fist
        ┌────┐             ┌──────┐
L-R     *L-R     R-L     L           L-R     R-L     L-R      R↙
(FDP)''(RDP)''(FDP)''(RSP)…….(SDP)''(SDP)''(FDP)''(RSP)…..Repeat

DD      DD      DD      D…………….DD      DD      DD       D
```

Notice how rotating the fists (***L-R**) of the RDP has changed the leading fists of the second pattern in comparison to #1-B. Also, we could rotate the fists of the FDP after the RDP. *You can rotate them on any double fist pass through from: front-to-back, back-to-front, or side-to-front or side-to-back.* The fist order of (SDP)''(SDP) in the second pattern cannot be rotated.

We can also advance this by adding a third "echo" on to the second combination but in a more complex manner. Let's continue from the last pattern, after the right fist (**R**⤴) passes through in #1-C:

#1-D

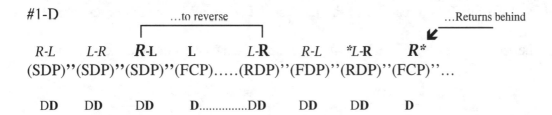

R-L   *L-R*   ***R*-L**   **L**   **L-R**   *R-L*   ***L-R**   ***R****

(SDP)''(SDP)''(SDP)''(FCP).....(RDP)''(FDP)''(RDP)''(FCP)''...

DD   DD   DD   D...............DD   DD   DD   D

Here, notice the pattern (SDP)''(FCP). The right fist (**R**) in the *SDP* simply extends out to the reverse position and waits for the left fist to go (FCP) and pass through to join it behind the bag for the RDP, which begins the next echo pattern. **Now we create the same rhythm starting from *behind the bag*.** This echo ends with both fists behind the bag, because the left fist (**L*) stays behind and the Right (*R**) returns. Let's continue by using the Reverse-Side Double Punch. I will repeat #1-D to set this up.

#1-E

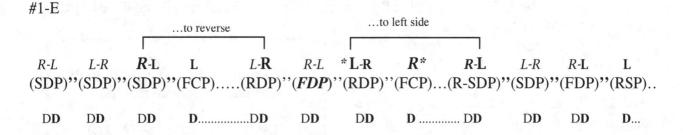

R-L *L-R* ***R*-L** **L**   **L-R** *R-L* ***L-R** ***R**** **R-L** *L-R* *R-L* **L**

(SDP)''(SDP)''(SDP)''(FCP).....(RDP)''(*FDP*)''(RDP)''(FCP)...(R-SDP)''(SDP)''(FDP)''(RSP)..

DD   DD   DD   D...............DD   DD   DD   D .... DD   DD   DD   D...

In the ***middle pattern***, notice the left leading fist (***L**) of the RDP. We can slip this out to the *left side* of the bag [brackets] while the right fist (**R**), which is the second fist of that RDP, links to the front where it immediately hits the FCP and passes through to the back of the bag (reverse position). Now the fists are in perfect position for the R-SDP. The last echo (third pattern) uses three different double punches. As written above, we could repeat starting from #1-A. But let's explore one other way to escape the situation of ending the pattern with both fists behind the bag. In the next example, the first pattern of #1-E with SDP's will remain the same, but starting with the (RDP) in the middle pattern, we can use a (**SDP**) instead of the (***FDP***).

#1-F

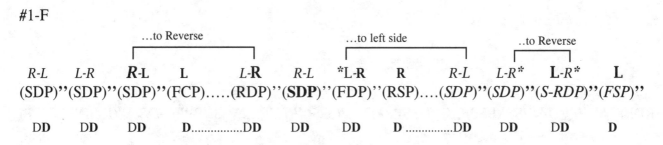

R-L *L-R* ***R*-L** **L**   **L-R** *R-L* ***L-R** **R**   *R-L* *L-R** **L-R*** **L**

(SDP)''(SDP)''(SDP)''(FCP).....(RDP)''(**SDP**)''(FDP)''(RSP)....(*SDP*)''(*SDP*)''(*S-RDP*)''(*FSP*)''

DD   DD   DD   D...............DD   DD   DD   D ....DD   DD   DD   D

In #1-F, beginning with (RDP) we go to the **SDP** instead of the *FDP*. Notice the left (*L) which leads the next FDP. It extends out to the side while the right fist connects in the FDP and links to the RSP and returns to lead the *SDP* which begins the last (or third) echo. Then notice the Right (R*) fist in the second SDP of the last sequence [brackets]. It must go from the right side to behind the bag for the second fist of the S-RDP. To do this, just extend your right elbow, which will put it in correct position. Compare the last four techniques *(all underlined)* with the first four and we see how the S-RDP can fit easily with SDP's, and the main difference is how to create the single punch technique. The first one in #1-F gets our hands behind the bag and the last one finishes in the front (after the FSP.) The remarkable thing about these combinations is they **all** happen with only two rebounds inbetween. There is no triplet rhythm in the sequences. Example #1-F ends with the left fist (L) doing a FSP and passing behind

Continuing after the left fist goes to the back, let's continue the echo in a totally different way.

#1-G

			...stays behind				Quick split fist					
L-R	*L-R*	↘**R**-*L*	**L***	*R*-**L***	*L-R*	*R*-**L**------ **R**	*R-L*	*L-R*	*R-L*	*R*
(R-SDP)''(S-RDP)''(FDP)''(RSP).....(S-RDP)''(SDP)''(SDP)''(SSP)....(FDP)''(R-SDP)''(SDP)''(FSP)
DD   DD   DD   D.................DD   DD   DD   D ....DD   DD   DD   D

In this last pattern, I have used more Reverse-Side and Side-Reverse Double Punches. In the first section, notice the FDP. The lead fist (↘R) drifts out to the right side to lead the next (**S-RDP**), while the left fist passes to the RSP (L*). The left fist [brackets] then re-circles from behind the bag for the second fist of the (**S-RDP**). At the end of the second pattern, there is quick split fist combination (L ---- R) in the underlined SDP''SSP .

The key to using the faster double bounce rhythm, and the echo's you can produce, is understanding the options we have in linking techniques from all sides of the bag. All five double punch techniques allow three linking options to other double punches with only two rebounds inbetween. These options are displayed in **[FIG 11A]**.

It is also important to know that we can use any "double strike" technique, such as the Outward-Double Elbow Strike (O-DES), or Downward-Double Elbow Strike (* D-DES) as we see below:

#1-H (* **Remove eyeglasses**)

**Double Punch combination options
in a double bounce rhythm**

FDP ''	RDP,	R-SDP,	S-RDP
RDP ''	FDP,	SDP,	S-RDP
SDP ''	FDP,	SDP,	S-RDP
R-SDP ''	SDP,	FDP,	S-RDP
S-RDP ''	FDP,	SDP,	S-RDP

FIG 11A

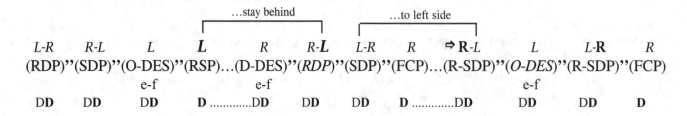

		...stay behind					...to left side				
L-R	*R-L*	*L*	**L**	*R*	*R*-**L**	*L-R*	*R*	⇨**R**-*L*	*L*	*L*-**R**	*R*
(RDP)''(SDP)''(O-DES)''(RSP)...(D-DES)''(RDP)''(SDP)''(FCP)...(R-SDP)''(O-DES)''(R-SDP)''(FCP)
e-f   e-f   e-f
DD   DD   DD   D ....DD   DD   DD   D ....DD   DD   DD   D

This is the most complex echo of this rhythm yet. There are some key features to figuring this out. *One secret is in the changeover from the first pattern to the middle pattern.* The left fist (*L*) does a RSP followed by the right elbow-fist D-DES. *Raise the right arm up in position for the* D-DES *as the left does the* O-DES''RSP. If you wait until the RSP to set up the right arm Downward Elbow Strike, you will be late. Also, notice the (*RDP*) after the D-DES. The left fist (*L*) is the second fist. *It is already behind the bag for the RSP.* Just hold it out [brackets] and wait for the right fist to hit D-DES and pass through. The third echo is set up by the right fist performing (FCP) and passing through to lead the R-SDP. *The secret to these combinations is the movement of the right fist (⇒R).* After it leads the first R-SDP it passes to the front of the bag, then must go to the right side to enter as the side fist in the next R-SDP. The tricky part is that it is going out to the side **while** the left arm is doing the *O-DES*.

This is just one example of "Echoing" a beat all around the bag. We can advance this by using a Triple Elbow Strike at the beginning and create a new rhythm by adding an extra beat.

Echo pattern #2-A

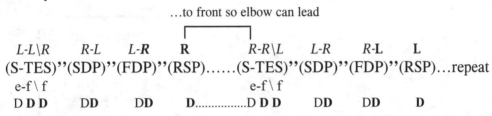

This is a snappy echo pattern that smoothly rotates the leading arm. Notice the RSP in the first pattern by the right (**R**) arm [brackets] and how its elbow leads the **S-TES** in the second pattern. Following this RSP we can use any triple elbow technique, such as the * D-TES. (* **Remove eyeglasses**)

#2-B

```
                    …to front so fist can lead          lead fist

L-L\R    R-L    L-R    R          R\L-L    L-R    R-L    R
(S-TES)''(SDP)''(FDP)''(RSP)……(D-TES)''(RDP)''(FDP)''(RSP)…repeat
e-f \ f                        f \ e-f
D D D    DD     DD     D...............D D D    DD     DD     D
```

We could keep varying the Triple Elbow strike used and rotate the fists all around the bag. I will demonstrate this below. (* **Remove eyeglasses for Downward Elbow strikes**)

#2-C

```
R\L-L    L-R    R-L    L        L-L\R    R-L    L-R    R        R-R\L    L-R    R-L    L
(D-TES)''(RDP)''(FDP)''(RSP)….(O-TES)''(RDP)''(FDP)''(RSP)….(S-TES)''(SDP)''(FDP)''(RSP)
f \ e-f                        e-f \ f                        e-f \ f
D D D    DD     DD     D.............D D D    DD     DD     D.............D D D    DD     DD     D
```

Here we have three triple elbow strikes being used to create this rhythm. Let's change this rhythmic echo by offering one other alternative. In the middle pattern beginning with the O-TES, we linked from the **RDP** to a *FDP*. We could go to a **SDP** instead, as shown below.

#2-D

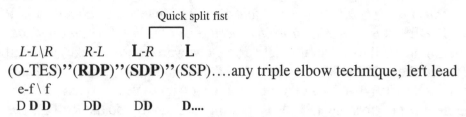

Quick split fist

*L-L\R   R-L   L-R   **L***

(O-TES)''(**RDP**)''(**SDP**)''(SSP)....any triple elbow technique, left lead

e-f \ f

D **D D**   DD   DD   **D**....

Notice after the **RDP** we switched to the **SDP**. Also, we split the fists after the **SDP**. The lead fist of the SDP (**L**), passed to the other side for a SSP. What happens is the right fist (second fist of SDP) hits the right side of the bag followed by the left fist on the left side. This combination is a little more difficult but looks fascinating since the arms are making opposite inward circles in the combination.

Another advanced manuever is to "rotate the fists" of the **RDP** (*L-R below) and change the lead of the next **SDP**, as the next example illustrates. Notice how the SDP''SSP fist order is changed.

#2-E

Rotated fists

*L-L\R   *L-R   R-L   **R***

(O-TES)''(**RDP**)''(**SDP**)''(SSP)....any triple elbow technique, right lead

e-f \ f

D **D D**   DD   DD   **D**....

> **Remember:**
>
> *Downward* Elbow Strikes are bad for your Eyeglasses !
>
> Take them OFF

With practice you can keep this same pattern and rotate the SDP lead from side-to-side. There are many ways to vary this pattern. This next exercise will demonstrate three different ways to create this echo rhythm. As usual, several key points will be highlighted.   (* **Remove Eyeglasses**)

#2-F

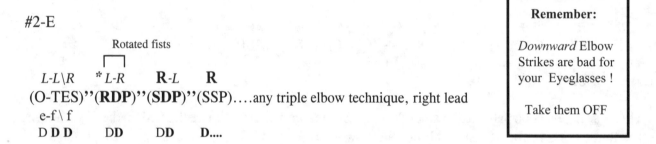

Rotated fists   ...to side   ...elbow to lead

*L-L\R *L-R   R-L   L   L\R-R   R-L   L-R   L   L-L\R   R-L   L-R   L*

(O-TES)''(**RDP**)''(FDP)''(RSP)....(D-TES)''(R-SDP)''(**SDP**)''(SSP)....(S-TES)''(SDP)''(FDP)''(RSP)

e-f \ f   f \ e-f   e-f \ f

D **D D**   DD   DD   **D**.............D **D D**   DD   DD   **D**.............D **D D**   DD   DD   **D**

In the first sequence, I rotated the fist order of the **RDP**, (*L-R .) Then the second fist (L) of the FDP passes to the RSP. As the Left hits RSP, raise the right arm up in position for the D-TES. After the D-TES, notice the left (L) fist moves over to the left side of the bag to enter in the R-SDP. The **right** arm connects *elbow-fist* in the D-TES and the fist passes to the back to lead the R-SDP. The underlined SDP''SSP techniques are a quick split-fist combination. After the left fist connects the SSP, the left elbow now leads the S-TES of the last sequence. Finally, the first fist of the FDP links to the RSP. After this, any triple elbow strike could be used that leads with the left arm.

The two previous patterns all occurred in the faster two bounce rhythm. We can add in a triplet (3 rebounds) "break" to stutter the rhythm and add variety to the echo. Let's create this using a triple elbow pattern.

Echo Pattern #3-A

Note triplet rhythm ↓   Note triplet rhythm ↓

```
L-L\R    R-L    L-R    R              R-R\L    L-R    R-L    L
(S-TES)''(SDP)''(SDP)''(FCP) ''' ......(S-TES)''(SDP)''(SDP)''(FCP) '''
e-f \ f                              e-f \ f
 D D D    DD     DD    Ddd.................D D D   DD     DD    Ddd
```

This rhythm has a nice triplet break in the middle which sort of breaks the tension. Let's continue it on and change the techniques used. (* **remove eyeglasses**)

#3-B

```
L-L\R    R-L    L-R    R              R\L-L    L-R    R-L    L
(O-TES)''(RDP)''(SDP)''(FCP)'''......(D-TES)''(RDP)''(SDP)''(FCP)'''
e-f \ f                              f \ e-f
 D D D    DD     DD    Ddd.................D D D   DD     DD    Ddd
```

We are almost forced to use a Front Circle Punch (FCP) for the triplet technique, because the elbow techniques can only begin from the front and any other single punch technique (RSP, SSP etc) links with the elbow strikes after two rebounds. Let's continue this pattern but jazz it up a little and add another triplet rhythm. (* **remove eyeglasses**)

#3-C

```
           ...to left side                           ...to left side
        ┌─────────────┐                           ┌─────────────┐
↻  L-L\R     R-L    L-R    R      L      ↻  L\R-R     R-L    L-R    R      L
(O-TES)''(R-SDP)''(SDP)''(FCP)'''(FSP)''''....(D-TES)''(R-SDP)''(SDP)''(FCP)'''(FSP)'''
e-f \ f                                      f \ e-f
 D D D    DD     DD    Ddd    Ddd.................D D D   DD     DD    Ddd    Ddd
```

This pattern, using the R-SDP, is a little more difficult. Note that the first fist of the Triple Elbow Strike (↻ L) and [brackets], drifts to the side position while the second fist (larger **R**) links behind to set it up. The FSP adds an extra triplet rhythm which creates a pleasant pause in the beat. Let's finish this whole echo combination with a Fist Roll at the end.

#3-D

Note triplet rhythms
↓   ↓

```
L-L\R    R-L    L-R    R      L          L\R-R    R-L    L-R    R-L-R-L-R L......
(S-TES)''(SDP)''(SDP)''(FCP)'''(FSP)'''......(D-TES)''(RDP)''(SDP)''(F-Roll)
e-f \ f                                 f \ e-f
 D D D    DD     DD    Ddd    Ddd.................D D D   DD     DD    DDDDDD...
```

The ending Fist Roll kind of climaxes the rhythm to a close. Continually repeating #3A-D one after the other creates more or less of a "cadence" around the main beat (echo) of the triple and double accented techniques. We are just playing with the sounds and the beat….and we can make up thousands of them.

I want to close with one more catchy echo rhythm that really demonstrates the diversity of the techniques. This is one of the most complex and fascinating echo's I have found yet, but it is an excellent rhythm to teach the endless variety of combinations on the bag.

Echo pattern #4-A

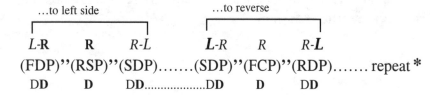

In the first pattern, notice the second fist of the FDP (**R**) passed through to RSP and returned to lead the SDP, and the left fist goes out to the left side. In the second pattern, the left fist (larger *L*) leads the SDP and goes to the side. To do this, (simply extend the left elbow, straightening the arm) waiting for the right to perform FCP and pass behind the bag and join it. As written, the double punch techniques move from the front area, to the left side, then right side, then behind the bag.

Also, the single punch between them rotates from behind the bag to the front. The most amazing thing about echo pattern #4-A is the *fist order* of entry. Neither fist ever enters from the same striking area (front, left side, right side or behind) twice in a row! Look at the left fist…it enters from the front of the bag, left side….right side, then from behind. The right fist, which is more active, enters from the front of the bag, behind, left side…right side, front, and from behind. Both fists are **constantly linking to different sides of the bag.** (Using the linking symbols for writing each change would be a nightmare.)

Interestingly enough, after #4-A you can repeat * these two in ANY order. The first pattern can be repeated by itself because it ends with a SDP which can return to a FDP on two rebounds. The second pattern can be repeated by itself, *OR* you can go back and repeat the whole sequence because after a RDP we can go to either a FDP or SDP after two rebounds. Let's continue the rhythm of echo #4-A, after the RDP, but change the combinations entirely.

#4-B

```
                              …to right side
                            ┌──────────┐
 L-R      L       L-R       R-L*     R       R-L
(FDP)''(RSP)''(FDP)………(RDP)''(SSP)''(SDP)……
 DD       D       DD…………………DD       D       DD
```

The first FDP of #4-B easily follows the RDP in #4-A. In the first pattern, we let the lead fist (L) pass behind to the RSP. After the last FDP, both fists pass under to create RDP in the second pattern. Notice after the RDP the lead fist (larger *R*) links to the right side for the SSP [brackets] and then leads the last side SDP. The left fist (*L**) motion in the second pattern RDP is slightly awkward, because it moves "in" toward the chest, then to the left side. You can "sync" the left fist to your right by letting it go to the left side as the right fist performs the SSP. Then they are moving together in the same direction.

After the final SDP in #4-B, when can repeat the first pattern because FDP follows a SDP on two rebounds. However, the second pattern can not repeat because a RDP follows a SDP on three rebounds. Let's continue the echo by moving to the other side…

#4-C

```
                    ...to left side
                  ┌─────────────────┐
L-R      L      L-R        R-L      R      R-L
(SDP)"(SSP)"(FDP)........(R-SDP)"(SSP)"(FDP)....
 DD      D      DD.....................DD     D      DD
```

This pattern opens with the lead fist (**L**) of the SDP passing to the other side for the SSP. This combination creates a subtle "split fist" action between the second fist of the SDP and the left SSP (the underlined *R* **L**). The most difficult combination occurs moving from the first pattern to the second, or: (FDP)"(R-SDP). After the L-R of the FDP, the left fist must move to the left side as the right fist is passing to the reverse position. In the second pattern, the right fist (larger **R**) leads the R-SDP and moves to the right side for the SSP. Here again, a "split fist" occurs between the left fist (the second fist of the R-SDP) coming from the left side, and the right fist (noted by L   R).

Pattern #4-C also rotates the double punches to different areas and splits the single strikes between the left and right side. Also, neither fist enters from the same side twice in a row. Let's continue and create one more "double punch-single punch" echo.

Echo pattern #4-D.....(2nd pattern is most difficult)

```
                    ...to right side
                  ┌─────────────────┐
L-R      L      L-R     ↘R-L*     L      L-R
(RDP)"(SSP)"(FDP)......(R-SDP)"(FCP)"(R-SDP)
 DD      D      DD.................DD     D      DD
```

This pattern opens with a RDP, which naturally follows the FDP ending #4-C. We have the lead fist (**L**) linking to the SSP and then leading the FDP. Both the L-R fists must change positions after the FDP to set up the R-SDP, exactly as in #4-C. The right goes behind and then out to the right side.

The last pattern is created by some of most complex fist movements yet. After the initial R-SDP, the second fist (larger **L**) links from the side to the front (FCP) and passes through behind the bag to lead the last R-SDP. What is tricky is the right (↘R) is moving from behind the bag to the right side *at the same time* as the left fist is doing the FCP. Here is precisely what happens: After the initial R-SDP, both fist are momentarily in front of the bag together, chin high. As the left fist (**L***) returns to go FCP, the right fist must move sideways. At this point, the fists are going in different directions, but *the secret is realizing that both arms are simply extending the fists*. The left fist extends through the bag and the right extends a little more "out" to the right side. Then they flex back in to complete the last R-SDP. Amazingly, again no fist has entered from the same area twice in a row.

This is not the last way to create this echo. There are numerous other combinations to do this with just the fists, and we could push the difficulty by *rotating the fists* of any FDP or RDP. The more complex a rhythm gets the more we have to concentrate on fist control. My intention, though, is not to show every possible combination but to illustrate how the techniques flow together.

I will conclude this section by showing this same rhythm echo using several elbow techniques. After the last R-SDP of #4-D, we can do this:

Echo Pattern #4-E   Using Outward-Double Elbow Strike

```
    R        R      R-L          L        L       L-R
(O-DES)"(RSP)"(SDP)......(O-DES)"(RSP)"(SDP)....
    e-f                       e-f
    DD        D      DD...............DD       D       DD
```

This combination is relatively simple compared to the maze of linking fists in the previous examples! Here we are rotating an Outward-Double Elbow Strike from the right arm to the left arm. (Note that we must use the SDP to set up the left O-DES. The second fist (**L**) of the SDP is coming from the side, which links to a front technique on two rebounds. Using a FDP would force three rebounds before another front technique, because of the bag angle of rebound. A small, but important, difference.

Pattern #4-E can repeat itself but let's look at one more Double Elbow Strike to create this echo continuing from the last pattern, after the last SDP. This one will be a little more difficult.

Echo Pattern #4-F Using Downward-Double Elbow Strike   (* **remove eyeglasses**)

```
                    ...to reverse area
                      ┌─────────────┐
    L        R      ⬃ R-L          R        L       L-R
(D-DES)"(RSP)"(SDP)......(D-DES)"(**RSP**)"(SDP) ....... can repeat #4E  or  #4F
    e-f                       e-f
    DD        D      DD...............DD       D       DD
```

Following the last SDP of #4-E, we can complete a D-DES. We have to anticipate this technique and "set up" for it just before and here is the secret. (***Notice that the same combination* SDP...D-DES** *occurs within the #4-F pattern and I will use these as the example.*) The first fist (⬃ R) of the SDP will create the downward elbow technique. As the second fist (*L*) connects in the SDP, the right arm must be moving up to position the D-DES so it can be completed after two rebounds. Also notice that the **RSP** that follows the elbow technique is performed by the "other", or left fist. Again there is a secret to make it easier. As the fists complete the SDP they are both in front of the bag. The inward motion of the left fist coming from the side will bring it to the chest. *As the right arm begins the D-DES, let the left fist move with it, only lower under the bag*. As the right fist makes contact, the left is already behind ready to enter after two rebounds. (a perfect "drift 1/2 and re-enter)

If you perform this entire echo, #4-A all the way thru #4-E, you will use almost every "advanced" topic developed. There are lots of other ways to create this and other "echo" patterns and I encourage you to develop your own.

To me, "echoing" is probably the best way to learn the techniques because creating them forces study and concentration on how the they all blend together. About 90% of my own knowledge about the speed bag came through creating more and more complex echo patterns. I also notice that when "hitting" in the gym, most of the people who approached were fascinated by "...that one rhythm you were doing." It was usually an echo I was practicing on. I have also found echoing to be a valuable teaching method.

Speed Bag Training To Music

If creating rhythm echo's is one of the best ways to learn the speed bag techniques, then hitting to music has to be one of the most enjoyable, and expressive ways to *use* them. Imagine it sort of like a hanging "bongo drum". You hit the bag in time to the music, creating syncopated rhythms along with the beat of the song. (For those who haven't studied music, *syncopated* means accents that fall off of, or inbetween, the main beats of a song.) All we really need is (1) some music and (2) a way to play it. I will focus on the music later. First let's look at how we can play it.

The speed bag is fairly loud by itself, and we have to get the music volume over the sound of the bag. This can be done in several ways. One way is by a personal tape or CD player which can be worn on a belt or placed in a pocket, as shown in shown in **[FIG 11A]**. This is the most practical method, especially in a public work-out area such as a health club. Notice the wire to the headphones runs up the back of the shirt, but it can be in front. Just keep it out of the way of your arms.

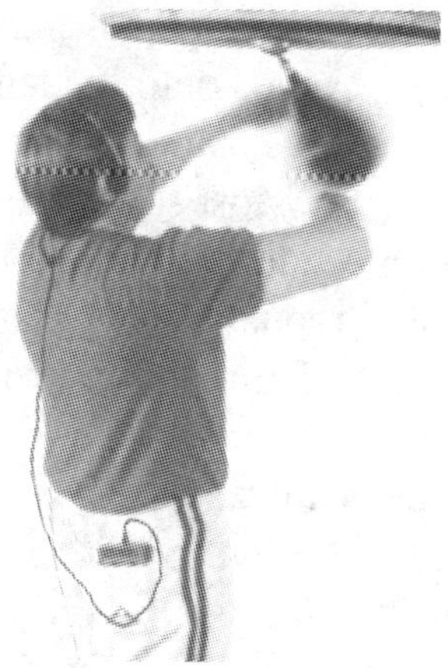

Fig 11A Small player

Another way to do this is by using a portable tape or CD "boom box" shown in **[FIG 11B]**. This method is only practical for the home because of the volume needed to hear the music. The further away the speakers are from you, the louder the music has to be. Notice how the tape player is set right under the board. Even this close, you may have to turn it up almost to full volume. Alone, I prefer this method, because it is much easier to adjust volume or change CD's or tapes. (…however, other household members and your neighbors may prefer the other method.)

Fig 11B Boom Box

You can hit to any type of music, such as Rock, Top 40, Disco, Techno, Classical, Military Marches, and other types not listed. I could not begin to list all the music that can be used, because this is a matter of personal taste and preferences. However, I have included a short list of my favorite songs at the end of the chapter along with a much larger list in the appendix.

There are a few secrets to know about musical choices for speed bag. The best music has a lot of **individual notes**, with distinct separation between them. It is much easier to hit to *four individually played notes*, (one on each beat), than *one note* held for four beats. More notes means more sounds to help tell *you* where you are in the rhythm. Some rock & roll songs *hold one guitar note* for several measures, giving no beat separation or noticeable melody to follow. Some of the newer jazz flamenco guitar music has incredible note separation, along with other sounds that are easy to hear.

> Hitting to slower music creates excellent fist control. Hitting to faster music is physically more demanding and gives a harder physical work-out.

The **pitch** of some instruments are easier to hear than others. Any sounds within the same pitch as the rebounding bag will usually not be heard as you punch, including the lower bass drums, long held guitar notes, or the bass guitar. Horns, piano, tenor sax, violin, etc. are easier to hear above the bag.

Vocals in music are usually louder than the instruments. Most popular music mixes both singing verse with instrument solo's. The instrumental sections will be harder to hear. With pre-recorded tapes there is not much you can do about this, but when recording your own music you can adjust the input levels of the music *as you record it*. Record the voice parts of a song at one level and *raise the level* for the longer instrumental interludes. Raising the input levels during recording programs the needed volume changes onto the tape. Music editing software allows you to do this for songs on CD.

Using music allows you to "program" your work-outs for any amount of time, and desired level of intensity. Most songs are 3-7 minutes long, which is a long time for *non-stop* speed bag work - at any tempo. Start out with a few slower songs to warm up. Leave 10 or 15 seconds between each one for rest. Gradually record faster paced music, which increases your punching intensity. On a 90 minute tape, each 45 minute side will have about 30-35 minutes of punching time with short rests in between.

It does not take great speed bag skills to hit to music, and you can do it with just the two techniques of the Basic Rhythm. Regardless of your innate rhythmic sense, you can learn to keep a speed bag beat to music. Every single combination presented in this book can be *either* a routine speed bag practice combination, or a snappy rhythm, letting you jam along with your favorite tunes. The interpretation is up to you. To teach this concept, I will develop two types, *or styles*, of using bag beats to music. The first one will be geared to learning to *feel the basic beat* with music. It is the learning mode. The second will expand on the first and set the natural rhythm in your bones free.

1. Hitting "on the Beat" (Straight Time Punching)

All music has a rhythmic pulse or *groove*. You tap your foot or snap your fingers to it. So does the speed bag. Begin with the two techniques that make up **The Basic Rhythm** (Front Circle Punch-FCP & Front Straight Punch-FSP, pg. 21). Hitting just the front of the bag, the Basic Triplet Rhythm can be used by *having the fists contact the bag "on the beat"*, (ie....every time you tap your foot, a fist hits the bag.) Four foot taps would be four punches. The fist hits directly on the beat. Now you are punching

> **Bag Size** *(and Speed), and* **Music Speed** *will effect how you can hit to it. Experiment with big and small bags to get the full effect of how these two interact.*

directly in "straight time" to the music. Depending on the speed of the music, you can vary this by punching either faster of slower. For instance, *for slower music you can hit faster*, doubling the number of punches. For every four foot taps, eight punches land. Think of this as hitting "Double time". You will find this works particularly well if hitting to slower music on a fast bag. Hitting to slower music with a fast bag allows you to perform the Basic Rhythm faster than the perceived rhythm of the music. Hitting twice as fast corrects for this and keeps your punching rhythm "on the beat" in *double-time*.

For faster music you hit can hit slower, or for every four foot taps, only two punches land. Think of this as hitting in *"half-time"*, and it works well when hitting a larger slower bag to fast music. Many popular dance songs are too fast for straight time punching on every beat. Punching on every other beat in the music corrects for this, and you are still "on the beat" - Just every *other* one.

In this way, you may always have *three* punching speed options: Hitting either directly on the beat, (straight time) or twice as fast (double time) or half as fast (Half-time). You usually can not do all three to the same song, but at least one, sometimes two, will always work with the Basic Rhythm. Just start with the Basic Rhythm and see which way you need to go. *Adjusting bag size can also dramatically effect which methods will work on any given song.*

It sounds complicated, but as long as your punching speed is adjusted evenly in time to the music, the accented fist contacts (punches) will be in sync with the music beat, and the "extra" bag rebounds will add variety and color to the sound! Actually, all four front fist techniques can be used. To use the **Front Double Punch**, time the technique so the *second* fist (accented) lands when your foot taps. **Front Fist Rolling** is easy to rhythmic sync with the music, but it is usually in Double-time.

All of the Elbow Strikes can be used. You can use continuous alternating Outward or Downward -Triple Elbow Strikes to the beat of most music by having the *last fist* of the technique hit the bag *directly on the beat* of the song The leading elbow or fists will create "pick up beats". You will be swinging pretty fast to complete this. However, when you change to some other techniques you will have to slow your swinging down to stay in time with the music, because you will not be adding the extra "stutter" beats. One way to do this is to use "advanced front fist rolling" (page 123). **When front punching only it is easier to change swinging and bag speed with Fist Rolling than any other technique.**

Below are few front punching "rhythm" combinations for hitting on the beat. The **bold underlined Fists** indicate where the imaginary beat of the music would be. As you read or try them, tap your foot in a *slow* beat. Try and feel how the last fist falls in with your tapping foot. *Certain combinations will be underlined to indicate repetitive sounds that work well together.*

$$\textbf{R} \quad \textbf{L} \quad \text{L-}\textbf{R} \quad \textbf{R} \quad \text{R-}\textbf{L} \quad \textbf{L} \quad \text{L-}\textbf{R} \quad \textbf{R} \quad \text{R-}\textbf{L} \quad \text{L-}\textbf{R}$$

1.......(FCP)'''(FSP)'''(FDP)'''(FCP)'''(FDP)'''(FCP)'''(FDP)'''(FCP)'''(FDP)'''(FDP)'''..repeat

$$\textbf{R} \quad \textbf{L} \quad \text{L-}\textbf{R} \quad \text{R-}\textbf{L} \quad \text{L-L\\}\textbf{R} \quad \text{R-R\\}\textbf{L} \quad \text{L-}\textbf{R} \quad \text{R-L-R-L-R-L-}\textbf{R}$$

2 ....(FCP)'''(FSP)'''(FDP)'''(FDP)'''(O-TES)'''(O-TES)'''(FDP) ''' (F-Roll)'''...repeat
      e-f\ **f**   e-f\ **f**

FDP is a great technique to use because the first(lead) fist acts as a *pick up* beat. This double beat "D**D**" sound is a rhythmic variation used a lot in music. In #2, notice the last F-ROLL. The first and last fist will be on the beat. The other punches within may or may not, depending on your Rolling speed. You can vary this to match the music by speed up or slowing down.

Linking in straight time "on the Beat".

We can also hit "on the beat" when passing the fists through the bag to any of the three reverse techniques. The speed bag rhythmic *sounds* are different for linking fists through the bag, but the principle is the same. The accented fists will contact the bag "on the beat".

Actually, a Single Fist figure-[8] (FCP) '' (RSP) is easy to use with music, for the " 1-2-1-2" bag beat is more like the standard or 2/4 or 4/4 music tempo. This combination also adjusts readily to *half* or *double time*, and the accent will most naturally fall on the FCP if you started the linking on that punch.

Both single and double fist linking can be used, and the key is to get the main "beats" of the bag (accented fist) to fall exactly on, or directly inbetween, the main beats of the song. Although you are trying to keep a steady *tempo* with the music you do not necessarily maintain constant swinging or fist speed. For instance, when doing a (FSP) '' (RSP) split fist combination, you can choose between two rebounds or four rebounds. This changes the accented sounds of the bag along with the speed of your fists. Doing 5 Split-Fist Punches with 4 rebounds inbetween is a great combination with any song.

Slight changes in punching speed are also required when mixing straight Basic Rhythm punching to linking with reverse techniques. It seems easier to go into both a half-time and double-time beat when passing to the reverse techniques - especially with FDP''RDP combinations.

How you can flow from front punching to reverse punching again may vary with music speed, bag size and your ability to control and manipulate the bag's speed. You may find combinations that seem impossible on one bag size work very easily with another. It is interesting to note that the combinations of (FDP)'''(FDP), or (RDP)'''(RDP), and (FDP) '' (RDP), can all be used to keep the same beat to music, and the last variation sounds completely different than the first two. But as long as the *second* fist of each technique connects on the beat, they all work equally well.

All of the side techniques can be used for punching "on the beat", although it takes a little practice to feel the double bounce and triplet rhythm changes required when linking around the bag. However, the principle is the same - in that every accented punch (second fist in double punches, last fist in triple elbow strikes) fall directly on the beat.

Here are a few practice rhythms for *Linking on the beat*. Again, the **bold underlined Fists** indicate where imaginary beat of the music would be. Bag rebounds are shown but do not change where the accents fall. Start from the Basic Rhythm.   (be aware of Reverse and Side techniques)

$$\text{R} \quad\quad \text{L} \quad\quad \text{L-}\textbf{R} \quad\quad \text{R-}\textbf{L} \quad\quad \text{L-}\textbf{R} \quad\quad \text{R-}\textbf{L} \quad\quad \text{L-}\textbf{R} \quad\quad \text{R-}\textbf{L} \quad\quad \text{L-}\textbf{R}$$
3 ....(FCP)'''(FSP)'''(FDP)'''(FDP)'''(FDP)''(RDP)''(FDP)''(RDP)''(FDP)'''...repeat

$$\text{R} \quad\quad \text{L} \quad\quad \text{L-L\textbackslash}\textbf{R} \quad\quad \text{R-}\textbf{L} \quad\quad \text{L-L\textbackslash}\textbf{R} \quad\quad \text{R-}\textbf{L} \quad\quad \text{L-}\textbf{R} \quad\quad \text{R-}\textbf{L} \quad\quad \text{L-}\textbf{R}$$
4 ....(FCP)'''(FSP)'''(O-TES)'''(FDP)'''(D-TES)''(RDP)''(FDP)''(RDP)''(FDP)...Repeat
        e-f\ **f**   f\e- **f**

$$\text{R} \quad\quad \text{L} \quad\quad \text{L-}\textbf{R} \quad\quad \text{R-}\textbf{L} \quad\quad \text{R} \quad\quad \text{L} \quad\quad \textbf{R}^* \quad\quad \text{R-}\textbf{L} \quad\quad \text{L-}\textbf{R}$$
5 ....(FCP)'''(FSP)'''(FDP)''**(RDP)**''''(FSP)''''(RSP)''''(FSP)''(RDP)''(FDP)'''...Repeat

In this last exercise, notice the middle Split-Fist combinations. It all starts with the **(RDP)**, where the lead fist (R) returns to the front for the First underlined FSP. The Left fist stays behind. Then the **R*** fist passes to the back to lead the next RDP. This sounds great with four rebounds inbetween instead of two. Two rebounds makes it twice as fast. Either way, just have the punch land on the beat of the music.

$$\text{R} \quad\quad \text{L} \quad\quad \textit{L-}\textbf{R} \quad\quad \textit{R-}\textbf{L} \quad\quad \textit{L-}\textbf{R} \quad\quad \textit{R-}\textbf{L} \quad\quad \text{L-L\textbackslash}\textbf{R}$$
6 ....(FCP)'''(FSP)'''(FDP)''(RDP)''(SDP)''(SDP)''(O-TES)'''...repeat
        e-f\ **f**

Number six is a really nice rhythmic combination. The sounds of FDP-RDP-SDP-SDP fits to just about any song on the planet, in either half time, regular time or double time speeds.

These six samples are just a few of the hundreds of possible combinations available to hit *directly "on the beat"* with the speed bag. Any technique that *sounds* like another can be substituted, such as (D-DES) or (O-DES) for (FDP), or (D-TES) for (O-TES). Also, Triple Elbow Strikes can substitute for any double punch, just remember to adjust your speed and force so that the last (accented) punch is directly on the music beat. Once you feel how the speed bag sounds become a regimented drum part with the music, it is a lot more fun. You may even start marching along as you punch. Actually, military marches are perfect for this type, or "style" of punching with music. It is very precise and easy to follow. But it is not the only way to hit to music. Let's move on to the next.

2. Hitting in a "Syncopated Beat".

The previous "on the beat - straight time" punching works for all types of music, but does not allow for much freedom of expression. Think of a military marching band. They move in strict formation with little individual originality. No one does the funky chicken or some unrehearsed steps. Everything is perfectly in time, which is alright - except it gets boring after a while. It has no *swing*. In fact, I love a good Sousa March as well as the next guy, but I'm not going to dance to it.

Rhythmically, we can dance on the speed bag! We can vary from the regimented, more structured "straight time" beat - to a more expressive, improvisational punching to music. I call it hitting in a *syncopated beat*, where many of the punching accents will land "off" the main music beat. But, after a few techniques a main punching accent *will* land directly on the beat and you are still in rhythmic sync with the music. And every few measures of music you will come back in on the ***Down Beat.*** For the non-musicians or rhythmically challenged, it may easier to understand by explaining a few basics of music rhythm structure and just how this relates to the speed bag (Sorry…it's the drummer in me ☺)

In a measure of music there are a number of beats, say four as an example. As you tap your foot you may count this as **1**-2-3-4, **1**-2-3-4..etc. The Number "**1**"is often referred to as the downbeat, and is usually sensed as the heaviest beat. Or, you may count this as **1**-2-**3**-4. Either way, beats "..2 -3 -4" are still ongoing, and they are all spaced evenly apart. There is also a *space* (or amount of time) *inbetween the beats*. Accents, notes, etc. may also fall anywhere within this space between the counted rhythm. Accents (or punches) landing directly at the halfway point are still sensed rhythmically as "on the beat" (This is what allowed us to go into double-time or half-time on the bag earlier). Beats (accents) that do not fall **evenly** within these spaces are called syncopated, or slightly "off the beat". The combinations in this section will create rhythmic patterns where punching accents consistently land either off the beat (syncopated) or on beats 2, 3, or 4 for a few measures of the song. Then a slight variation will put your fist right back in on the downbeat, just like you were off doing a cool improvised drum solo. Guess what…..you will be. And it is awesome when done correctly.

Where the first style of hitting (on the beat) was like a Military March, think of this as Dixieland/ Jazz/Blues and Funk. The main difference will be adjusting your punching speed. For any particular song, you will have to either *speed up* or *slow down from the Basic Rhythm beat* to go into a syncopated style. Which way you go depends on music speed, bag size and your punching ability. Below are a few short syncopated rhythm combinations that will work with any type of music. I will explain these as if the music was in a normal 4/4 time. I may also put the musical beat number over the punch for clarity. If that means nothing to you, don't worry. "Feeling" the beat is much more important than counting it.

1. **Three Front Single Punches + Three Reverse Single Punches** (3+3) As shown below:

1			**3**			**1**			**3**		
R	ʀ	R	**R**	ʀ	R	**R**	L	L	**L**	L	L
(FCP)'''(FCP)'''(FCP) ''			**(RSP)**'''(RSP)'''(RSP) ''			**FCP**'''FSP'''FCP ''			**RSP**'''RSP'''RSP''		

The underlined version uses just one arm, and the second uses a basic rhythm punching change over. The interesting feature is we are putting six punches in the space of four beats. In each sequence, the **first front punch(Bold)** usually starts on the "1" beat, and the **first Reverse technique** starts on the "3" count. the other punches fall inbetween the other beats, but never directly on them. The secret is adjusting your punching speed to make this work. The other punches are syncopated around the other beats.

2. **Five Front Single Punches + one Reverse Single Punch.** (5+1) as Shown below.

1				4		1				4	
R*	R	R	R	**R**	R	**R**	L	L	R	**R**	R
(FCP)'''	(FCP)'''	(FCP)'''	(FCP)'''	**(FCP)** ''	(RSP) ''	**(FCP)**'''	(FSP)'''	(FCP)'''	(FSP)'''	**(FCP)** ''	(RSP)

Again, the underlined version uses just one arm, and the second uses a basic rhythm punching change over. Here we once again see six punches put in the space of four beats, and you have to punch fast to do it. The **first front punch** usually starts on the "1" beat, and the 5th punch is on the "4" count. You can go from the first 3+3 to this 5+1 smoothly by allowing the **First FCP** (**R***) in each sequence to start the next one. * You can fudge on this combination sometimes by using 5,6,or 7 front punches before the RSP. You may need to do this when you find yourself off the beat slightly, or if you enter this combination on the wrong beat. In a measure or so the rhythm will be right for the RSP.

   Remember: To get back to the Basic Rhythm (straight time punching) from this combination you will have to either go faster, or slower. This is true for all of these rhythms.

3. **Single Fist pass through to Front Double punch.**   as Shown below

	2			4	
L	**L**	L-R	R	**R**	R-L
(FCP) ''	**(RSP)** ''	(FDP) '''	(FCP) ''	**(RSP)** ''	(FDP)''' Repeat.

This is a super combination with any song. It just fits, and is very versatile. Here the accented punches usually lands on the "2" and "4" count. this fits very well with the first two rhythms. It is easy to get into this from #1, (3+3) by allowing the last (third) FCP to be the first FCP of this combination. Also, you can can out of this by allowing the *last fist of the FDP* to begin #2 (5+1).

4. **Front Double punch, pass through to two RSP's.**   as Shown below

	1			3	
L-R	**R**	R	R-L	**L**	L
....(FDP)''	**(RSP)**'''	(RSP) ''	(FDP)''	**(RSP)**'''	(RSP)''...repeat

The accented fist here normally falls on the "1" and "3" count .This works especially well with number one (3Front +3 Reverse). Just let the *second RSP in #1* act as the *second RSP here in #4*. Follow it with a FDP and go right into this combination #4. Also, you can let the Second fist of this FDP be the first fist of the 5+1 combination #2. You can also mix it with combo #3. It takes a little modification though. After the FDP in number #3, use a FCP instead of the FDP, (single fist pass through) to the two RSP's in#4 (it is easier rythmically). Then you stay right on beat, no problemo.

   This next one is a snappy syncopated rhythm that works great with music, but it is a little longer and more complicated, demanding some control from the reverse position. It is actually an echo rhythm off #3, and I will re-write #3 to show it. I will add a bottom sound line with "D" to highlight the sound. Remember, **the bolded letters** are where the music beat usually falls in this combination.

5.   Variation of #3 to Reverse echo.   as Shown below   ↓

2				4			2			4	
L	**L**	*L-R*	*R*	**R**	*R-L*	*L-R**	**R***	*R-L*	*L-R*	**R**	*R-L*
(FCP)''	**(RSP)**''	(FDP) '''	(FCP)''	**(RSP)**''	(FDP) ''	(RDP)''	**(FCP)**	''(RDP)''	(FDP)''	**(RSP)**''	(FDP) '''...repeat.
D	**D**	DD	D	**D**	DD	DD	**D**	D D	DD	**D**	DD

The new part is the underlined section, after the second FDP. Here both fists then pass behind and create a sound echo from behind the bag. Notice that after the first RDP, the second (*R**) Fist passes to the front for the **FCP**. The left stays behind, waiting for the next RDP. After the second RDP, both fists return to the front, for the next FDP. Then the second fist (**R**) again passes to RSP, and returns to lead the final FDP, and then start over again with exercise #3-or #5 after three rebounds. You can get out of this in a lot of places and go to the other rhythms. However, one advanced way is to exit on the RSP (arrow) to either Rhythm #1 (3+3), or #2 (5+1), starting from behind.

Another similiar combination works well off of Rhythm beat #4.

6.   Variation of #4 to Reverse echo.   as Shown below, with #4 repeated.

1				3			1			3	
L-R	***R***	*R*	*R-L*	***L***	*L*	*L-R*	*R*	*R-L*	*L-R*	***R***	*R-L*
(FDP)''	**(RSP)**'''	(RSP)''	(FDP)''	**(RSP)**'''	(RSP)''	(FDP)''	**(RSP)**''	(FDP)''	(RDP)''	**(FCP)**''	(RDP)''..repeat
DD	**D**	D	DD	**D**	D	DD	**D**	DD	DD	**D**	DD

Again the underlined section creates the same exact rhythm variation as #5, we just got into it from a slightly different set up rhythm. In fact, Rhythms #3 and #4 are just playing with the predominate sound of the Double Punch, and the sound variation in #5 and #6 above are the exact same rhythm echo featured earlier in 4-A, pages 162-165. All the echo combinations work as syncopated rhythms to music.

One last syncopated rhythm will feature A variation using A Triple Elbow Strike sound.

7.   Variation of #3 with Triple Elbow strikes.   as Shown below, with #4 repeated.

L	**L**	*L-R*	*R*	**R**	*R\L-***L**	*L*	*L\R-R*	***R***	*R*	***R***	*R-L*
(FCP)''	**(RSP)**''	(FDP) '''	(FCP)''	**(RSP)**''	(D-TES)''	(RSP)''	(D-TES)''	**(RSP)**''	(FCP)''	**(RSP)**''	(FDP)
					f \e-**f**		f \e- f				

This begins and ends with Rhythm #3. The underlined part is a rhythmic variation using the Downward Triple Elbow strike. The O-TES could also be used. *We could add a third TES in this pattern (any of them) and let the last fist act as the first punch of Rhythm #2 (5+1), because* **it would land on the DownBeat**, (1). Because of that, we could also come out after the a third triple elbow strike into hitting in straight time, (and speeding up or slowing down to find the correct speed.) Lastly, We can get into a syncopated rhythm with triple elbow strikes just as easily after the first RSP in rhythm #3 - (FCP)''**(RSP)**''(FDP).

By mixing just these seven examples together, with slight variations, you can easily hit to any and all types of music in the syncopated rhythm. You just gotta feel the beat.

Mixing "On the Beat" and "Syncopated" Punching Rhythms together

Eventually, you will not have to concentrate on hitting in either the "straight" or "syncopated" rhythms, and you will naturally use both together automatically adjusting speed and power to create whatever rhythm sound you want, no matter where your hands are around the bag.

There are two ways to start punching to a new song. First, try the Basic Triplet Rhythm in "straight time". Some songs will be either a *little too fast* or a *little too slow* for the bag you are using. Punch faster to try double time, or go slower to find the half-time speed. One of the three speeds should work.

The second way is to begin a single fist linking rhythm, with **1**-2-**1**-2 bag sounds. When you find the right speed on the beat, start trying a few double punches and see how they sound. It also works well to let one fist do a drift-[1/2] and re-enter (pg 129) to a RDP. The lead fist is a "pick-up" beat. Also, try the FDP''RDP, for six to eight pass. This makes a sound that fits most songs. Then move to some other techniques and combinations, adjusting the speed of your punching to keep in time with the music. When you lose it, or fall off the beat, either go back to single fist linking or perhaps Front-Fist Rolling.

For songs that demand a very fast, powerful Basic Rhythm to keep up, you will have to slow down slightly to find the correct *syncopated* punching speed. For songs that demand a very slow Basic Rhythm, you will have to speed up to find the correct speed. The reverse is also true. In many songs you will find the *accents of the melody* will match with bag rhythms. For instance, in *Mortal Combat theme*, the main melody is 5 accented notes and a stutter to start over again. The syncopated 5+1 fits this perfectly.

Many songs have moments when the rhythm or music stops completely for an instant, and then either an instrument solo, or spoken phrase starts it again. Several of my favorites examples are: "The Rhythm Is Gonna Get You" and "Live For Loving You" by Gloria Estefan, along with "Batdance" by the performer who used to be called Prince. Just before the music stops there are usually 3 or 4 heavily accented beats. Repetitive Hook Punching works perfectly on these heavy beats. So does front - reverse split fist punching with four rebounds inbetween.

You may find yourself developing certain "routines" to your favorite songs, as you get better. You can punch along, stop the bag occasionally (in time to the music) and take off again. You may catch yourself singing along, and dancing as you punch. Step back and do your best James Brown imitation for a few measures before returning to the bag. Move your head and shake your butt. Step to different sides of the bag and get down with the beat. Bob and weave, Juke and Jive..... - YOU BE JAMMIN'!

A Few of my Favorite songs for the Speed Bag

TITLE	Artist	TITLE	Artist
Jammin' (Slow, Hot Sax)	Candi Duffer	Oh Yea	Essential Yello Album
Rhythm is Gonna Get You	Gloria Estefan	Call it Love (cool drums)	Yello " "
Get on Your Feet!	Gloria Estefan	The Hunt (Planet Drum)	Micky Hart
Turn the Beat Around (yes!)	Vicky Sue Robinson	Ooh Ahh, Just a little Bit	Tina Marie
Danger Zone (hang on!)	Kenny Loggins	Bang the Drum all Day	Todd Rungren
Red Hot (..it is!)	Vanessa Mae	Get Ready for This	2 Unlimited
Mission Impossible Theme	Movie Soundtrack	Shake (you will!)	Otis Redding
The Immortals Mortal Combat	Movie Sountrack	Satisfaction	Otis Redding
Space Jam	Movie Soundtrack	Baby Work-Out	Jacki Wilson
Total Eclipse of the Heart	Nicki French	Jumpin' Jack (it is!)	Big Bad Voodoo Daddy
The TV Song	Blue Man Group	BatDance	Prince (?)
Rods & Cones	Blue Man Group	William *Lone Ranger* Tell	Rossini

See Appendix D for a more comprehensive song list

CHAPTER 12

Special Training & Martial Arts

The previous chapters covered the techniques for "continuous" non-stop striking. Although this is super exercise and great for hand-eye coordination, it is not the only method to use a speed bag. It can be used to train for specific punching or striking techniques and combinations used in boxing or the martial arts. It is a fantastic tool for learning "in-fighting", or throwing techniques in very close quarters.

The speed bag is mostly viewed as a piece of boxing equipment, but it is has the same value to anyone training their hands and feet, either for sport or self-defense. Virtually every boxing gym has a speed bag, but very few martial art schools do. Most martial artists are unfamiliar with it simply because they have not been exposed to it....or found reliable information on how to use it.

I generally refer to boxing under the heading of martial arts. I do not separate "boxing" and "martial arts" techniques, because each discipline uses many of the same movements. Martial Arts (I am including all styles) uses all the boxing techniques, but perhaps by different names. Pure American boxing uses only a small percentage of the techniques available to martial artists. For instance, boxers do not use elbow strikes, knife hands or spinning techniques.

This chapter will focus on specific speed bag training for whatever discipline you are in. The exercises are general in nature and will teach you the basics of how the bag can increase your own technique and combination ability. IT IS NOT A BOXING OR MARTIAL ARTS TRAINING MANUAL. It will not replace qualified instruction in boxing or the martial arts.

I am assuming you already have a basic understanding of the techniques used in this chapter. If you do not, then proceed cautiously because technique "mechanics" will only be discussed if a variation adds economy of movement to an exercise on the speed bag. The techniques described will be the same hand and elbow strikes used in most martial art styles, however not ever style may have each one...or may call it by a slightly different name.

Fig 12A Fighting Stance

One of the main differences between regular speed bag training and this "special" training is the beginning stance used. Previous chapters use a full open stance, facing the bag, which is great for speed bag practice, but a lousy choice for fighting. Martial Arts have many different stances. The exercises here will all be completed from the normal "fighting" stance **[Fig 12A]**.

In whatever stance you use, you will have a "leading" fist (furthest away from your body) and a fist closer to your body (sometimes called the "back" or second "fist. For our training purposes, it does not matter which hand is forward and which is back. Martial Artists usually fight either way, and most boxers always train either "orthodox" (left hand forward) or "Southpaw" (right hand forward.)

Along with the stance, there are a few other differences. Height adjustment of the board is not as crucial because we will not be "linking" one fist through to the other side. Bag height is more keyed to the height of an opponent . We will also have to "measure the distance" between ourselves and the bag. (This does not mean with a ruler. This is a phrase used to "give yourself enough room to complete a technique or combination". In some exercises we will be "closing" distance between ourselves and the bag, (ie…spinning backfist.) Everything else is the same including the "rules of rhythm" discussed earlier and counting the rebounds between techniques. I will also use the same method for technique abbreviations, (see chapter 3).

Fig 12B-1 Backfist

Hand Techniques

We will focus on 9 hand only techniques. Some are fist punches and some strike the edges of the hand. Several of the punches were covered in earlier chapters but are quickly reviewed here.

Punches

The **Backfist**, symbolized by (**BF**). This is gener- ally thrown with the leading hand. There are several

Fig 12B-2 Backfist

ways to do a backfist. The "traditional" method, is seen in **[Fig 12B-1]**. Here we see the fist has rolled over to strike the back of the fist. The contact point is near the large knuckles of the hand. **[Fig 12B-2]** demonstrates another method which modifies this slightly and keeps the palm pointed down, eliminating the "rolling" over to strike the back of the hand. This method is a little easier particularly when performing 3 or 4 striking combinations on a small fast bag. Hit the large knuckle over the little finger (see the "Front Circle Punch, in chapt. 4.)

The **Jab**, symbolized by **(JAB)**, is thrown by the leading arm and also contacts the front of the fist over the large knuckles **[Fig 12C]**. It's the most used lead punch in boxing.

The **Front Straight Punch** is identified as **(FSP)**. This is related to the reverse punch in some styles, or a straight right in boxing. Either way, you are striking with the "back" fist, or the fist that is under your chin. The bag contacts the front of the fist, over the last three large knuckles **[Fig12D]**.

The Jab and Front Straight Punch can be put together (much like the Front Double Punch) with only one rebound inbetween. You could also combine the Backfist with the Front Straight Punch in this way.

Fig 12C Jab

Fig 12D Front Straight Punch

The **Hook Punch**, shown as **(HP)** enters from the side of the bag and connects over the large knuckles of the fist **[Fig 12E]**. It is a very versatile technique in that it can be thrown by either fist. This technique can create some rhythmic variations because individual differences in execution may cause the fist to travel straight in from the side of the bag, or the rear-side or the front-side. This will change the angle of the rebound resulting in a different number of rebounds before the next technique (see chapter 9, **PG**. 94).

The **Hammer Fist**, symbolized as **(HF)**, makes contact in a downward direction and connects the side of the fist over the large knuckle of the little finger **[Fig 12F]**. It is usually thrown by the "back" fist under the chin. Care must be taken when practicing this technique on the speed bag, because it is possible to hit the rebound board with the edge of the fist. I recommend adjusting the board to where the bag is at least level with the mouth, or slightly higher. You can also modify the swing by keeping the elbow lower during the movement.

The **Uppercut Punch**, symbolized by **(UPC)**, is very similiar to the hook except it is thrown in an upward direction **(FIG 12g)**. It must contact the bag just after it rebounds from the board. It can be thrown by either fist.

Fig 12E Hook Punch

Fig 12F Hammer Fist

Fig 12g Uppercut

Ridge Hand striking

Ridge Hand striking is also adaptable to the speed bag. There are two types of Ridge Hand strikes, depending on the direction of the movement.

The **Inward-Ridge Hand** strike, symbolized by **(I-RH)**, is called this because the direction of movement is "in" toward the chest or center of the body. The palm is facing down and the bag contacts

Fig 12H-1 Inward-Ridge Hand

the hand on the large knuckle of the index finger **[Fig. 12H-1]**. The key is to close the thumb over the palm of the hand. Like the Hook Punch, variations in execution may find the technique contacting different points on the side of the bag and change the rebounding angle. (If you use this same movement but keep the hand closed in a fist, you would have the Side Single Punch used in the earlier speed bag section.)

The **Outward-Ridge Hand**, identified as **[O-RH]**, connects the same part of the hand as the Inward-Ridge hand, but the technique moves "out" from the chest and the palm is facing up, as shown in **[Fig12H-2]**.

Fig 12H-2 Outward-Ridge Hand

Knife Hand striking

Like the Ridge Hand strikes, there are two methods of Knife Hand Striking-both inward and outward. The **Inward-Knife Hand** strike, symbolized by **(I-KH)** **[Fig 12i-1]**, (Next page), moves "in" toward the center of the chest with the palm up. It connects the edge of the hand on the side of the little finger.

The **Outward-Knife Hand** strike, **(O-KH)** seen in **[Fig 12i-2]** contacts the same part of the hand but has the palm down and moves "out" from the chest.

Fig 12i-1 Inward-Knife Hand

PRACTICE EXERCISES

There are hundreds of possible combinations of these hand techniques. By using the abbreviated symbols for each technique, it is easy to write practice exercises showing technique combinations and the exact number of rebounds inbetween. The following are only a few examples. Practice each one until you can perform it quickly with snap.

Every technique is a singular attack and can be practiced by itself on the speed bag. To do this, assume your fighting stance and simply repeat each striking technique by itself with three (or five) rebounds inbetween. The following examples are assuming the "orthodox" stance, with left leg-and-left arm forward. Then repeat them with the right arm and leg forward.

Repeating techniques by themselves

     L   *L*   *L*
1. (BF)'''(BF)'''(BF)…change lead

     R   *R*   *R*
2. (I-RH)'''(I-RH)'''(I-RH)…change lead

     R   *R*   *R*
3. (I-KH)'''''(I-KH)'''''(I-KH)…change lead

     R   *R*   *R*
4. (HF)'''(HF)'''(HF)…change lead

178

Fig 12i-2 Outward-Knife Hand

Notice how each technique follows itself after three or five rebounds. Exercise #3 uses five rebounds because of the stance and re-positioning needed. You may also need five rebounds if you smash the bag too hard. The exercises show only three repetitions due to space. Work each technique up to at least ten continuous strikes, and do the same with all of the techniques listed.

Of course we will not always follow a technique with the same technique. The beauty of having an "arsenal" of techniques is mixing them together in different combinations. Most of the time we will attack by mixing two or more techniques together. The following combination exercises will mix two, three and then four techniques together, often coming from different sides of the bag. They arc only a guide to help you get the feel of the bag and how combinations flow together. Remember, individual differences in execution may change the number of rebounds.

Two Tech Combo # 3 L-BF / R, I-KH

Two Technique Combinations. (notice * one hand combinations)

   L   *R*   *L*   *R*   *L*   *R*   *L*   *R*
1. (BF)'''(FSP)   2. (BF)'''(I-RH)   3. (BF)'''(I-KH)   4. (BF)'''(HF)

   L   *R*   **L*   *L*   **L*   *L*   *L*   *R*
5. (BF)'''(HP)   6. (BF)'''(JAB)   7. (JAB)'''(BF)   8. (JAB)'''(FSP)

Two Tech Combo #5   Left-BackFist (BF) / Right-Hook Punch (HP)

   L   *R*   *L*   *R*   *L*   *R*   *L*   *R*
9. (JAB)'''(I-RH)   10. (JAB)'''(I-KH)   11. (JAB)'''(HP)   12. (JAB)'''(HF)

  *L   *L*   *L*   *R*   *L*   *R*   *L*   *R*
13. (O-KH)'''(BF)   14. (O-KH)'''(FSP)   15. (O-KH)'''(HP)   16. (O-KH)'''(I-RH)

   L   *R*   *L*   *R*   *L*   *R*   *L*   *R*
17. (O-KH)'''(HF)   18. (O-KH)'''(I-KH)   19. (O-RH)'''(I-RH)   20. (O-RH)'''(I-KH)

   L   *R*   *L*   *R*   *L*   *R*   **L*   *L*
21. (O-RH)'''(HF)   22. (O-RH)'''(HP)   23. (O-RH)'''(FSP)   24. (I-RH)''''(BF)

   L   *R*   *L*   *R*   *L*   *R*   *L*   *R*
25. (I-RH)''''(FSP)   26. (I-RH)''''(I-RH)   27. (I-RH)''''(HP)   28. (I-RH)''''(I-KH)

Two Tech Combo #8 Left-Jab, Right-Front Straight Punch (FSP)

All of the proceeding combinations began with the lead (front) hand. We can also "lead" or begin a combination using the second, or "back" fist under the chin.

    R   *R*   *R*   *R*   *R*   *L*
1. (FSP)'''(BF)   **2**. (FSP)'''''(I-RH)   **3**. (FSP)''''(HP)

    R   *R*   *R*   *R*   *R*   *L*
4. (FSP)'''(O-RH)   **5**. (I-RH)'''(BF)   **6**. (HP)''''(HP)

Three Technique Combinations (Notice * = back hand lead)

    L   *L*   *R*   *L*   *L*   *R*   *L*   *R*   *L*
1. (BF)'''(BF)'''(FSP)   **2**. (BF)'''(BF)'''(I-RH)   **3**. (BF)'''(FSP)''''(UPC)

    L   *R*   *L*   *L*   *R*   *L*   *L*   *L*   *R*
4. (BF)'''(I-RH)''''(I-RH) **5**. (BF)'''(FSP)''''(HP)   **6**. (BF)'''(JAB)'''(FSP)

    L   *L*   *R*   *L*   *R*   *L*   *L*   *R*   *L*
7. (JAB)'''(JAB)''''(FSP) **8**. (JAB)'''(FSP)''''(I-RH) **9**. (JAB)'''(HF)''''(UPC)

          L   *L*   *R*   **R*   *L*   *R*   *L*   *R*   *L*
10. (JAB)'''(BF)'''(HP)   **11** (I-KH)''''(I-RH)''''(HP)   **12**. (JAB)'''(FSP)'''(HP)

Three Tech Combo #5 Left-BackFist, Right-Front Straight Punch, Left-Hook

Three Tech Combo #10   Left-Jab, Left-BackFist, Right-Hook

Three Tech Combo #12   Left-Jab, Right-Front Straight Punch, Left-Hook

Four Technique Combinations (Notice * = back hand lead)

$$\quad\quad L \quad\quad L \quad\quad R \quad\quad L$$
1. (BF)'''(BF)'''(I-RH)''''(I-RH)

$$\quad\quad L \quad\quad L \quad\quad R \quad\quad L$$
2. (BF)'''(0-KH)'''(FSP)''''(I-RH)

$$\quad\quad L \quad\quad R \quad\quad L \quad\quad R$$
3. (BF)'''(FSP)''''(HP)''''(HP)

$$\quad\quad L \quad\quad R \quad\quad R \quad\quad L$$
4. (JAB)'''(HF)'''(BF)'''(HP)

Four Tech Combo #3   Left-BackFist, Right-Front Straight Punch, Left-Hook, Right-Hook

      L   L   R   R   *L   R   L   R*

5. (JAB)'''(BF)'''(I-RH)''''(BF)   **6**. (JAB)'''(FSP)''''(HP)''''(HP)

      L   R   R   L   *L   R   L   R*

7. (O-KH)''''(I-RH)''''(BF)'''(I-RH)   **8**. (I-RH)''''(FSP)''''(HP)''''(I-RH)

      L   R   L   R   *R   R   L   R*

9. (O-KH)'''(I-KH)''''(I-RH)'''(HF)   **1O**. (FSP)'''(BF)'''(HP)''''(I-KH)

Elbow Striking Techniques

    Elbow strikes can be devastating. When executed with speed and control, they deliver tremendous power on contact. They are excellent for "close quarters", or "in" fighting, and they are extremely difficult to block. The secret to them is short, rapid snapping motions from the shoulder coupled with body rotation. We will use three elbow techniques on the bag. The name of the elbow strike techniques describe the direction of the elbow movement. (Since I have describe numerous elbow striking techniques in this book, I will use the same names for consistency.)

Outward-Single Elbow Strike (O-SES)

    The Outward-Single Elbow Strike is abbreviated (**O-SES**). We bring the fist of the elbow striking arm under the opposite ear during the set-up and direct the elbow "outward" from the body, bringing the upper arm point of the elbow into the bag. **[Fig 12J-1]**. If executed from a normal fighting stance it is much easier to complete with the lead arm. If you use the rear arm (usually near the chin), there is a greater degree of torso rotation but it follows a Front Straight Punch very naturally.

FIG 12J-1 Outward-Single Elbow Strike

Inward-Single Elbow Strike (I-SES)

    In this technique the elbow will move "in" toward the chest, striking the bag with the forearm point of the elbow. The power comes from the shoulder motion and hip rotation. We can do this technique with either arm, but it is more commonly used by the "rear" arm.

The Inward-Single Elbow Strike is abbreviated as **(I-SES.)** The technique is demonstrated by the rear arm in **[Fig 12J-2a]**. As the point of the elbow is thrust into the bag, we must rotate from the waist. This body rotation leaves us in a slightly awkward position very close to the bag. And it is difficult to recover smoothly within three rebounds.

FIG 12J-2a **Inward-Single Elbow Strike**
Back Arm (Right)

FIG 12J-2b **Inward-Single Elbow Strike**
Lead Arm (Left)

The Inward-Single Elbow Strike can also be executed by the lead arm **[Fig 12J-2b]**. There is not as much distance for the elbow to travel, so the swinging action is more of a "winging" forward thrust with the elbow. If you are proficient at the Hook Punch, then use the same hip thrust and body turn. With practice, this is a very powerful technique which can be devastating in close (a foot or two away-where there is no room to jab or punch.)

Downward-Single Elbow Strike (D-SES)

In the Downward-Single Elbow Strike, abbreviated **(D-SES)**, the elbow moves into the bag in a downward motion. The key to this is the set-up, which brings the arm up into a position much like throwing a baseball. As shown in **[Fig 12J-3]**, the right arm is brought up into position and then the elbow is brought down into the bag. Care must be used to avoid having the fist hit the board. You can avoid this by raising the board higher or by keeping the elbow flexed, leaving the forearm resting very close to the upper arm. *Take off your eyeglasses when doing Downward Elbow techniques. The fist comes dangerously close to the frames.*

FIG 12J-3 Downward-Single Elbow Strike

ELBOW STRIKING PRACTICE COMBINATIONS

There are many possible combinations using the elbow strikes. Before using them with the fist techniques, Let's practice each one by itself, and then with each other...(note the number of rebounds.) You may want to adjust or reverse your stance to change the leading arm. (* notice back arm lead)

     L   *L*   *L*
1. (O-SES)'''(O-SES)'''(O-SES)

          R   *R*   *R*
2. (I-SES)'''(I-SES)'''(I-SES)

     R   *R*   *R*
3. (D-SES)'''''(D-SES)'''''(D-SES)

          L   *L*   *R*
4. (O-SES)'''(O-SES)'''(I-SES)

     L   *R*   *R*
5. (O-SES)'''(I-SES)'''(O-SES)

          L   *R*   *R*
6. (O-SES)'''(D-SES)'''(O-SES)

    *R   *R*   *L*
7. (I-SES)'''''(O-SES)'''''(I-SES)

        *R   *R*   *L*
8. (I-SES)'''(O-SES)'''(D-SES)

Elbows only Combo #7   Right-(I-SES) , Right-(O-SES) , Left-(I-SES)

Two Technique Combinations of Fists and Elbows (Notice * = BACK HAND LEAD)

    L   *L*   *L*   *R*   *L*   *L*   *L*   *R*
1. (BF)'''(I-SES)   2. (BF)'''(D-SES)   3. (BF)'''(O-SES)   4. (JAB)'''(I-SES)

Fist-Elbow Two Tech. Combo #1 L-(Bf), L-(I-SES)

     L   *L*   *L*   *R*   *L*   *R*   *L*   *R*

5. (JAB)'''(O-SES)   **6**. (JAB)'''(D-SES) **7**. (O-KH)'''(I-SES)   **8**. (O-KH)'''(D-SES)

     L   *R*   *L*   *R*   *L*   *L*   *R*   *R*

9. (I-RH)''''(I-SES)   **10**. (I-RH)''''(D-SES) **11**. (I-RH)''''(O-SES) **12**. (FSP)'''(O-SES)

Fist-Elbow Two Tech. Combo #4 L-(Jab), R-(I-SES)

Fist-Elbow Two Tech. Combo #5   L-(Jab), L-(O-SES)

Three Technique Combinations of Fists and Elbows (Notice * = BACK HAND LEAD)

	L	R	R
1.	(BF)'''(FSP)	'''(O-SES)	

	L	R	R
2.	(BF)'''(HP)	''''(O-SES)	

	L	R	R
3.	(BF)'''(D-SES)	'''(O-SES)	

	L	R	R
4.	(BF)'''(I-SES)	'''(O-SES)	

	L	L	R
5.	(BF)'''(O-SES)	'''(I-SES)	

	L	L	R
6.	(BF)'''(O-SES)	'''(I-RH)	

Fist-Elbow Three Tech. Combo #5   L-(BF), L-(O-SES), R-(I-SES)

Fist-Elbow Three Tech. Combo #6   L-(BF), L-(O-SES), R-(I-RH)

    L   *R*   *R*   *L*   *L*   *R*   *L*   *L*   *R*

7. (JAB)'''(I-SES)'''(O-SES)   **8**. (JAB)'''(O-SES)'''(D-SES)   **9**. (JAB)'''(O-SES)'''(HF)

    *R   *R*   *L*   **R*   *L*   *R*   *L*   *L*   *R*

10 (FSP)'''(O-SES)'''(I-SES)   **11** (FSP)''''(I-RH)''''(I-SES)   **12** (I-RH)''''(0-SES)'''(HP)

Four Technique Combinations of Fists and Elbows (Notice * = BACK HAND LEAD)

    L   *L*   *R*   *R*   *L*   *L*   *R*   *R*   *L*

1. (BF)'''(FSP)'''(O-SES)'''(I-SES)   **2**. (BF)'''(HP)''''(O-RH)'''(I-SES)

    L   *L*   *R*   *R*   *L*   *R*   *R*   *L*

3. (BF)'''(O-SES)''''(FSP)'''(0-SES)   **4**. (O-SES)'''(I-RH)''''(BF)'''(I-SES)

    L   *R*   *R*   *L*   **R*   *R*   *L*   *L*

5. (JAB)'''(D-SES)'''(O-SES)'''(I-SES)   **6**. (FSP)'''(O-SES)'''(JAB)'''(O-SES)

    *R   *R*   *L*   *L*   *L*   *L*   *R*   *R*

7. (I-SES)'''(BF)'''(D-SES)'''(O-SES)   **8**. (I-SES)'''(O-SES)'''(I-KH)''''(O-SES)

    These are just a few combinations we can put together with fists and elbows. Emphasize control first, then speed. Concentrate on the body rotation needed, angles of attack, and be sure to use correct hand positions for ridge-hand and knife-hand strikes. Practice these written combinations and then make up your own. Use all the techniques and change your stance. With time, I guarantee your "in" (close quarters) fighting will become a non-stop flow of controlled attacks.

SPINNING FIST TECHNIQUES

Spinning Fist techniques are not truly *separate* techniques, but techniques that are executed at the end of a body spin. The keys are timing the spin and judging the distance. Spinning techniques generate a tremendous amount of power due to the torque of the body spinning around and the added distance the fist travels. There are several ways to "spin" before a technique. One way is by taking a forward (advancing) step with the back leg as you spin. This method closes the distance between you and the target. Judging the stepping distance is crucial. Another way to spin is twisting only from the waist by a quick torso rotation. This method does not "step in" and close the distance so it is easier for distance judgement. The speed bag is great for practicing both methods.

Besides the need to judge the distance, spinning techniques quickly emphasize how much we use our eyes in hitting the bag. Even though we can use the number of rebounds to tell when to punch, our eyes are tracking the bag and we see the angles of rebound. The lose of visual contact with the bag, even for an instant, disrupts this information. Even if you spin very quickly, and snap the head around to spot the bag, there is not enough time to gauge the angle of rebound. This will magnify the slight differences of exact fist contact on the bag. For example, a Backfist may hit the front, front-side, or side of the bag. The rebounding angles of the bag are very different for these points of contact. Normally, we can see this and compensate by making slight adjustments in the next technique, but when spinning we lose this ability. There is very little control of where the fist hits the bag after a spin but most of the time the fist enters from the front-side, or directly from the side. We must hope that the rebounding angle of the *previous technique* was correct.

Also, many times a spinning technique seems to work equally well after an even or odd number of rebounds. This is due to the exact moment of fist contact on the bag, as well as the rebounding angle. Regardless of the angle of rebound, there is always a point when the bag is pointing straight up and down. If your fist hits at that moment, it does not matter from what angle it got there. The bag is straight and ready to be hit from any direction. This seems to happen a lot with spinning techniques...(kicking also.)

Spinning Backfist

A "Spinning Backfist" is nothing more than a Backfist executed at the end of a spin. We can use the Knife-hand, Ridge-Hand and Elbow strikes from a spin, but the Backfist is probably the most common spinning technique. Let's begin with the *Step and Spin Backfist*, abbreviated (**SS-BF**) and shown in **[FIG 12K-1]**. Some people call this a "180° spinning backfist" or "turning backfist". It begins from a normal fighting stance, left leg and arm forward. Notice how the turn is "clockwise". If the right leg and fist were forward, the spin would be counter-clockwise. (The best way to remember which way to spin is to bring your rear leg around to the front by turning your back to the bag.) As we spin and step, the right fist uncoils from its position by the chin and extends out, striking the bag as the right shoulder comes directly in line with it. The fist strikes more from the side of the bag. This is an extremely powerful technique and when it is done with any speed, the bag will rebound so fast that it is difficult to get the fist out of the way. You must retract it quickly.

FIG 12K-1 Step & Spin Backfist

To practice this technique, first we have to measure the distance for the spinning-step movement. This is the trickiest part. Experienced "spinners' will have no problem, but for those new to spinning, here is a simple way. Do [Fig 12K-1] backwards, or from right to left. Assume the *finishing position* (left leg forward and left arm extended with the back of the fist on the side of the bag.) Imagine a straight line on the floor going from your front foot, through your back foot and extending several feet behind you. Pivoting on the right foot, step clockwise {turning your back to the bag} with the left foot and place it on the imaginary line. You have actually rotated about 180° degrees. Your should now be the correct distance for your spin-step. To do the technique, simply retrace this motion. As you begin the spin, snap your head around to "spot" the target and help judge the range.

Since this technique covers so much distance, it is difficult to use it after a leading jab or regular Backfist. As the arm extends, the fist will usually go way past the bag and you'll hit your forearm or elbow. You adjust the distance by either reducing or enlarging the extension of the arm or the size of the step. With practice, you will gauge how far the step should be.

The practice exercises start from a left arm, left leg forward fighting stance. Many techniques can follow this one after it connects. Some examples are offered below. (**notice * = one hand combinations**)

     * R   R   R   L   R   L   R   L

1. (SS-BF)'''''(BF)   **2**. (SS-BF)'''''(I-RH)   **3**. (SS-BF)'''''(HP)   **4**. (SS-BF)'''''(FSP)

     * R   R   * R   R   R   L   R   L

5. (SS-BF)'''''(O-SES) **6**. (SS-BF)''''(I-RH)   **7**. (SS-BF)'''''(I-KH) **8**. (SS-BF)'''''(I-SES)

Even with minimal speed and power, the above combinations occur very quickly. That is why I used 5 rebounds. When you can do them with only three rebounds, you are smokin' !

Distance management is the key to this technique. If your spin-step is too big, you can adjust by using the Outward-Elbow Strike instead of the backfist. Just substitute **(SS-OSES)** for the backfist in the last examples. Another possibility is to follow with the next type of spinning backfist.

The *Waist-Spinning BackFist,* abbreviated **(WS-BF)**, is demonstrated in **[FIG 12K-2]**. Notice that only the upper body twists around from the waist. The feet do not move. As you spin, get the head around first to spot the target. This method works best when you are already in close to the target, but want the added power of the spin. This technique can follow numerous other leading techniques, as demonstrated in the next few exercises. The begin with a left arm, left leg fighting stance.

FIG 12K-2 Waist Spinning Backfist

     L   R   L   R   L   R   L   R
1. (Jab)'''(WS-BF)   **2**. (BF)''''(WS-BF)   **3**. (O-KH)''''(WS-BF)   **4**. (I-RH)'''(WS-BF)

The last four combinations finish in an awkward "cross-legged" stance. This is not a good position to be in. One solution is to quickly spin (rotate) back into the normal fighting stance, or…another Waist-Spinning Backfist with the other hand.

     L   R   L   L   R   L   L   R   L
5. (Jab)'''(WS-BF)''''(WS-BF) **6**. (HP)'''(WS-BF)''''(WS-BF) **7**. (BF)''''(WS-BF)''''(WS-BF)

In the above examples, the second (WS-BF) could be changed to several different techniques, such as an Outward-Elbow Strike, Outward-Knife Hand or Outward-Ridge Hand.

WS-BF Two Tech. Combo #2   L-(BF), R-(WS-BF)....then step back into stance

There are many different combinations available off of these spinning techniques. Add them in with the one, two, three and four punch and elbow combination exercises. The Waist-Spin method will probably work better. Focus on distance and control. Speed will come later.

Another WS-BF Combo   R-(WS-BF), L-(WS-BF)

FIG 12K-3a Retreating Backfist - Spin (turn) Back

Retreating Backfist

The two previous Spinning Backfists moved us "toward" the bag. We can also use a "retreating spin" away from the target. Assume the normal fighting stance fairly close to the bag. To retreat-spin, step clock wise with the front (left) leg (turning your back to the bag, but moving away-not toward it.) As you spin-step, [or turn] back, get your head around to spot the target. Your right fist will snap out with a Backfist as you complet the motion and right shoulder comes in line with the bag **[FIG 12K-3a]**, above.

FIG 12K-3b Retreating Backfist - Stepping Back

We can also retreat by *stepping* back counter-clockwise with the front (left) leg **[FIG 12k-3b]**. It is not so much a "spin" as it is stepping back. Better yet, we do not turn our back to the bag (or opponent.) Swivel on the right foot, and step back with the left leg. As your right shoulder comes in line with the bag, snap out a quick Backfist with the right hand. As you retract the right fist, you can follow this by stepping in with the right leg and throwing an Outward-Single Elbow Strike after three (or five) rebounds. Numerous other techniques can be used in this combination.

KICKING

A speed bag is a terrific tool for practicing several kicking techniques of the martial arts. They are not necessary advertised as a kicking target, but I have found it is a great replacement to needing a partner to stand and hold a focus mitt. It's also great for working out by yourself at home. Most non-martial artists don't think about kicking the bag, and it usually rubs boxers the wrong way. The power generated by the kicks far surpasses the fists and elbows, but I have never seen a bag "blow" from a kick

---

This section is offered for experience martial arts students. It is not intended for a general fitness workout. Poor kicking technique can cause injuries such as pulled muscles in the hips or legs. Particularly if you are not flexible enough to kick comfortably at face level. Please seek certified instruction in these techniques before attempting these kicks. ☯

SAFETY FIRST

Kicking a speed bag brings up equipment and safety issues. Contacting the bag with your foot does not hurt…but contacting the board does, and can cause serious injury to the foot. This is especially true with crescent kicks that make contact with an upright foot position, or hook kicks that have a downward snap rather than parallel.

I highly recommend you extend the distance between the board and your foot by doing one of several things. First, use a larger, longer bag, (10" x 13".) This lowers the target (belly of the bag) from the board. Second, by adding an "S" hook into the swivel connection **[FIG 12L]**. With proper precaution the Roundhouse, Hook and Crescent Kicks can all be practiced effectively.

FIG 12L "S" hook in Swivel

The kicking practice exercises offered are only the *basics* to familiarize you with potential of speed bag training. There are advanced methods for each kick, such as jumping or 360° spinning, but these are not developed here. The advanced martial artist can easily adapt the bag to those techniques.

Again, If you do not know the difference between these kicks and the proper body positions to do them, please do not attempt the following pictures or practice exercises.

ROUNDHOUSE KICK

FIG 12M-1 Front Leg Roundhouse Kick

The Roundhouse Kick, (or Round Kick) is one of the fastest and most often used kicks. It can be thrown by either the front leg, abbreviated **(FL-RHK)** or the back leg, abbreviated **(BL-RHK.)** We need to adjust the distance from the bag depending on which leg we will use.

Let's begin with the Front Leg Roundhouse Kick **[FIG 12M-1]** from the standard fighting stance of the left leg and arm forward. (Fig 12M-1 shows the right leg forward for a better view.) After each exercise, reverse the stance and repeat the combinations. (Remember, individual differences in the angles of the foot or fist entering into the bag may change the number of rebounds between techniques.)

Several *front leg* Roundhouse Kick practice exercise include:

    L   *L*   *L*
1. (FL-RHK)''''(FL-RHK)''''(FL-RHK) The key to this is a fast retraction of the foot. (If the bag rebounds into your foot, think of it as being grabbed.) It is harder than you might think because the bag is really moving. This retraction is needed in all the combinations.

    L   *L*   *L*   *L*
2. (FL-RHK)''''(BF)''''(FL-RHK)''''(BF) The front leg will extend further than the front fist. You may have to lean in for the Backfist (BF) because when you are distanced properly to land the foot on the bag the fist is almost too far away.

    L   *R*   *L*   *R*
3. (FL-RHK)''''(FSP)''''(FL-RHK)''''(FSP) The foot and fist enter on opposite sides

    L   *L* *R*   *L*
4. (FL-RHK)''''(BF)'''(FSP)''''(FL-RHK)

You can vary these by substituting other hand techniques or elbow strikes. One flowing combination I really like to do is:

L $\qquad$ L $\qquad$ L $\qquad$ L

5. (FL-RHK)''''(O-SES)'''(BF)''''(FL-RHK) After the first FL-RHK, you will lean in for the elbow strike. Then start leaning back for the BF, and keep going back into your chamber for the final kick.

It is almost impossible to add a back leg Roundhouse Kick into these combinations because by the time we chamber the knee into position, the foot would extend well past the bag. We must adjust the distance, moving several feet back. An easy to find the correct distance is to use the desired leg for a FL-RHK, then step back with it 180°, making it the rear, or back leg. (As an example, use the right foot in the *front* position and find the comfortable range for a Front Leg Roundhouse Kick. Now just step back with it (clockwise 180°) until it is the *back* leg. (Actually, you may need to scoot back a little more than this, because the act of kicking seems to extend the kick a little further as the base foot swivels.) We are now out of range for most hand techniques (except spinning.)

The Back Leg Roundhouse Kick **(BL-RHK)** is demonstrated in **[FIG 12M-2]**. Several practice exercises are given next.

R $\qquad$ R

6. (BL-RHK)'''''(FL-RHK) In this combination, the right leg is back and we execute the Roundhouse. Because of the body turning with the kick, it becomes the front leg. Holding it in the chamber after a speedy retraction, kick again with the same leg. Work this up to 10 or more repetitive kicks.

R $\qquad$ L

7. (BL-RHK)''''''(BL-RHK) In this combination, the right leg kicks from the back position then lands in front. Hold that stance and adjust the distance for the left leg to kick from the back position. *The secret to this is knowing how far back to adjust.* If you put your *front leg* (now the right) just a little further back than your *back leg's* (now the left) position, you will be just about right. The six rebounds shown allows time for this adjustment.

FIG 12M-2 Back Leg Roundhouse Kick

R $\qquad$ R

8. (BL-RHK)''''(BF) This is exactly the same as exercise #2. The only difference is the origination of the kick from the rear position. Once the body has turned and the kick lands, than any fist technique can be used that follows a front leg Roundhouse Kick.

R $\qquad$ R $\qquad$ L

9. (BL-RHK)''''(BF)'''(WS-BF) This combination takes a little concentration, because there is a lot of body movement. We chamber the leg and turn counter-clock wise for the back leg round kick, than land and spin counter clockwise from the waist for the spinning backfist. You may need five rebounds between the backfists, and the angles of entry may change the rebounds to an even number (four or six.)

These are just a few of the possible kicking combinations possible with the Roundhouse Kick. Most martial artists have several "favorite" combinations. Try and develop them on the bag.

Hook Kick

The Hook Kick (sometimes called a Heel Kick) has several modes of delivery. Either by the lead (front) leg or the rear (back) leg. We can also hook with the back leg by spinning 180°. All can be practiced effectively on the speed bag.

> Extra caution is needed if your hook kick snaps in a downward angle rather than parallel. You do not want to get your foot above or even with the rebound board where the downward angle can snap your heel into the board. Raise the board and use a larger bag.

FIG 12N-1 Front Leg Hook Kick

The Front Leg Hook Kick, abbreviated **(FL-HK)** usually enters from the rear-side of the bag **[FIG 12N-1].** Again, we need to adjust the distance to execute the kick. From the fighting stance, left leg and arm forward, here are a few practice combinations.

      L   *L*   *L*
1. (FL-HK)'''''(FL-HK)'''''(FL-HK) This combination is almost impossible to do on three rebounds because of the power generated and the time needed to re-chamber, extend and kick again.

$$\quad\;\; L \qquad\quad L \qquad\quad L$$
2. (FL-HK)''''' (BF) or (O-KH)

$$\quad\;\; L \qquad\quad R \qquad\quad R$$
3. (FL-HK)''''' (FSP) or (I-RH)

$$\quad\;\; L \qquad\qquad L$$
4. (FL-HK)'''' (FL-RHK)   This exercise is one of the most beautiful and efficient double kick combinations on the bag (or in sparring for that matter.) The snapping retraction of the Hook Kick brings it into perfect chamber position for the Roundhouse Kick. **Anyone who has seen Bill "super foot" Wallace fight has marveled at this combination, as many of his opponents will testify.** (Many years ago, at Memphis State University…now the University of Memphis…he would do this on the speed bag.) This combination can also be reversed as seen in the next exercise.

$$\quad\;\; L \qquad\qquad L$$
5. (FL-RHK)'''' (FL-HK)   The secret to this combination is quick re-chamber after the roundhouse kick. Also, be careful as you extend for the Hook Kick, otherwise the foot may hit the rebounding bag.

FIG 12N-2 Back Leg Hook Kick

Back Leg Hook Kicks can be done several ways, either by moving forward into a front chamber or by spinning backward 180°. We will address the spinning hook kick in a later section. Here we will focus on moving forward into a front chamber (sidekick) position with the rear leg **[FIG 12N-2]**. I abbreviate this **(BL-HK.)** It requires the body to turn and chamber the kick, so more distance is needed. A few practice examples are offered

     R   *R*

6. (BL-HK)''''(FL-HK)   This combination begins with the right leg back. After the first Hook Kick is executed, it lands and is now the front leg. Care must be taken not to allow the snap of the hooking leg to pull it back out of position. The bag helps build this control. Notice it is a **one leg** combination.

    Once the back leg has performed the Hook Kick, exercises #2 and #3 and #4 can be used as long as the hooking leg lands in front.

    The next three practice combinations will have the back leg Kicking and returning to the back, or rear, position. We will then follow with another kick. One key to controlling distance in these combinations is by adjusting the placement of the rear foot after the first kick is executed

     R   *R*

7. (BL-HK)'''''(BL-RHK)   In this combination, the back leg (right) performs a Hook Kick and returns to the rear position. Notice this is written with six rebounds because of the time needed to return the right foot to the rear but they enter from different sides of the speed bag. Notice it is also a **one leg** combination.

     R   *L*

8. (BL-HK)'''''(FL-RHK)   This is another combination where the back leg kicks and returns to the rear position. But now the front leg (left) performs the Roundhouse Kick. In this combination, both kicks enter from the same side, so the number of rebounds between is an odd number (5). One way to control distance in combinations like #7 & #8 is by adjusting the placement of the rear foot after the first kick is executed. Another example is given below.

     R   *L*

9. (BL-RHK)'''''(FL-HK)   Once again the rear leg kicks and return behind. Let the lead leg (left) pull up in the chamber as the right lands. Notice the front leg (left) connects from the *same* side.

Spinning Hook Kick

    The Back Spinning Hook Kick, is demonstrated in **[FIG 12P-3]** and is abbreviated **(S-HK).** Exercises here only address the 180° spin (and not the more advanced 360° spin), so we will always be executing this kick with the back leg. This is one of the most powerful kicks and the force of the spin can easily return the leg to the rear position again. Again, we will start from the normal fighting stance, left leg forward.

     R *R*   *R*

10. (S-HK)''''(S-HK)'''''(S-HK)   There is no time to waste during this combination. As soon as the right foot touches the ground you will have to spin again. This combination helps develop a controlled spin. Creeping forward with the spin may have the bag hitting near the calf instead of the heel. Targeting and spin control are vital.

FIG 12N-3 Spinning Hook Kick

> R   R

11. (S-HK)'''''(BL-RHK)   Again the rear leg returns to the back and performs the Roundhouse Kick. You may have to adjust your distance back slightly for the Roundhouse.

> L   R

12. (FL-RHK)'''''(S-HK)   Here we have the front leg (left) doing a Roundhouse Kick followed by a spinning hook. You will have to adjust your distance after the first kick by sliding back slightly.

> R   R

13. (S-HK)'''''(FL-RHK)   This is probably one of the most advanced combinations offered. It is almost exactly like exercise #4, except it takes tremendous body control throughout the spinning movement. As you spin clock-wise, you must spot the target, execute the hook kick and stop the spin. After the Hook Kick, do not allow the body to complete the turn and *do not land the leg in front*. Keep the right leg chambered up and execute the Roundhouse Kick.

This last exercise will combine a spinning Hook with a Waist-Spin Backfist. It will take some distance management. You will also be going around twice. Be careful you don't get dizzy!

> R   R

14. (S-HK)'''''(WS-BF)   Here we spin, kick and land behind. Begin the waist spin as soon as the right leg returns to its rear position. Try to time this so there is no jerking inbetween.

CRESCENT KICKS

There are several types of crescent kicks, including the Outward-Crescent Kick, and the Inward-Crescent Kick. Both can be performed by either the front or back leg. They can also be done with spins, so they offer tremendous variety. We will focus on the most common and easiest crescent kicks.

> *Crescent Kicks are the most dangerous kicks on a speed bag because of the upright foot position passing under the board. Do not attempt these techniques without proper guidance and instruction.*

Outward-Crescent Kick

This kick can be done with the front leg or back leg. A front leg Outward-Crescent Kick is abbreviated **(FL-OCK)** and demonstrated in **[FIG 12o-1]**. We will start from the normal fighting stance, left leg and left arm forward. You may have to adjust the distance. Several practice exercises include:

FIG 12o-1 Front Leg Outward Crescent Kick

1. (FL-OCK)''''''(BF) Here the front leg crescent kick lands in the front and is followed by a left Backfist. Since they both hit the from the same side, an odd number (five) of rebounds is used. These two can also be performed in the reverse order.

L   R

2. (FL-OCK)''''(I-RH)   Again the left leg lands in front and is followed from the same side by the Inward-Ridge Hand after three or five rebounds.

L   R

3. (FL-OCK)''''(FL-OCK)   In this combination the front leg (left) performs the Outward-Crescent Kick and lands behind. Let your body turn with the force of the kick to reverse your stance, which puts your right leg in front. You may need to adjust your distance toward the bag for the second kick.

L   L

4. (FL-OCK)''''(BL-RHK)   In this combination, the front leg kicks and lands behind. The left leg then executes the Roundhouse Kick. Adjust your distance back for the second kick.

    The Outward-Crescent Kick performed by the back leg, is abbreviated **(BL-OCK)** and shown in **[FIG 12o-2]**. The only difference between this kick and the Front Leg Outward-Crescent Kick is from the stance to the chamber. When we chamber the rear leg up to the front, we tend to move forward and close the distance. We do not advance forward as much when we pull the front leg up into a chamber.

FIG 12o-2 Back Leg Outward-Crescent Kick

R   L

5. (BL-OCK)''''(FL-RHK)   In this sequence, the back leg (right) leads with an Outward-Crescent Kick and lands behind. The left leg then does a Roundhouse Kick. You may need to adjust your distance back for the second kick.

R   *R*

6. (BL-OCK)''''''(WS-BF) Here the back (right) leg does an Outward-Crescent Kick and lands behind. The body motion of landing behind initiates the turn of the waist-spin. Distance judgement for the Backfist is a key for this. You may have to extend the arm out all the way, or bend the elbow (if the bag is closer to the body.)

Inward-Crescent Kick

This kick can be done with either the front or back leg, but we will concentrate on the back leg, as shown in **[FIG 12o-3]**. It is abbreviated **(BL-ICK)**. We will start from the normal fighting stance, left leg and left arm forward.

Several practice exercises include:

R   *L*

1. (BL-ICK)''''''(BF) Here the back leg crescent kick is performed and returns to the back position. Then, follow with a left backfist. Since they both hit the from the same side, an odd number (five) of rebounds is used. They can also be performed in the reverse order.

R   *R*

2. (BL-ICK)''''''(I-RH) Again the left leg returns to the rear and is followed from the same side by the inside ridge hand after three or five rebounds.

R   *R*

3. (BL-ICK)''''''(BL-OCK) In this combination the back leg (right) performs the Inward-Crescent Kick and lands behind. You may need to adjust your distance for the second kick.

FIG 12o-3 Back Leg Inward-Crescent Kick

4. (BL-ICK)''''(FL-RHK) In this combination, the rear leg (right) kicks and lands behind. The left leg then executes the Roundhouse Kick. You may need to adjust your distance back for the second kick.

5. (FL-HK)'''''(BL-ICK) In this sequence, the front (left) leg does a hook kick, and lands front. Adjust your distance and let the back leg (Right) follow with the Inward-Crescent Kick. It requires an odd number of rebounds

6. (S-HK)''''(BL-ICK) Here we start with the back (right) leg performing a back spinning 180 Hook Kick and land behind. At that point, stop your body motion and follow with the Inward-Crescent Kick after four or six rebounds.

7. (FL-RHK)''''(BL-ICK) This is a very smooth combination. You can vary this by throwing two or three Roundhouse kicks before the Inward-Crescent Kick.

Spinning Outward-Crescent Kick

The Spinning Outward-Crescent Kick, abbreviated **(S-OCK)**, can also be performed by the back (rear) leg after a 180° backspin. It may also be called a "back spin crescent kick". From the normal fighting stance, with the left leg forward, turn back clockwise by swiveling on the front foot, (much like the spinning Hook Kick.) As the swivel-turn starts, chamber the rear leg (right), and snap it out in the Outward-Crescent Kick **[FIG 12o-4]**. It is an extremely powerful kick and slams the bag sideways.

This is one of the most dangerous techniques to practice on the speed bag because the back spin gives only an instant to sight the bag and commit to the kick or bail out. *Please **do not attempt** this technique*

FIG 12o-4 Spinning Outward-Crescent Kick

if you are not properly trained. The spin will close the distance between you and the bag, so judging this is vital. If your stance is too close, then the foot in the upright position, can hit the board.

Several practice combinations are given below

    R   *L*
1. (S-OCK)'''''(FL-RHK) After the spinning crescent, the right leg lands behind. Adjust back and follow with the Front Leg Roundhouse Kick, which enters from the same side.

    R   *R*
2. (S-OCK)'''''(BL-RHK) Here the right leg performs the Roundhouse Kick as soon as it lands behind.

All of the previous kicking exercises are guides to help you become familiar with kicking on the speed bag. With time you will develop you own variations and favorite combinations.

PRACTICE VARIATIONS

There a numerous ways to add variety to your training. Besides using the written hand and kicking exercises, hit "freestyle," using no set rhythm or number of rebounds. Have the bag swing slowly while you move; duck, bob and weave, as if sparring. Let the bag bounce from two to six times while picking your shots by sight more than sound. Do not pre-plan the order of techniques. Move around and execute by feel and position as you close in and move out. Flowing between kicking, hand techniques and elbow strikes creates excellent distance management. Vary the striking intensity from several quick repeating punches, to harder finishing straight punches or ridge hands. After a harder punch, use the extra rebounds to move back and fire a kick when the bag is in position. Also, use the boxing tips in the next section.

Board Breaking

The bag is excellent for practicing board breaking techniques, **[Fig 12P]**. Focus on a non-swinging bag and execute the technique all the way through the target area. This is great for beginners who need a more forgiving target than wood. Be sure and keep the fingers tight together.

  FIG 12P Inward Knife Hand "Breaking"

When used correctly, the speed bag can be a valuable training aid for the Martial Artist. It can help you develop targeting ability and hand speed, which is essential for *both* punching and blocking. It can develop increased power for "in" fighting. And it can also increase your combination ability. Regardless of your Martial Arts style - purposeful speed bag practice can improve all your techniques.

For the martial artist that really likes speed bag training, I would suggest learning some of the techniques covered in chapters 4-9, for continuous non-stop speed bag work. You might find the Front Double Punch and all the "double elbow strikes" can be useful techniques for close quarters

Boxing Workout Tips.

The speed bag is associated much more with Boxing than with karate, and it is considered a vital part of the daily boxing workout. There are some specifics for boxing that need to be addressed. *The following information was gathered in conjunction with Mr. Kenny Weldon, Internationally recognized boxing coach and trainer of young champions. He also has many fine boxing training programs available for those interested in serious boxing training. The author is very appreciative of his input and cooperation.*

Traditionally, when boxing "camps" were large outside facilities the speed bag was mounted above the center of a "ring" or platform. In this way, the fighter would punch while using his footwork to move *all around the bag*. The fighter never stood still or punched without footwork. This is an undesirable position, and boxing training emphasizes footwork. However, when training facilities moved inside and space was a premium, a speed bag "ring" was not possible,- and it was mounted on the wall, which eliminates half of the potential moving radius! This gave rise to the commonly seen modern practice of standing still while punching the bag, which is not relevant to actual "in-the-ring" boxing. Therefore, it is vital to the competitive boxer to **emphasize footwork** when hitting the speed bag. Once you learn punching skills and gain bag control, begin hitting the bag while using your normal slide-shuffle footwork.

Hanging on the wall, or floor stand, creates three (3) sides, or areas to move to (front, left and right). You can slide clockwise and counter-clockwise around the bag. Do this while constantly jabbing. Then add in a straight punch with the Jab. Move forward, then back. Slide left, then right; in and out. Mix it up, all the while hitting the speed bag from the front. This will feel strange at first, because your range and distance from the bag may be constantly changing. Practice "walk-overs" to another side of the bag, which is following your punch (usually lead arm/jab) and moving to a completely different side (or area) of the bag. Some people call this stepping through. Be sure and *not cross your feet or turn your back to the bag*. It will take some practice but this is a great way to learn to swivel quickly and re-position on the balls of you feet. To do this, you may have to let the bag rebound four or five times before punching again with either a jab or straight punch. When done correctly, it is similiar to a spin move in the ring. Practice it going left and right, as well as after a jab, a Straight Punch or a Hook. Once you are adept at this, you can step though to *any* side of the bag, *after any punch*, without stopping your punching rhythm. Regardless of the speed bag's position, there is a possible boxing punch to hit it.

Another important point for boxers is to emphasize and practice what you need *in the ring*. Many techniques for total speed bag mastery are illustrated in this book, but some are *not actually relevant*, (most double punches and reverse punches), *legal*, (all elbow striking) *or purposeful movements* (side single punch) in the actual boxing ring. Emphasize the Jab, (also Front Circle Punch which is like a flicking jab), the Front Straight Punch, the Hook and the Upper-cut. For variety, perhaps throw in a Front Double Punch and Front Fist Roll....but keep it basic to what you will use in the ring. Forget about fancy linking and passing the fists through to the back. Why? Because to pass the fist through successfully *the elbows must be raise up close to parallel, and this is disasterous position during a boxing match*! Your sides, and ribs are exposed to be hit. (I emphasize the high elbow position for speed bag fitness and creative expression,...and it is vital to pass the fists through the bag. But the bag does not try to hit back!) So, **for the competitive fighter, keep the elbows down** close to sides for protection. But be careful and not let your hands drop, for the lowered elbow position tends to allow your fists to drop and swing from the waist. Strive to keep your hands up.

Most trainers have their boxers use the speed bag as part of a training circuit, where each piece (heavy bag, rope jumping, shadow boxing etc.) is utilized for the length of time of their matches. This can vary from 1.5 - to - 3.0 minutes, depending on their age and skill level. If this is your training intent, then you may need a timer, or perhaps tape some music the exact length of your training interval (page 165).

Adjust the bag to different heights for variety. Utilize a larger, slower bag for punching power and stamina. Use the lighter, smaller bags for more speed. Remember the smaller bags need smaller punching movements to get your hands in position. Also, you do not have to punch at full power all of the time! Slow down, work your favorite combinations, such as "flicking" your Jabs, double hook punches, Uppercuts, etc. Many like to time their swing to *pin the bag* up against the board, so it does not rebound. Occassionally, throw a much harder punch and be ready for the bag to go much faster. React to this as you would a ring opponent...for he/she will most likely not be moving at a constant speed either.

Lastly, let the speed bag help you overcome your weak points. Work you weakest or worse techniques in high repetitions. Emphasize proper start position, footwork and body movement, pin-point targeting and correct follow through. Then set up and do it again, time after time. then add in your footwork, moving left and then right. Utilize your speed bag time to hone your ring skills.

Roger Hoover	Kenny Weldon	Alan Kahn
Referee	Boxing Trainer	Speed Bag Demo

National Silver Gloves Tournament, 1997   Kansas City

Chapter 13

Teaching the Speed Bag

One of my favorite activities is showing other people how to use a speed bag and I take teaching it very seriously. That is why I wrote this book. I really love to see people learn the "secrets" and discover how simple and enjoyable it can be. However, teaching can be very time consuming and not everyone wants to spend time "watching someone else" hit the bag. But as your own skills on the bag become more advanced get ready to hear….."how do you did that?" If you do not particularly care about teaching others, then please show them this book and let me teach them. But if you are a "coach" or trainer\consultant….or just a person who enjoys teaching others…then this chapter is for you. Regardless of your ability you can always show somebody what you know. And the only secret to helping others is having some basic knowledge about the bag, and *knowing what to look for*- how to spot and fix problems, when they are hitting. Having taught many people over the years, I have found the right and wrong way to do this. This chapter will describe some helpful hints and teaching guidelines.

Using the above example of "..how did you do that", most people will approach for one of several reasons. Either because you are using your elbows, doing machine gun fist rolls, or because you are hitting from behind the bag. When someone first approaches, find out how much experience they have on the bag. Most people will fit into one of three "levels". Those who are an absolute beginner with no experience on the bag, those of limited experience (…or are not very good at it yet) and those who are very skilled, showing excellent rhythm and timing. You can usually size this up pretty quickly by asking them if they have ever hit one. You will usually get one of three answers. One, "none whatsoever", two "a little…but I'm not very good" or three, "Yeah, I have hit it a while" or some other comment indicating they are fairly experienced. Let's say at this point they have no experience, so they are a beginner.

The Beginner with no experience

Everyone has to begin somewhere. Those with no experience do not have to "unlearn" improper swinging. There are no bad habits to break. Besides their limited exposure, beginners are particularly dependent on the equipment they *first* use. The most important thing for us, as their helper, is to be sure the equipment will not be a barrier to them. A good review of the equipment chapter is helpful, as well as hand protection. But I have found the single most important feature is the *height of the bag*. (A close second for importance is the size of the bag.) Because this is so important, I will spend a few lines to explain some of the problems learning on a speed bag set to an incorrect height for the individual.

A Bag set too high or too low will have terrible effects on the correct swinging motion . Each creates its own special problems, so let's examine them separately.

If the bag is set too high, **[FIG 13A]** then the belly of the bag will be up too high (…even at forehead level). In the correct stance the fist will hit too low on the bag or make a "glancing" blow. The bag will seem to slip off the fist, making a weak rebound. A person may adjust to this by raising the elbows up and making a higher circle. Or they may start swinging in an up and down motion from the shoulder, which I call "pawing the bag." Here they will hit the "top" of the fat part (belly) on the downswing, or hit the bottom of the bag on the upswing. Passing the fists from front to back on a bag that is too high is almost impossible. The fist may travel upward to the bag at such an angle that it will hit the bottom of the belly, and drive it up into the swivel. If correct contact is made at the front, then the fist is usually traveling "through the bag" in a upward (instead of straight) direction, and will be closer to the rebound board at the end of the swing (…when the arm is extended.) The bag will not have enough room to drop over the fist. Some people try to raise up on their tip toes to hit a bag that is too high, which makes balancing tough.

FIG 13A Bag too High

If the bag cannot be brought down any lower, then it is better to create a raised platform to stand on, as demonstrated in **[FIG 13B]**. Here a piece of plywood is laid on top of several 1x4's, but any type of platform would work as long as it is stable.

FIG 13B   Raised Platform

FIG 13C Bag too Low

When the bag is set too low **[FIG 13C]**, the belly may be at the bottom of the chin or throat level. To compensate, they will swing "down" onto the top part of the bag. This is a very awkward swing angle and they may hit the board with their fist. After a while, if the bag is much too low, they may try and squat down in an attempt to line up better…and the thigh muscles will complain severely. Again, linking from front to back is impossible because of the swing arc. The fist may hit too high on the bag (close to the lacing) and never make it through. Or, it will be lower at the end of the swing (arm extended) and as it returns, it will usually hit the bottom of the bag, driving it up into the swivel.

210

The best correction for all these problems is to get the bag to the correct height **[FIG 13D]** and eliminate learning to swing wrong. If the board does not adjust anymore, or there are no wrenches available, then you may be able to get the right level by changing bags. If the bag is too high, a larger bag will lower the belly by an inch or so. You can raise the belly by using a smaller bag, but this can also cause the next problem for beginners.

FIG 13D Correct Height

The second biggest problem most beginners face is using a bag that is too small. There is a point where the bag is too fast for a beginner to learn on. I have personally found this to be the 9"x 6".

This size (or smaller) takes such precise swing and fist control that it is very unforgiving and exasperates a beginner. It rebounds much too fast from a blow of "normal" force, to count the rebounds. Frustrated,they will try to swing faster, which guarantees they will hit harder....and the bag goes even faster! Soon they are totally frustrated.

If there is not a larger bag to use, a few secrets can help. First, let some air out of the bag (not much...Do not let the leather crease.) This makes the bag a little mushier, and slower. Also, the correct swing adaption is to make *smaller* fist movements, not faster one's. A smaller circle of movement can get the fist into the correct hitting position faster, without using more force. Remember....it is the *force* of the punch which adds speed to the bag. A beginner may not understand the theory behind this, but trust me...it works. Swinging in smaller movements with less force usually fixes all problems caused by a bag that is too fast.

Besides these equipment issues, we want to emphasize the most basic and simple skills with beginners. Start with the proper stance, (fist and elbow position) swinging movements (small circles) and Basic Rhythm (three bounces between each front technique). The Front Circle Punch is the easiest one to begin with. If you have to, stand behind them and hold your hands gently under their elbows to keep them up so they can "feel" the correct position   **[FIG 13E]**.

Front Straight Punch   **Front Circle Punch**   **Inward-Single Elbow Strike**

Fig 13E Supporting the Elbows

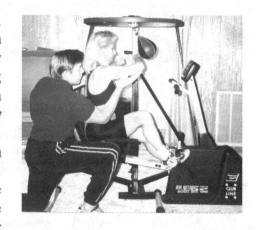

Emphasize SLOW swinging and hitting lightly, for many beginners will blast away much too hard. (Teach them to "count" the rhythm. Counting makes them slow down because it is impossible to do fast.) Get them going on the first few techniques. It is usually best to tell them how many "setup" techniques to do before trying the *new* technique. For example, if teaching the Front Fist Roll, have them perform three Front Circle Punches and then do the roll. Most people hesitate on new techniques, trying to anticipate when to throw it. Usually they will be late with the movement, or will do 15-20 repetitions while they stand there "anticipating." Giving a pre-set number of preliminary movements eliminates the guesswork for them. It also helps establish the rhythm and speed of the bag, but three reps does not let them race out of control.

Generally, beginners can handle the Basic Rhythm (Front Circle Punch and Front Straight Punch), Front Double Punch and Front Fist Roll in one session. Sometimes I will throw in the outward elbow techniques if that is what really fascinated them. More than three or four techniques in one lesson is usually a waste of time because there are so many combinations with each technique that they can not remember. After three or four techniques, with both fists leading, their shoulders usually give out.

Of course, some people want to try that "fancy stuff from behind the bag" or "hitting it with the elbows". Usually, I will demonstrate a couple "fancy" things and let them try it. Amazingly, many beginners will find these are not too difficult. This is because each *technique* is not really that difficult to do and it is *combinations* that are more challenging. (I do not like to teach elbow techniques first off, because they demand the proper stance with the fist and elbows up and most beginners can not maintain it. This can cause lots of "break downs", and loss of eventually lack of confidence.)

But a beginner may pick up really fast. Occasionally I will find a gifted person who can pick up much more than just two or three techniques. These folks are challenging because they learn so fast, and it is very rewarding too see them quickly get so much better.

It may boggle the mind of a beginner to consider 24 techniques to learn. Make it easier by explaining there are *only seven (7) speed bag swinging movements*. They are: 1. Front Circle Punch, 2-Front Straight Punch, 3-Reverse Single Punch, 4-Hook Punch, 5-Outward Elbow, 6-Inward Elbow, and 7-Downward Elbow Strike. Everything else is just adding these seven movements together. (The Side Single Punch is nothing more than a variation of the Reverse Single Punch with the elbow position moved back. The circling arm motion is the same. A technique like the Outward-Triple Elbow Strike joins the Outward elbow motion and the Front Straight Punch motion. All the techniques work like this.
Also, try the optional beginner *four-step work-out program* on page 32. It is much easier for some folks.

PEOPLE WITH SOME EXPERIENCE

The main difference between "some experience" and "beginner" is usually the bad habits learned through experience. They can vary widely in their skill levels. Ask them to hit the bag a little. Do this to see their swing motion and basic arm position. (Universally it is poor...half moon swinging, low fists, elbows down). You also want to get a feel for their timing. People who have used a bag before usually have some "feel" for the triplet rhythm. They can do several techniques and combinations but they may lack control. The rhythm gets faster and faster, (because they are swinging harder and harder). When they finally run out of control, they are blasting away. Often, after three strikes.....they're out!

This demo quickly tells you their ability. If they can barely keep the bag going in a triplet cadence (all front techniques), and do not keep a fairly constant rhythm…you are probably wasting your time to teach them complex linking combinations. Go back to the basics.

It does not matter how many different techniques they can do. If they can keep a good controlled rhythm, begin teaching them a few techniques and watch them practice to gain control by leading with both the right and left fist. It is important to stress a variety of combinations. When they can do the seven "beginning" techniques from the front, then get them to explore going from every reverse technique to every front technique. This adds a lot of variety and begins planting the seed of creating many more combinations than they might do otherwise.

As you teach, it is best to use a logical pattern of technique development. This book presented all the techniques in a precise order, which allows every movement (technique) to be understood through the practices exercises. Every technique is a preliminary setup for the next technique. That is why the Outward-Single Elbow strike leads to the Outward-Double and then the Outward-Triple Elbow strike. That is why we learned all the Double-Elbow Strikes as a preliminary to the 4way Elbow Strikes. You do not have to re-invent the wheel. Use the practice exercises written in this book. They work for anybody.

TEACHING ADVANCED PRACTITIONERS

Once in a while a person will show up who is amazingly good on the bag. You can tell by the "sound and rhythm" that they are gifted. They can hit powerfully for long periods of time at a constant, controlled speed. They may use their elbows and appear to be very relaxed when hitting. They can pick up everything you show them and quickly add it to their routine.

I have found people like this "by accident"…sometimes even a beginner with little or no experience, who just seems to absorb everything they see. Almost everyone can learn the physical techniques and hit the bag adequately, but not everyone "feels" the beat. Every advanced practitioner I have met hits and learns by the "sound and rhythm" of the bag. (Drummers do this very well. They "feel" a rhythm and reproduce it.) Also, they have the discipline to practice. Not every technique or combination is easy for them but they will practice until they get it. The key for these folks is challenging them with new rhythms and combinations. Emphasize multiple linking combinations and all the areas covered in the chapter of advanced combinations. My personal favorite teaching tool is "echoing", because it creates total fist control and understanding of how the bag works. The more you (the teacher) can understand about how rhythm and the bag work, the better you can teach it. And, the more creative expression and enjoyment they get in their workout.

More General Teaching Tips for Everyone

1. Anyone of any age or sex can learn to hit a speed bag. It only demands knowledge and practice. I have taught many women and young teenagers to make a speed bag stand up and walk. There is nothing inherently "male" about using a speed bag, anymore that there is about riding a bicycle.

2. Emphasize BASICS….Bag height, stance, elbow position and swinging motions. **The single most important factor on a speed bag is** *control*. Speed is secondary (…and impossible without control.)

3. Try to figure out how someone learns the best, either by watching, listening or counting. Some people do best by imitating swing movements. They will reproduce what they see you do. Others will pick up

by reproducing the "sound" and beat of the bag. Some people learn best by using the counting method. After someone has a certain amount of skill the counting method is more difficult because the more complex linking combinations usually get the bag going faster than they can count. It takes exceptional control to do multi-elbow fist linking slow enough to count. Try teaching different ways and see what works. Most people will benefit from all three. If one method is not working….switch.

4. Linking to the three reverse punching techniques is usually the most challenging skill area. Most people, particularly beginners, may be afraid of attempting this because they think they are "reaching" behind the bag, and they see how close the bag comes to the nose. It takes some time to learn to judge the correct distance, and they may have trouble getting the fist movements correct. But there are a few "secrets" to doing them safely. One is stepping, or leaning, to the side. For instance, when doing the Reverse Single Punch with the right arm, step or lean *slightly* to the right side of the bag. Have them push the right shoulder forward (which turns the face away from the board) and out of the way. This also keeps a good bend in the elbow and makes it easier. Another "secret" is to vary the fist angle to hit the side-reverse borders, which will *make the bag rebound towards the left or right front of the board*. This works particularly well with the Reverse Double Punch. Reverse Fist Rolling is the most difficult. The natural reaction is to lean back much too far. This is the wrong fix because it will straighten the arms and the elbows must stay bent to roll the fists. I have found the best way to protect the nose when reverse rolling is to lean back *slightly* and catch the bag *just after it hits the front of the board*. This creates a sharper hitting angle, and keeps the bag slightly *above the nose*. This also takes good control, so expect a little trouble.

Be sure they are hitting the belly, or lower part of the bag. Hitting higher makes linking (passing the fists through) impossible. *Reversing the order of the techniques can often help*. If someone is having trouble linking from the front- to-back, have them do the reverse technique first. As an example, it is sometimes easier to learn to do: (R-Roll)-[1/2]-(F-Roll) then to do the Front Fist Roll first. This usually works for any new combination. Put the most difficult technique first on the non-moving bag, then go to the easier one. On some techniques, you may find it easy with the bag already slowly moving.

5. Standing directly to the side is the best place to watch the arm motions. From this position, watch the elbows. If they are waving up and down, (pawing the bag) then the person is swinging from the shoulders, not the elbows. If the fists are dropping below the waist, they are making too large of a punching motion. You can also see if they are *resting* the fists at the waist, rather than up in the ready position. The natural swinging motion should bring the fists back to the chin, (not the waist.) But a natural consequence of keeping the fists up at chin level is letting the elbows sag down to the sides. Linking is very difficult to do with the elbows down.

Standing behind someone allows you to better see the body-torso motions. Also, it is a good place to see if the elbows are kept up in proper position to allow linking. Standing behind and supporting the elbows in the correct "up " position (seen in **Fig 13B & 13D**) is a very effective way to teach the "feel" of the arm position, particularly for multi-fist linking.

6. Learn as much as you can about how the bag works. Understand the differences between techniques and combinations. A complete breakdown of all speed bag techniques by Names, Areas of the bag, Punching variations and Elbow Striking Techniques is listed on page 216. The order I used for teaching techniques in this book is a logical progression of one technique movement getting you ready for the next technique. For example, it is more difficult to initially learn the Outward-Triple Elbow Strike as one motion than to progress from the Outward-*Single*, to Outward-*Double* and finally Outward-*Triple* Elbow Strike. Also, the order of the techniques in this book generally go from the most simple (easier to learn), to the most difficult. It is hard to comprehend, let alone do, a Reverse-Side Double Punch if they can not control reverse punching or side techniques. However, you may find an order that works best for you, such as all the fist techniques, then the elbow techniques, etc.

7. Always emphasize safety. Check the equipment to make sure it is in good repair. Although I emphasize hand protection, most people will often hit without it. Keep an eye on the knuckles…particularly the little finger. Untrained hands can really take a beating over long periods of use. If someone complains of the "sides" of their fingers hurting the culprit is usually a "loose" fist. This will let the fingers bang together on contact.

    The bag, or fist, can hit back. It is not uncommon for the bag to graze the tip of nose when learning the reverse techniques and linking. Tell people it may happen. I have never seen anyone get away with NOT getting bonked once or twice. A missed Reverse Single Punch may also hit the chest. *The biggest safety feature is taking eyeglasses off*, especially when doing downward elbow strikes, or a downward fist will remove them for you.

8. Teach only what you know. If you are not a trained martial artist, please do not try to teach these techniques on the bag. Especially kicking. Lots of things can go wrong and if you do not understand how the kicks are done someone is asking for injury. The normal head-high bag is much higher than most untrained people can kick. A ripped groin or hamstring muscle is a costly price to pay. Put the bag at a comfortable height, like at the shoulders or waist. Use a large bag. No amount of training will ever replace common sense and I have never witnessed a rebound board broken in a kicking demonstration.

9. Last of all-have fun teaching. There is no better feeling than watching someone become proficient at the bag because of your guidance. Most people are fascinated by advanced speed bag ability and many have said they "…could never do that". Proving them wrong is a joy to watch. In a few lessons they are making up rhythms and dancing when the do it. During lighter moments, run some down-&-out patterns. The bag holds an excellent spiral in a forward pass.

    In almost 30 years of using and teaching the speed bag, I have had the pleasure to teach a wide variety of people, including seasoned athletes, senior citizens, teenagers and a variety of people that are "challenged" with physical or emotional disorders. I have also had the opportunity to help persons who were blind, deaf or restricted to a wheelchair. Regardless of these challenges, I have not found one person *who can not learn how to hit it*. The rhythm is infectious and it only takes a little determination and practice. It offers more personal enjoyment and self-expression than any other type of repetitive exercise. And, once you learn to hit the speed bag, it does not go away. After years of lay-off, it only takes a few minutes to shake off the rust.

    Whether you are an occasional or avid speed bag practitioner, boxer, martial artist or teacher, I hope some of the information and training exercises in this book has been of help to you and your use of the *Amazing Speed Bag*.   **Now - go put a lot of Rhythm in YOUR Work-Out!**

…Just Hit It !

Breakdown of 24 Speed Bag Techniques

TECHNIQUE NAMES & ABBREVIATIONS

1 Front Circle Punch	(FCP)
2 Front Straight Punch	(FSP)
3 Front Double Punch	(FDP)
4 Front Fist Rolling	(F-ROLL)
5 Outward-Single Elbow Strike	(O-SES)
6 Outward-Double Elbow Strike	(O-DES)
7 Outward-Triple Elbow Strike	(O-TES)
8 Reverse Single Punch	(RSP)
9 Reverse Double Punch	(RDP)
10 Reverse Fist Rolling	(R-ROLL)
11 Inward-Single Elbow Strike	(I-SES)
12 Inward-Double Elbow Strike	(I-DES)
13 Inward-Triple Elbow Strike	(I-TES)
14 Downward-Single Elbow Strike	(D-SES)
15 Downward-Double Elbow Strike	(D-DES)
16 Downward-Triple Elbow Strike	(D-TES)
17 Out & Down 4way Elbow Strike	(O-D 4way)
18 Out & In 4way Elbow Strike	(O-I 4way)
19 Side Single Punch	(SSP)
20 Side Double Punch	(SDP)
21 Side-Triple Elbow Strike	(S-TES)
22 Hook Punch	(HOOK)
23 Reverse-Side Double Punch	(R-SDP)
24 Side-Reverse Double Punch	(S-RDP)

General Technique Information

12 Punches.................(Fists only)
12 Elbow Strikes..........(Elbow & fists)

Areas of Bag Contact

15 Front....... (FCP, FSP, FDP, F-ROLL,
O-SES, O-DES, O-TES, I-SES,
I-DES, I-TES, D-SES, D-DES,
D-TES, O-D 4way, O-I 4way)

3 Reverse....(RSP, RDP, R-ROLL)

6 Side..........(SSP, SDP, HOOK, S-TES,
R-SDP, S-RDP)

Variations of Punches

5 - Single Punches (One Fist)....
(FCP, FSP, RSP, SSP, HOOK)

5 - Double Punches (Two Fists).....
(FDP, RDP, SDP, R-SDP, S-RDP)

2 - F-Rolls......(F-ROLL, R-ROLL)

12 ELBOW STRIKING TECHNIQUES

3 - One Elbow only   (O-SES, I-SES, D-SES)
3 - One Elbow + One Fist   (O-DES, I-DES, D-DES)
4 - One Elbow + Both Fists   (O-TES, I-TES, D-TES, S-TES)
2 - Both Elbows + Both Fists   (O-D 4way ES, O-I 4way ES)

Seven Speed Bag Swing Movements

1 - FCP   2-FSP   3-RSP   4-HOOK Punch

5 -Outward Elbow   6-Inward Elbow   7-Downward Elbow

Appendix A-1

Advanced Fitness Speed Bag Work-Outs: SET UP

The Speed Bag is a great workout for the shoulders and arms, but it does not effect the legs. For the individual who wants either advanced cardiovascular conditioning or coordination training, the following ideas are offered. *Follow the safety proceedures that are included with all exercise equipment.*

WARNING: These are much more intense than speed bag training by itself.

By combining the Speed Bag with several other types of fitness aparatus the benefits of both can be greatly expanded. This works with both a stationary cycle and a stepping exercise machine. I call these new fitness programs: PUNCH & RIDE © and STEP & PUNCH©.   Two types of Stationary Cycle set-ups are shown below.

UPRIGHT CYCLE and **Wall Mounted Speed Bag Platform**

Short wheeled cycle can go forward or sideways. If forward, space the wheel at least one inch from wall. Less stable than recumbent. *Side techniques not recommended* (can sway bike). Saddle seat uncomfortable.

Regardless of bike style, align the cycle under the board where it is level and stable. This is extremely important. Be sure it does not rock sideways or "creep" forward as you pedal. Injury can result from falling.

Balance is needed on a standard upright cycle as shown to the left. Be careful!

Set Cycle under Board,   Bag position

DO NOT STAND UP AS YOU RIDE OR YOUR HEAD WILL CONTACT THE REBOUND BOARD!

RECUMBENT CYCLE and **FREE STANDING FLOOR FRAME**

Bike must go sideways or cannot reach bag. This is the most stable set-up and most comfortable due to chair seat of the Bike. Can do all techniques without problems. Authors favorite style and preferred workout.

Lower Board   Set cycle underneath   Cycle ready   bag in position   Punch & Ride
it is highly recommended to use three support straps as mentioned on page 8, along with weights.

Appendix A-2

Beginning Punch & Ride© Work-Outs

PUNCH & RIDE © workouts allow a Speed Bag and a Stationary Cycle to be used either individually or together at the same time to create four (4) potentially different types of training sessions:

1. Speed Bag Punching. You do not have to stand up to hit the speed bag effectively. Sitting on the cycle, simply do normal Speed Bag punching. Do not Pedal.

2. Riding Cycle Normal Stationary Cycling workout and do not use the Speed bag. Most of the cycling programs will work, but *DO NOT STAND UP AND PEDAL.*

3. Interval Training Ride for specified time, (3-5 minutes) stop and Punch Speed Bag for specified time (1-3 min.) or number of Punches (50 - 100) Repeat x2 or 3

4. Punch and Ride Punching with Arms, at the same time, Pedaling cycle with legs. The legs and arms will often find a natural "sync", where they both adjust to each other for speed or force. The legs tend to dominate because it is the largest muscle group.

There are several variables that can be changed, such as *speed* of movement or *force* required. Speed Bag size allows these to be manipulated for the arms, and pedaling speed and pedal resistance allow these to be addressed for the legs. Again, leg speed or force tends to predominate. Most cycles have a simple method to change pedal resistance while you are riding, but you will have to stop and get off to change speed bag sizes. Therefore, It is best to select bag size before you start. Speed and Force can also be used to create some advanced focused workouts. For **ADVANCED PUNCH & RIDE WORKOUTS, see Appendix A-3**. (**Warning: these are extremely intense)**

STEP & PUNCH©

This is an advanced workout and not for *Speed Bag* or *Step* beginners. Skill and Balance are demanded!

An extremely intense and coordination focused workout is possible by joining a speed bag and a stepping type exerciser. This is a very physically demanding activity requiring: good speed bag control, excellent balance and coordination and good to excellent cardiovascular fitness. *This is potentially dangerous because the board is directly overhead, and you must be positioned so your head is outside the board so it will not interfer with your stepping. Support straps are mandatory on a free standing floor frame speed bag unit, due to the height of the board. (see pg. 8)* Because of the required safety distance from the bag, only front punching on a small bag are recommended. The same variables in Punch & Ride © can be manipulated, however, this demands more coordination and is much more physically intense.

Raise Board   **Set Stepper underneath in position**   **Adjust bag**   **Step & Punch**
it is highly recommended to use three support straps as mentioned on page 8, along with weights.

Appendix A-3

Advanced Punch & Ride© Workouts

Below are 16 different Punch & Ride Settings designed to create wide variations between punching speed & punching force -vs- Riding speed and Riding force. They isolate the upper and lower body against each other in both speed and resistance. Bag Size can influence punching speed & force. You can punch slow & easy, or fast & hard. Likewise you can ride slow or fast with no resistance, or do the same with full resistance. It is much more physical with full pedal resistance. They also require (and build) coordination.   Train Safely!

WARNING: These Are extreme Physical Work-outs. Be Careful and do not overexert!

Possible Punch & Ride Advanced Variations, due to:

1. *Bag Size*   (x2 - Large=12x9 or 11x8 &   Small =9x6 or smaller: (Size effects resistance or force needed)
2. *Punching Speed*   (x2 - Slow/easy & Fast/Hard/Forceful. (Need good control on a small bag)
3. *Cycle Riding Speed*   (x2 - Slow/easy & Fast)
4. *Pedal Resistance*. (x2 levels - None & Maximum) full pedal resistance requires Leg force. Pedal Hard.
5. *Advanced Focus*   Extreme variations between Arms and Legs movement, with both Speed & Force required

	BAG Size	PUNCH Speed	RIDE Speed	Pedal Resistance	Advanced Focus
1	LG	Slow/Easy	Slow/Easy	None	Warm-Up
2	LG	Slow "	Slow "	Maximum	Tone/Coord/Fit
3	LG	Slow	Fast/Hard	None	Coordination
4	LG	**Slow**	**Fast "**	**Maximum**	**Fitness**/Coord.
5	* LG	Fast/Hard	Slow/Easy	None	Fitness/Coord
6	LG	Fast "	Slow "	Maximum	Fitness/Coord
7	LG	Fast	Fast/Hard	None	Fitness/Coord.
8	LG	**Fast**	**Fast "**	**Maximum**	**Extreme Fitness**

* Large Bag, Fast speed = More Force on Arms. Builds Power & Endurance

****

	BAG Size	PUNCH Speed	RIDE Speed	Pedal Resistance	Advanced Focus
9	SM	Slow/Easy	Slow/Easy	None	Warm Up
10	SM	Slow	Slow	Maximum	Tone/Coord
11	SM	Slow	Fast/Hard	None	Coordination
12	SM	**Slow**	**Fast**	**Maximum**	**Fitness**/Coord
13	* SM	Fast/Hard	Slow/Easy	None	Coordination
14	SM	Fast	Slow	Maximum	Coord/Fitness
15	SM	Fast	Fast/Hard	None	Coordination
16	SM	**Fast**	**Fast**	**Maximum**	**Extreme Fitness**/Coord

* Small Bag, Fast speed = Emphasize Speed & Quickness

* All *Maximum Pedal Resistance* settings are most difficult. Use caution.

Appendix B-1

Songs for the Speed Bag

Slow to faster speed Music.

TITLE	ARTIST - Album	NOTES / SUGGESTIONS
Boxer	Simon & Garfunkle	Slow Basic Rhythm or syncapted punching beat
I can't wait to be King	Jason weaver (Lion King)	Slow Syncopated punching beat
Oops Up	Snap (world power album)	Slow Syncopated beat
I got the Power	Snap " "	Slow Syncopated beat
Cult of Snap	Snap " "	Slow Syncopated beat
Gonna Make you Sweat	C&C Music Factory	Cool for syncopated punching rhythms
Principles of Lust	Enigma (MCMXC aD)	Cool & funky. great slow music for syncopation
Mea Culpa	Enigma " "	Syncopated beat " "
Rivers of Belief	Enigma " "	Syncopated beat " "
Theme from Rocky	Bill Conti (Rocky)	Slow Basic works well for warm up or Double time to smoke.
Mama Said Knock You Out	L.L. Cool J.	Very slow Basic or Double time. Easy to syncopate beat
Sax A-Go-Go	Candy Duffer	Syncopated beat and dance along too.
Pick up the Pieces	Candy Duffer	Syncopated beat and fun to jam with
Open your Heart	Madonna	All Madonna's Dance music is good for syncopated or Basic
Express Yourself	Madonna	
Cherish	Madonna	Double Punch rhythm works well FDP"RDP on this one.
Vogue	Madonna	Strike a pose and a speed bag at the same time. fun to hit to.
Get into the Groove	Madonna	
Bustin' Loose	Chuck Brown & soul searchers	pretty slow, syncopated and funky beat.
Relax	Frankie goes to Hollywood	Fast Basic to driving beat. can syncopate also
Marines' \Yankee Doddle	Bill Conti (Rocky Soundtrack)	great for straight time punching and cadences
Burn Rubber On Me	The Gap Band	syncopated punching seems to work best with off-beats in disco.
River of Dreams	Billy Joel	Nice easy syncopation or good double time basic rhythm.
Wanna Be Starting Something	Micheal Jackson (Off the Wall)	
Don't Stop Till Get Enough	Micheal Jackson	All his dance music is great for Syncopated punching
Pure Energy	Information Society	Syncopated beat fits drums in perfectly in parts
Live For Loving You	Gloria Estefan	Syncopated beat to all Gloria's Music. great stuff for bag!
Colony Bogey (March)	John Phillip Sousa	Basic Rhythm or on-beat punching for marches
Physical	Olivia Newton John	Driving Basic Rhythm or Syncopated beat
If You're not in it for Love	Shania Twain (Woman in Me)	Basic Rhythm or Syncopated with the cool drums.
You win my Love	Shania Twain " "	
No one needs to know	Shania Twain " "	Basic Rhythm & FDP"FDP
Barcelona Nights	Ottmar Liebert (Nouveau Flamenco)	Syncopated beat to Latin and World Music
2 the night	Ottmar Liebert " "	" "
Snake Charmer	Ottmar Liebert (The hours between night & day)	" "
Havana Club	Ottmar Liebert "	" several on this album can be used.
Mario takes a Walk	Jesse Cook (Gravity Album)	Syncopated beat to Latin Music
Brio	Jesse Cook "	Hang on to this one. unreal guitar
Gipsy	Jesse Cook "	How does he do this? gotta hit to it!
Tempest	Jesse Cook (Tempest Album)	Get the "Vertigo" album also. Jesse Rocks!
Cupids Dance	Robert Michaels (Paradiso Album)	Syncopated Beat
Sunset Samba	Robert Michaels "	
Where's the Love / MMMBop	Hanson (middle of Nowhere)	good syncopated speed bag tunes!

Appendix B-2

TITLE	ARTIST - Album	NOTES / SUGGESTIONS
Land of 1000 Dances	Wilson Pickett (Greatest Hits)	get the album. Punch or Dance to it.
Everybody needs somebody to love	Wilson Pickett " "	Basic Rhythm to most songs on album.
Here Comes the Sun	Richie Havens (Sings Beatles &Dylan)	Hit to this one and listen to the rest
Rock & Roll Pt II	Gary Glitter	Basic Rhythm to good old Rock & Roll. Not funky, but fun
Pretty Woman	Roy Orbison	Great for both Basic Rhythm & Syncopated Punching
Show Me	Joe Tex	Old school Rock & Roll. Fast Basic Rhythm
Heat Wave	Martha & Vandellas	Old school Rock & Roll. Fast Basic Rhythm
Wipe Out	Beach Boys	Fast Basic Rhythm. Try to syncopate on drum solos
Twilight Zone	2 Unlimited (Get Ready)	Syncopated beat sometimes follow melody line
Contrast	2 Unlimited Syncopated	"there's no limit to what this beat can do!"
Don't Lose Your Head	Queen (a kind of Magic)	Quick syncopated beat or slow Basic Rhythm
Beat it	Micheal Jackson	Driving Basic Rhythm or medium syncopated
Crank it up	Peter Brown	Syncopated beat to this and most disco music.
Pinball Wizard	The Who	Easy Basic Rhythm or syncopated
Can't Touch This	M.C. Hammer	Syncopated punching all the way. can't touch this!
Cantina Band	Geo. Lucas (Star Wars)	Don't Laugh, this is a great ragtime tune!
Tootsie Roll	69 Boyz	Fist Rolling city with Tootsie Roll. syncopated!
JellyHead	Crush	Syncopated punching or medium syncopated
Thunderer (march)	John Phillip Sousa	Slow Basic Rhythm or medium syncopated
Stars & Stripes Forever (march)	John Phillip Sousa	" " depending on bag size.
Semper Fidelis (march)	John Phillip Sousa	" "
Washington Post (march)	John Phillips Sousa	" "
Nasty Boys/ Rhythm Nation /Alright	Janet Jackson (Design of Decade)	Syncopate the whole album!
I would die for You/Baby I'm a Star	Prince ? (Purple Rain)	Fast Basic Rhythm. Hang On!
Trust	Prince ? (His Batman album)	Trust me.....it's fast Syncopate it.
Footloose	Kenny Loggins (footloose)	Fast Basic Rhythm. Hang On!
Holding out for a Hero	Bonnie Tyler " "	Holding out for the end is more like it!
Raise your Hands	Bon Jovi	Fast Basic Rhythm or syncopated Punching
Who are You	The Who	Fast syncopated punching, with some basic also
Final Bell	Bill Conti (Rocky)	Fast Basic & wait for the final bell
Reel around the Sun	Billy Whelan (River Dance)	start at 4:38 into the song & test your rhythm
Jump, Jive an' Wail	Louis Prima	Fast Basic Rhythm or slow syncopated punching
Zoot Suit Riot	Chill Pill Dancers	Fast Basic Rhythm or slow syncopated punching

Pictures

Over the years I have had the good fortune to demonstrate the speed bag at numerous trade shows relating to the sporting goods or health/fitness industry and boxing tournaments around the country. Along the way I have met an interesting array of people, and some of the most dedicated speed bag fans on the planet. Many send me pictures and video's after they begin using this program and I appreciate the feedback. Here are a few interesting pictures, as well as some of my many speed bag friends.

NationalSporting Goods Association (NSGA) Chicago

demonstrations of hitting the speed bag to music.

Martial Arts Seminar, Waco TX

Thomas "Hitman" Hearns
supershow, Atlanta, GA.

Dr. Roy Schroeder, MSU

They don't come any nicer than **Bill Pearl**
Mr. Universe, Gold's Gym Convention

Marcus Allen, K.C. Chiefs
Supershow, Atlanta, GA

Working out - yrs ago!

He's learning!- Las Vegas fitness Expo

Northwest Texas Regional Fair, Longview TX

Gene Lund, Michigan

Sports, Health, Fitness Expo Dallas, TX

Big Ben Kniffen & family   Ericka,   Brenda,   Kyle & "F-Roll" C.J.

My Wife Elizabeth

Friend,   John Baca Kevin Simmons   (author)

Quiet on the Set..

Dick O'Leary, Wisconsin

Scott Ryan, Atlanta, GA.

John Brown, owner - Ringside Boxing
Silver Gloves National Tournament

John Baca, CMH

John is a close friend and a certified speed bag fanatic. He is also a true hero. On Feb. 10, 1970, while under heavy enemy fire in Vietnam, he displayed unbelievable courage. With total disregard for his own safety he took actions that were responsible for saving the lives of eight (8) American soldiers. Few men pass this kind of test. Surviving horrific wounds, he was awarded the United States of America's highest award - the Congressional Medal of Honor.

Never forget the sacrifices made by our men and woman in military service. Men like John (and those who do not return) allow men like me to write books like this in a free society.   There was a great price paid for this freedom.

Wes Campbell, dummy, Joe Ryan, Atlanta GA

Christy, Jennifer, Trish, Marge, Iris,
George & Roy, Honolulu N.YMCA

Index

Index

Index

ABOUT THE AUTHOR

The author was born in 1950 in Brooklyn, New York and graduated from South High School in Grand Rapids, Michigan. A music/percussion major in high school, He has a B.A. in Psychology, and Master's degrees in both Vocational Rehabilitation Counseling and Therapeutic Recreation Administration, all from Memphis State University (now The University of Memphis.) He is a certified rehabilitation counselor (CRC) and a certified therapeutic recreation specialist (CTRS). He has taught classes in Therapeutic Recreation at Northwest Jr. College in Senatobia, Mississippi and Baylor University in Waco, Texas. He also spent almost 5 years working for the Muscular Dystrophy Association in Memphis, Tennessee and Columbus, Georgia. He currently works as a Recreation Therapist in Waco, Texas.

Fairly uncoordinated in most sports, He competed for the Memphis State University Racquetball team, and has been active in the martial arts for many years. He holds a Black Belt in Korean Hapkido under Grand Master Kyong Sik Song of O.H.T.C. Martial Arts in Dallas, Texas. He has published articles concerning speed bag training in the May 1991 issue of Black Belt Magazine and the July 1998 issue of Martial Arts Training. He is proud to be a member of the *Team Ringside* advisory panel of boxing.

An active speed bag enthusiast for almost 30 years, he uses speed bag training as a rehabilitative activity with a wide variety of sensory-motor disorders, as well as emotional and behavioral problems. He also has "trial-by-fire" experience… using the speed bag in recovery from neurosurgical reconstructions of his own cervical spine.

Past personal appearances performing speed bag demonstrations and training seminars at:

**The National Sporting Goods Convention, (NSGA) in Chicago, Illinois
The Gold's Gym National Convention, Las Vegas, Nevada
The Fitness Expo, Las Vegas, Nevada
Martial Arts Training Seminar, Waco, Texas
A Night of Boxing, West Palm Beach, Florida
The Super Show, Atlanta Georgia 1996
The 1996 Olympic Games, Atlanta Georgia
The Sports, Health & Fitness Expo, Dallas, Texas
The National Silver Gloves Tournament, Kansas City, Kansas
The Northeast Texas Regional Fair, Longview, Texas
The SuperShow, Las Vegas, Nevada, Feb 2001**

Grandkids are the best!

The Speed Bag Bible ©
ORDER FORM

I would like to order the following item(s):

_____ Copie(s) of **THE SPEED BAG BIBLE**

($21.95 per copy. Order 5 or more for $19.95 each.) **BOOKS** $ _____

The Speed Bag Bible is now on Video. There is a **four-tape series, (Tapes 1-4)** which covers all topics in great detail, with many demonstrations in real time and slow motion. Throw in some inside secrets and it adds up to almost *eight hours* of instruction! AND, there is also a lesser **TWO (2) HOUR** video, covering most topics (not advanced). These video's are the best way to *see & hear* the awesome rhythm of the bag. **ALL VIDEO'S are VHS,** unless special ordered, requiring pre-pay in advance.

_____ **TAPE 1** **Chapter 4** (Front Fist Punches) and **Chapter 5** (Reverse Punching & Linking)

_____ **TAPE 2** **Chapters 4, 6, 7 and 8** (All Twelve Elbow Striking Techniques *on one tape*)

_____ **TAPE 3** **Chapter 9** (Quick Review of tapes 1&2 - and Side Techniques)

_____ **TAPE 4** **Chapters 10** (Review & Advanced Combinations) and **Chapter 11**

_____ **TAPE 5** **Punch Drumming** ("secrets" of hitting the speed bag to music!)

_____ **2 Hr Comprehensive Speed Bag Training** (Covers most topics in *The Speed Bag Bible* such as, Rhythm, 24 Techniques, many combinations and Linking from all areas. Some slow motion and narration. THE "ULTIMATE" PRIVATE SPEED BAG SEMINAR

_____ **Rhythm & Rehab.** (How to use SPEED BAG in a rehabilitation program or clinic setting)

Tapes 1 - 4 Individually……….	$21.95 Each
TWO HR. comprehensive…….	$24.95
Tape 5, Punch Drumming…………	$24.95
Rhythm & Rehab video……………	$24.95
Video Tapes 1 - 4 ……………	$79.95 (Save $8.00)
BOOK & 2 HR. comp ……….	$39.95 (Save $7.00)
BOOK & All Tapes 1 - 4 ……….	$89.95 (Save $11.00)
ALL Video Tapes 1 - 5 ……….	$99.95 (Save $12.00)

VIDEOS $_____

SHIPPING & HANDLING

Books: $ 5.00 each. 5 or more copies, $4.00 each (Foreign $ VARY) $ _____

VHS Tapes: $4.00 each. (United States) (Foreign $ VARY, depending on country) $ _____

TEXAS Residents, please add 8% Sales Tax **of product total**: $ _____

TOTAL ENCLOSED $ _____

Cut

I would be interested in:

_____ Attending a Speed Bag Training Seminar by the Author

_____ Sponsoring a Speed Bag Training Seminar with the Author

_____ Promoting and/or Distributing The Speed Bag Bible program

Other: _____

SHIP OR MAIL ALL TO:

Your Name:_____

Address 1:_____

Address 2:_____

City:_____ State: _____ Zip:_____

COUNTRY (Int'l):_____ mail codes:_____

Telephone (if needed): (___) _____ Best Time To Call _____ __Am __Pm

FAX phone (if needed):(____) _____ extensions? _____

INTERNATIONAL Telephone (if needed): Country codes(_____) _____

internet e-mail address: _____

Please Ship By ____ UPS ____U.S. Mail Other:_____

Please Allow 3-6 Weeks Delivery. Personal Checks or foreign may take longer.

Send Order To: **THE SPEED BAG BIBLE**
Post Office Box 21103
Waco, Texas 76702-1103